BEN JAY CUNNINGHAM: DISPATCHES ON MY BRIEF VISIT TO EARTH

Ben Jay Cunningham: Dispatches on My Brief Visit to Earth

An Oral History

TRANSCRIBED AND EDITED BY
CATHY CRAMER

Catherine M. Cramer

Contents

This book is dedicated to all those whom I've loved and still love (you know who you are) -- But especially the stories in these pages are for my children and their families: Sam, Sean, Shane, Kristy, Peyton, Colwyn, Kenny, and my grandchildren Emma, Gabriella, Raquel, Wyatt, Ben, Mila, Tristan, Ana, Javan, Resa, and Gracyn. And to the children of the grandchildren and so on who might find themselves someday on this planet -- May your journeys on Earth be kind and happy.

- b.j.c.

Editor's Foreword

Since the day I met Ben, he has been telling me stunning, unbelievable stories about his life. I've long believed that he has lived the most interesting life of anyone I have ever known, and that his autobiography would be a fascinating read. But over time, it became clear that he would never write such a thing -- he is just not self-absorbed enough to find himself to be an interesting writing topic.

Then one day, after thirteen years of marriage, the answer came to me -- I would record him telling me stories about his life and then transcribe those stories to create a sort of biography/autobiography. And that is what this is.

We began the project in the summer of 2019, me recording him telling a few stories every few evenings. We both enjoyed this so much. And while Ben's stories are no doubt embellished to some degree, I am confident that they are all based on true events.

I tried to keep each story as true to Ben's words as possible, though I did do some editing when he strayed off in other directions (as he is wont to do). But, for the most part, these are the stories of Ben's life, in his own words. I hope you enjoy reading them as much as I enjoyed hearing them.

Chapter 1

Childhood: Birth to Age 11

Birth

Apparently, it was a bad birth. Something was all messed up in my mother, and they said that they might be able to save the mother but they didn't think they'd be able to save the child. And one of my parents' best friends, Jay Bannon, who I'm named after -- my middle name is Jay -- was there. He was the right blood type and they needed a blood transfusion, and they hooked him directly up to my mother in the operating room and were just transferring the blood directly from him to her. And he saved both mother and child.

They had told my parents before the birth that, if I did survive, I would be what they termed psychologically in those days, an idiot. And of course you know, I've often said that I think the jury is still out on that one. (Laughter)

First Memory

I must have been a little less than a year old. I was in a crib; I remember bars. I've never liked bars. Even though later I was

a cop and worked behind bars. But up on the wall was this little, these little wall figures, of Old King Cole and his merry old
men. His fiddler's three. Old King Cole and his fiddler's three.
And from where I was lying in my position, that's what my line
of vision was. So everyday I was looking at Old King Cole and
his fiddler's three. And sometimes my mother would sing to
me, or chant to me, the kind of song or chant that went along
with that. And so that's actually, that's my first memory of life.

Cockroaches

I must have been about three years old, maybe four, I don't
know, but I woke up in the middle of the night. I was going
to go to the bathroom, and I'm walking down the hallway, just
a regular little hallway, and all of a sudden things start flying
into my face, big things, horrible things. There was no light on.
They were hitting me in the face and all over, and I started
screaming, and one of my parents came and turned the light
on. And there were cockroaches everywhere. Everywhere. We
had a bunch of pine trees outside, and cockroaches are basically tree roaches, and somehow they had gotten into the
house. It created sort of a little bit of a trauma moment for me
every time I had to pad my way down the hallway to get to the
bathroom at night.

Quicksand

I was three or four, and I was at my Grandpa's farm. And while
the grown-ups were talking, I wandered down to the creek on
one of the paths. And I started to cross over to something I was
looking at, I can't remember what, and I stepped in quicksand
and started sinking. So I'm up to about, almost chest high, and
I'm thinking, "I know this is not good, I know I'm sinking under

something," and I'm scared. I guess. I don't remember that, but I'm sure I was, who wouldn't be?

So the next thing I know, it's up to about chest high, and in the distance, I hear the tractor, and here comes my mother and Grandpa on the tractor. She's hollering my name, and I start hollering back, and they pull up to the edge of the creek on the tractor, and my Grandpa gets out and throws me a rope, ties it to the tractor, tells me to put it around my head, under my arms, and he just backs the tractor up and pulls me out of the quicksand.

Almost Losing an Eye

When I was four, my father and my Uncle Jay, who saved my mother's and my life at birth, were hauling in a new bed to the house when I was old enough to sleep in an actual bed. And I was so excited, it was going to be a bed! And there was, well, what seemed to me like a long hallway, at the time. It was at 1435 Chippendale Street in Houston. It was not a long hallway, it was probably only about 20, 25 feet long. But they were taking in the bed railings, to set up the bed, and I was so excited. I was behind them, watching them do this, and I was running, and they had to stop for some reason, and I ran into one of the bed railings. And it hit me in the eye. And there was nothing but blood and screaming.

They picked me up, and quite frankly, I think it was my Uncle Jay, if I'm remembering correctly, who said -- who actually was in the army in World War II (my father was in the Navy in World War II) -- but I think it was Uncle Jay who said -- because people were screaming at that time, my mother was screaming -- but Uncle Jay threw me into the bathtub in the bathroom that was in the hallway, about as long as our hallway here at home, and they started letting me bleed in the bathroom. And I was bleeding like, it was spurting, it was crazy. And I thought,

"Woah, I didn't know there was this much blood in humans." I had pricked my finger before, or whatever, but this was a whole different experience. So they had me in the bathtub, and they were trying to staunch the bleeding, and they got the bleeding staunched, and they finally hauled me to the hospital.

And it happened to be the same doctor who had delivered me, his name was Nick Adamo. And they worked on my eye, and they said, "We've done the best we can. He'll probably only have about half vision in that eye. But that's the way it goes." That was my first big, first of two big eye injuries. But as it turned out, I didn't ultimately notice any difference in my eyesight. And apparently my eyesight was ultimately good enough for having me make expert marksman in pistols, rifles, and machine guns in the Army. So that little incident turned out a little better than anybody thought it might.

Vesta Jean Roberts

So Vesta Jean Roberts lived in the neighborhood when I was living over in Oak Forest at 1425, as I called it, "Chickentail" Road, but it was actually Chippendale Road. We went to school together, we were in kindergarten together, in Miss Lacrone and Miss Trimble's class.

And one of the things that I had an enormous problem with in those days was how to spell mouse. I mean, M-O-W-S-E, M-O-W-C-E, I couldn't grapple with it. Vesta Jean Roberts was sitting next to me in class and she finally at one point leaned over and said to me, "Here's the trick. You watch the Mickey Mouse Club?" And I said, "Yeah." And she said, "Think about the song." And I said, "What song?" And she said, "M-I-C-K-E-Y, M-O-U-S-E." And all of a sudden, the light bulb went off. And not only did the light bulb go off on spelling the word, but that was the first time I had noticed Vesta Jean Roberts.

So we became kind of buddy-buddy in school. But then in the first grade, I think, it was getting pretty hot and heavy. And so one day, I asked her, did she want to go to the snow cone stand down at the park. I'm buying. And oh, I thought that was kind of pretty bold for me. But it apparently went through different layers. She had to get permission from her parents, her parents tagged along at a distance, and we met up at the snow cone stand. And I bought her a snow cone, and we held hands, and we walked a little bit along the little bayou that was running through there, and the parents were keeping a safe distance. And then, all of a sudden, she reached up and kissed me on the cheek.

And that was my first date, that was her first date, and I don't know what happened after that, but nothing ever happened after that. But one of the things that I sometimes regret a little bit is, I moved away from Oak Forest over to Far West Houston, and when I moved back in high school, I didn't realize that she was going to the same high school that I was going to. And even though I saw her name a time or two, we never ever connected again. Until one day, she showed up on some high school website, and it turns out her birthday was either my birthday or the day before my birthday, and I sent her a hello -- and this was, I was probably in my fifties at that time -- and she replied, and she said, "I'll never forget our date at the snow cone stand."

Geraldine

Geraldine was our housekeeper, a black woman, which was not uncommon in those days. Although I think as an adult, most of the housekeepers that I've experienced have all been white. But that was a job that was for black people then, and it was a good gig. And Geraldine, of course, as you can imagine, given the state of my mother as I was growing up -- I think she prob-

ably came to work for us when I was about four or five -- and
she was more a mother for me than my mother at the time.
Although my mother was not off the rails at that time, my
mother was actually in pretty good shape, so it was almost like
I had two mothers. And that was a good period of time in my
life.

So one day, when I think I was in the first grade, I had heard
for the first time some little ditty that some kids were talking
about. And when I got home from school -- Geraldine was always the one who met me, and sometimes with my mother.
And I think my mother was there that day, they were both
together, and they were like, "How was your day? What happened?" And I said, "Well, I learned a new song!" And they said,
"Oh, what was it?" I said, "It was pretty funny!" And to me it
was the rhythm and everything, and I said, "It was, eeny, meenie, miny, moe, catch a nigger by the toe, if he hollers let him
go, eeny, meenie, miny, moe!"

And all of a sudden, Geraldine's face fell. I mean, really fell.
My mother's face fell. Tears were coming down Geraldine's
face. And my mother said, "I'm sorry to hear you heard that."
And she said, "Geraldine, please talk to him about this."
(Brushing away tears) So Geraldine explained to me how hurt-
ful that was, and both of them -- and I give my mother a lot
of credit for this -- (Brushing away tears) basically said, "This
is the first time and the last time we ever want to hear the N
word in this house, or anywhere else." So I would say that was
a pretty deep lesson. That was the moment that the existence
of racism came to me -- I didn't know about it before then.

Learning to Fight

I think I was about six years old, I think I'd gotten through
kindergarten. And Jimmy Payne lived across the street. Jimmy
Payne and I were really good buds, and we would traipse

around the neighborhood together, up and down the street. We once got in trouble -- we decided it would be fun to strip naked and ride our tricycles up and down the streets. So we bonded. And of course, Jimmy Payne's mother got a call from somebody that we were riding naked up and down the street, and called her, so she came and administered corporal punishment to both of us, because that's what good neighbors did to people. So that was Jimmy Payne.

Occasionally, he would get out of control. He had a bit of a tendency to be a bully. And one day, we got in some little tiff, I have no recollection of what that particular tiff was, but he bloodied my nose. And I ran home crying across the street. And on that day, my mother -- and this was, of course, before I had any inkling of her alcoholism or anything, and I think she was pretty straight in those days -- but she was all upset, and I was crying, and my nose was bleeding, and she said, "Okay, I have to teach you how to fight."

And I said, "What do you mean?" And she said, "You're gonna have to learn to hurt him." And I said, "I can't do this." And I remember this so clearly, I said, "I don't want to do that." And she said, "Why?" And I said, "Because I have a tender little heart." And she started crying, my mother did. But even so, she said, "Try to keep it. But I have to teach you how to defend yourself. Your father's not here. He wouldn't know anyway. So I'm going to teach you."

So she got down on her knees in the living room and she said, "Okay, show me your fist." And I went like that [showing fist with thumb on inside]." And she said, "No." And so she came and she said, "Here's what you do. The fingers go down to the middle of the knuckle, and your thumb comes across. Do that with both hands, like that." And I said, "Okay."

And I practiced it, and practiced it, and got it right enough for her. And she's on her knees, her head even with mine, and she said, "Okay, now, I'm going to try to hit you, what do you do?" And she reached back to start hitting me, and I ran back-wards. And she said, "No. You've got to learn how to block the punch coming in." So we sparred around like that, not anything serious, for a few minutes.

And then she said, "Okay, you're ready. Now, Tender Little Heart, you have to learn how to actually hit and hurt some-body." And I didn't know what she was talking about. I said, "Okay." She said, "Okay, hit me." I said again, "I can't do that." And she said, "You have to." And there were tears running down my mother's face. So I hauled off and hit her. And she said, "Good." She said, "When anybody comes after you, you know how to hit them. And you hit them, and you hit them, and you do not stop."

And so that was her lesson to me on fighting. That was the first lesson that I ever had on fighting.

Arson

Well, this was my one and only ever incidence of committing arson. It wasn't on purpose, but it was arson. I had a friend that lived about three doors down, I don't remember his name now, we were not real close friends but we'd been pal-ing around a little bit in the neighborhood. I was six-ish at this point, maybe seven. I had a toolbox that I'd gotten for Christmas, a little toy toolbox but it had real tools in it, and somewhere along the line, I got hold of a big box of kitchen matches in the house, the kind you can strike on anything, and I thought it would be fun to go down and get my friend and we could get on the dri-veway or something and start throwing matches at the, see if we could strike the matches on the driveway.

So I get down to his house and the garage is wide open, cars are gone but the garage is open, that wasn't uncommon in those days. I knocked on the door and everything and he wasn't there, and I thought, "Hmm, well, gee, I better not do this out front because maybe my parents will see me or something, somebody will see me and report me to my parents." So I just started striking matches on the floor of their garage. But unfortunately, they had all these gasoline cans and chemical cans, all these kind of flammable things in there, and there was a little leakage on the floor somehow, and whoof, it caught fire and just exploded.

I made it out of the garage but I was so scared -- not for my life, I was scared that I was in trouble -- I ran home, I snuck in the house, I went to my bedroom, I got in my bed, and meanwhile, the house was on fire. Firetrucks were coming. All these firetrucks were coming out there.

And my Uncle Benny and Aunt Icie, the methodist preacher and his icy spouse, were there visiting. So I'm just hiding in my room, and finally -- but I'm listening to the fire engines and everything out there, I'm looking at them through the window -- and my mother and Icie came into the room and said, "What are you doing?" And I said, "I'm looking at the firetrucks." And they were angry, they said, "No, you can't look at the firetrucks. You did that." I said, "No, no, I've been in my room!" But they said, "No, the neighbors saw you running back from there."

And so I was in big trouble. And the consensus was, from my Uncle Benny and Icie, was that I needed to be put away in an institution because I was an arsonist, I was a pyromaniac is what they said, "it's obvious that he's a pyromaniac." Fortunately, my mother had grown up with Icie and Uncle Benny and knew that they were just batshit crazy, so she started defending me. I explained what happened, that it was an accident, but Icie and Uncle Benny didn't believe that, they thought I was lying through my teeth. So that was my arson event.

Rattlesnake Bite

Don't think of this in terms of a giant Texas rattlesnake that's six feet long. This was in the garden of my house on Chippendale Road when I was maybe six or seven years old. My mother was working in the little garden. She was sober that day, or maybe not, I don't know, but she's working in the garden. And all of a sudden she hollers out because this little ground rattler -- which was probably no longer than about 10 inches, they're a special little kind of rattlesnake -- bites her. And I'm trying to grab her arm away, and it bites me. But most of its venom went into my mother.

And instead of, like, her hand that swelled up -- I mean, she had to go to the hospital, and everybody had to go to the doctor and whatnot -- her hand swelled up to about the size of a large softball. But my bite -- because there was very little venom left after the first, you know, insertion into my mother -- my hand just swelled up and was black and blue and everything.

And they never gave us any, there was no such thing as antivenom at that time. So we just had to suffer through it. And they said, "You might lose the hand, you might not, we don't know how these things really work." And this was back in the '50's, you know, early '50's, maybe 1955 or something like that, '54. And so they said, "Yeah, we don't know. But we've done all we can, good luck."

And, obviously, my mother survived it and I survived it. Now had that been the kind of rattlesnake that we think of here in Texas and West Texas and whatnot, that's like four or five or six feet long, that probably would have killed us. But these little ground rattlers were more of a -- I think of it in retrospect as, "Eh, just another little nemesis."

Near Drowning

I was maybe six or seven. Jimmy Payne, my best friend and sometimes bully/nemesis, lived across the street from us on Chippendale, in Houston. And they had gotten a swimming pool, an in-ground swimming pool.

So I went over to his house one day to see if he was there to play, and he wasn't there -- nobody was there, they were all gone -- and I wandered back to the back of the house to see if they were back there, nobody was there. So I'm looking at the pool, and somehow I fell in. And I couldn't swim, I never learned to swim until I was about 9 years old. So I fell in, and I'm drowning.

And the story goes, from my mother, that she was in the kitchen washing dishes looking out the back of the house toward the backyard, and all of a sudden she had this horrible, horrible feeling that I was in bad trouble, and she saw in her mind the swimming pool across the street. And the next thing I know, I'm underwater and I'm drowning, and she jumps in the water and yanks me out, starts banging on me and I'm spitting water out. But yeah, but for that premonition, I would have been a goner.

Phoebe

There was a kid two or three houses down that was, I think this was around when I was six years old. Six or seven. They were having a birthday party, and I was down in his house before the birthday party and I was just fascinated by this parakeet, Phoebe. What kids were there were all playing and having a good time, and I was just sitting there talking and just fascinated by this beautiful little parakeet. And the mom saw me and said, "Why aren't you playing with them?" And I said, "This bird is just amazing!"

Anyway, the birthday party was like two or three days later, and we get to the birthday party, and she announces that there's going to be a raffle for the bird. And I'm just so excited, there's a chance, there's a chance, that I could get this bird! The bird and the cage! But I thought, this is going to be really disappointing, because there's like 15 kids there at the party, somebody's going to get it.

As it turns out, miraculously, I won the bird! And it was no accident. She did that. That was one of the nicest things anybody ever did for me. And I had Phoebe for years and years and years.

I was probably 12 or 13 years old maybe by the time she died. She just died of a heart attack and fell down in her cage. And Cecil was the replacement bird. Actually, I think we had gotten him before, because I was thinking she needed a friend. So Cecil was the next bird.

Getting Scooped up by a Crane

I was maybe six, maybe seven. Jimmy Payne and I were off on adventures. About four or five blocks from our houses there was a little park, I think it was Oak Forest Park, I don't remember. They were building a swimming pool. It was a big, deep hole, and lots of fun to be playing around in.

But even more fun was the huge mound of dirt they were digging out of the swimming pool, that made a mountain in the flatlands of Houston. We were playing on the mountain, we were crawling up and we were going to make it to the top. And we made it to the top. And we're sitting there thinking, "God, we have, like, climbed Mount Everest," although we didn't know what Mount Everest was, but it was Mount Everest to us.

And we're sitting there, and then all of a sudden this machine cranks up, the big crane-bucket-bulldozer thing that was digging all the dirt out, and it had been dormant. I mean, it was dead, it was asleep, that's why we were playing, because there was nothing going on. But I guess, I don't know, the guy came back from his lunch break.

And dump trucks start showing up, dump truck after dump truck, there must have been twenty dump trucks. And all of a sudden this thing, bucket, comes down, and starts pulling the top of the mountain off. And the first one missed us -- there goes all this dirt into the deal, and we're going batshit crazy because we're thinking, "God, I think we're about to die." And the next bucket or two picks us up in the bucket, dumps us in the dump truck, and then more buckets are about to come.

And this part of the story was filled in later by my mother, but she was standing in the kitchen, washing dishes, and all of a sudden, she had this, again, one of a number of premonitions that something bad was going on, and she knew exactly where it was, and she headed down to the park. And we had already been dumped in the dump truck, and the next load was coming up to come down on top of us. And she was screaming and hollering, we could hear her screaming and hollering, at the crane bucket driver, and he stopped everything and the crane operator got up there and found out, here were these two kids, sitting in the middle of all this dirt, buried up to their necks, with the next load about to come down on them. And I guess I can say that this mama that I wasn't supposed to have survived birth with, she wasn't supposed to survive, I wasn't supposed to survive, but here she came after me again, and yanked us both out of there, and so we survived that little mountain-climbing adventure.

Beer in the Bushes

I was about six, seven, somewhere in there. And, you know, Jimmy Payne and I were off on our little daily adventures. We were off towards the park again.

Somewhere along the way, near the park or in the park, we found a full six-pack of beer, hidden in some bushes, that somebody had either hidden or gotten rid of or whatever. But of course they didn't have pop tops in those days, so one of us had to sneak home to get a churchkey. I don't remember which one of us scored one first, both of our households were probably big beer drinkers, so there were churchkeys everywhere. But snuck in, got a churchkey, and went off and got in the woods near the park, and we decided that we were gonna drink this beer.

And it wasn't actually the first taste of beer that I'd ever had. What I knew, from growing up with my Grandpa, first beer that anybody ever offered me was my Grandpa at the 3-2 Bar in Gonzales, Texas, when he said, "Here, take a taste of this." And from the first time I ever tasted beer, I never liked beer.

But we were determined we were gonna drink this beer. And I think we worked through about maybe a beer and a half, taking turns sipping it, but we got tipsy. And we made our way home, and all of a sudden we both got whippings, I think from Jimmy Payne's mother, who for some reason often liked to give me whippings. Maybe she was giving me discipline because she knew my mother was sort of out of it somehow. Anyway, she gave us whippings with, as I recall, don't remember if it was a belt or a switch, but she said, "This is what happens when you get drunk and come home and let us know about it." So we made sure, Jimmy Payne and I made a pact, next time, we'll make sure we don't come home and they don't know about it. (Laughter)

The Rolled Socks Club

So this was the second grade and I was in Oak Forest Elementary School. This was in a part of Houston that was, still had lots of pine trees. And across the street from the school was a little forest that for some reason or another still existed.

And I had started a club called the Rolled Socks Club, and we were known for rolling our socks down. So those of us that were in the club were in the Rolled Socks Club. And they all kind of bought into this. So there were like four or five of us.

And one day I said, "Okay, let's sneak over during school to the little secret forest across the street." So about four of us, I think, signed on, and we went over to the secret woods to play hookie. So we're in the woods and everything's going fine, except for one of the kids, I have no idea who he was now, but he really, really, really had to go to the bathroom, like number two. Like serious, serious business. And there was no toilet paper of course. I said he should use leaves, and he threw a little fit.

And so, on the other side of the woods and across the street was a grocery store. So we said okay, we'll go over there and get a roll of toilet paper. And so we went over there and got a roll of toilet paper. I think it cost 22 cents, 20 something cents, I want to say 22 cents. And we were able to cobble that together, out of the three of us that were there, because the other kid was back shitting in the woods, right?

So we get the toilet paper, we go back, and everything is fine, and then the police show up. Because somebody at the grocery store had called the school, and said, "there's some kids over there in the woods, and they just bought a roll of toilet paper." And so a cop showed up and hauled us back over to the school.

And the principal, Mr. Dishron, quickly figured out that I was the ringleader of this little Rolled Socks Club, and so he decided to paddle me, give me swats. This was the first swats

I'd ever gotten in school -- I got them all the way through high school. I was probably one of the "getting swats" kings of all time. But he gave me these swats, and it was like two or three swats, and it didn't kill me, it wasn't the worst thing that ever happened to me, but I was banned at that point from starting any clubs in school, and we were forbidden from ever going off campus with the threat of more swats. Fortunately, by the time I was in the fourth grade, we moved to another school district, where I received more swats. (Laughter)

First Cigar

It was coming close to Halloween. I was about 8 years old. And I wanted to be a hobo. So my mother said that a hobo has to have a cigar. And I said, "Okay." And she says, "You've got to smoke a cigar. You can't just have a cigar in your mouth. You've got to smoke it to make it realistic." And I said, "Okay."

So she gives me this big ol' cigar, not one of these cigarillos that I chew on these days. And we were outside the house, and I started smoking. And I'm smoking and smoking this cigar, and I'm getting sicker and sicker. And I start throwing up. But she said I had to keep going, so I kept smoking and kept throwing up. And by the time it got to Halloween night -- I dressed up as a hobo with a hat and a raggedy coat or whatever -- I was not smoking anymore. Because I'd gotten so sick.

So I got through that Halloween and decided after that -- you would think I would have decided that I'll never smoke again. But no, I had gotten somewhat addicted to the nicotine. I never wanted to smoke cigarettes because my parents and everybody I knew smoked cigarettes, and they were a mess. I thought, "Okay, I'll smoke cigars."

So I did. I never inhaled much. But by the time I got to the Army, I was still smoking cigars. And when I got to Vietnam, I realized that smoking cigars was hazardous to my health, both in terms of the lungs and in terms of people being able to find you. So I stopped smoking cigars in 1969, and after that, I never really smoked again, except a rare gift of a Cuban or something.

Grandma Bess

Bess was my mother's mother. Bess Eason. She had married my Grandpa, Sam Eason -- the one I grew up with on the ranch, the farm, chicken farm, cattle farm. Bess was another alcoholic on that side of the family. She was by all accounts very, very smart. She worked as a sort of high-level secretary at one point at Baker and Botts, as a legal secretary.

I have no idea about her education or upbringing, but when I knew her, as a young child -- I don't remember when my first memory of her was, but probably I didn't see her more than three or four times in my life. But at some point she came to Houston from wherever she was. But she was a terrible alcoholic, and my mother followed directly in her footsteps ultimately.

And at one point, when I was probably about six or seven, she got arrested for being drunk and naked under one of the bridges in Houston. I don't remember all of the details of that, except my father was extremely vocal about having to go deal with that situation. She seemed like a nice person when she was sober, like a lot of drunk people. But she had her problems. And it was not her first run-in with everything. She'd been in and out of the Austin State Hospital. Actually my mother, later on, was in and out of the Austin State Hospital, and various other facilities, rehab facilities.

I was twelve years old when Bess died. I think that was the first funeral I had ever gone to. Apparently, as I gathered the story up, she had moved to Austin and was living in some "flophouse" in Austin, and either fell or was pushed down a flight of stairs. The only thing I remember about the funeral was -- I think it was the first dead person I had ever seen -- and I couldn't quite figure out at that time why everyone involved in that funeral -- and there weren't many people -- but they all seemed to be relieved. And that was my Grandmother Bess.

School Newspaper

I would have to say that this little unfolding was probably the beginning of my writing life. I don't know why I was compelled to want to write stuff, but it happened early. I've never done much with it in the long run, but it's been a part of me.

I must have been in the third grade at Oak Forest Elementary School in Houston. And I don't know why, but I got this bug in my head that I wanted to do a school newspaper. There was no such thing!

So I went and talked to somebody in the, you know, administration office there at the school, and said, "Look, I want to do a school newspaper. Just put stuff in that's going on at school." And they said, "Oh! Well, that's a new thing!" (Laughter) They said, "Let's talk about it." And they said, you know, if I could type stuff up, for the newspaper -- and they approved it, or whatever -- they could mimeograph it. And I said, "What's mimeograph?" They said, "Well, we take the typewritten stuff, and we run it through this thing, with a crank, or whatever, and it just will print out as many copies as we want." And I said, "Okay!"

So I wrote a newspaper. I went around, gathering information here and there, I don't even know what. It was banal stuff. This was not me on some great trip of changing the world, this was me just having an idea and I wanted to see it come to fruition.

And I was gonna charge for it. And the deal I cut with the school was -- and they went along with it -- I was gonna charge a nickel for each little newspaper. I would get four cents and they would get a penny to cover all of the printing stuff.

So I started putting out this little school newspaper. I don't even remember what it was. It might have been the Oak Forest Elementary School Paper. Who knows? I don't even remember. There's no copies of it left in existence. And it didn't last very long, because it was not a real profitable enterprise (laughter) for anybody. But I put out probably -- over the course of a school semester -- I put out about one issue a month. And that was the beginning of my, certainly the beginning of my journalism career, which did actually evolve into something a little more substantive and valuable later on. But that was Ben Cunningham, Third Grade Cub Reporter and Editor and Publisher of his own newspaper.

Captain Midnight

When I was about eight or nine years old, I was getting hooked on all these superheroes, reading comic books, and so on. And I decided I wanted to be a superhero crime fighter. So one day, I called up the Houston Police Department -- they didn't have 911 in those days, it was some regular telephone number to get hold of them. And they answered and wanted to know what the problem was. And I said, "There's not a problem yet. I just wanted to let you know that my name is Captain Midnight" or Captain X, I don't remember what my name was. It was something like that. I had given myself a superhero name.

And they were very patient with me. (Laughter) They said, "What do you do?" And I said, "I'm going to be protecting the city." And they said, "Have you done anything to protect the city so far?" And I said, "I'm watching." (Laughter)

And I said, "I think there's crime in this town, and I'm going to be watching out for it, and I'm going to be reporting it." And they said, "Are you going to actually do anything about it?"

And I said something like, "Only if I have to, if the police don't show up in time." (Laughter)

They were very -- it was a very congenial conversation. And of course they could tell from my voice that I was just a kid. And afterwards, they said, "Thank you so very much. Keep us posted. Try to give us a call before you do anything."

And when I got off the phone, I was so embarrassed. I was thinking, "Well, that was stupid. If I'm going to be a superhero, why would I tell anybody about it?" I thought, "I hope I didn't mess everything up!"

Sniffing some Snuff

I think I was maybe 8 or 9 years old at the time. And my father had opened up a little apothecary -- not any kind of big drug-store, just a very small apothecary -- in North Harris County off of Hardy Road. Hardy Road at that time was way the hell out in the country. But he thought -- and he was absolutely right, but he was 20 years before right -- that that area of the county was gonna just grow like crazy. And it was very small -- maybe 1500 square feet. But he would get 4, 5, 6, 7 customers a day.

But there was all of this subterranean stuff going on between my mother and father even then, right? And I think this was one of these situations where my mother was saying, "You never spend any time with him. You need to spend time with him." And he said, "Okay, I'll take him to work with me." (Laughter)

So he took me to work with him one day, and of course, if I was going to work with him, I was going to work. So my job was to, like, sweep, and dust, and take out the trash -- whatever. So I'm spending my day doing that. And I filched an ice-cream sandwich out of the little freezer thing, you know. And a Coca-Cola. And Junior Mints.

So it's the most boring thing in the world, because I was gonna be there for 12 hours. Because it was open for 12 hours. So I've done everything there is to do, and I don't know what else there is to do. All I want to do is go do something, and there's nothing to do.

So I'm poking around the place, and he's back there -- he was also a compound, what was called a compound pharmacy. Doctors would send prescriptions to him that were not just out of a bottle, you had to compound them and build them. So he spent a lot of time doing that.

So I'm looking around for something to do, and he's got some, you know, cigarettes and cigars and chewing tobacco and snuff. And I'm looking at all that, and I'm thinking, "Snuff. Huh." And I filched one of the little round snuff boxes and I snuck out back into the little alleyway behind the pharmacy.

And I'm looking at it, and I'm thinking, "I wonder how people do snuff?" And I'm thinking, logically, "Oh, people must sniff snuff. Okay, I'll sniff it." So I opened the canister and I put it up to my nose and I inhaled deeply. And that's not how you do snuff, that's how you die. (Laughter)

All of a sudden I started sneezing, convulsing, flopping around on the ground. And somehow or another, my father found me out there in the alley, close to death. Or at least, I thought I was close to death. He threw a bunch of water in my face, and finally I kind of came to.

But that was my first and last ever experience with snuff.

David Collins

I had been transferred, I had moved out from Oak Forest to Spring Branch in the fourth grade. They had the choice of putting me -- because I was a mid-termer when I started school originally -- they either had to put me ahead a half a grade or back a half a grade. They put me back a half a grade so I would start out in the fourth grade, instead of the second semester. And my teacher was Miss Stencil, probably one of the best teachers I ever had in my life. But David Collins was -- we were crossways from the very beginning. And at some point, in the classroom, we got into a tiff, and we were pushing each other in the classroom, and it was disrupting the whole classroom.

And the classroom was -- at Woodview Elementary -- had these kind of big sliding doors in the classroom that opened up to the outside, you could open them up. And when Miss Stencil saw that we were getting crossways and disrupting the class, she stopped everything in the middle of her teaching, and she said, "That's it. We will not put up with this. If you guys need to fight, you go outside."

She opened up the doors, and we went outside, and we started to fist fight. Eh, it wasn't so much a fist fight as it was just sort of pushing, you know, wrestling and pushing. But we had a whole audience watching us, right? All the kids in the classroom, and Miss Stencil. So we were trying to, like, you know, start out hurting each other. But after a couple, three, four, five minutes, we were, like, thinking it's all pretty silly. And we started laughing. And we actually bonded and became good friends. After that, wrestling around, rolling on the ground, laughing, she said, "Okay, are you done?" And we said, "Yeah, we're done."

And we came back in the classroom and we were like her two best students for the rest of the whole semester. That was in the fourth grade. And of course, we became good friends, and so in the fifth grade, we did the Acme Brick thing.

Elder

Elder was an old black cowboy who lived in Gonzales County, and he would come out and help us when we were, you know, cutting steers, cutting bulls, making them steers, and rounding up cattle. He and I clicked immediately. I think I first met him when I was around five or six years old but by the time I was cowboying, you know, working cattle, I was probably nine or ten years old.

And there was sort of a rite of passage in that world in those days, and part of that rite of passage was learning how to castrate bulls to convert them into steers. And in those days, mostly it was done with pocket knives. Later it was clamps. But Elder was the one who was put in charge of teaching me how to cut a calf. And so with my old Case knife and his old Case knife, he taught me how to cut bulls, pull the testicles out. And the deal was that Elder got to take all the bull testicles with him -- it was a perk -- so they could cook them up and make what people call Rocky Mountain oysters.

But he was a great, great cowboy. I mean, at least in my mind, everybody in Gonzales County knew that he was one of the best cowhands ever that came down the pike. And he had a big family, but he took an interest in me, and we were close.

And we had a big pecan bottom down in Gonzales County, and every year we would let Elder and his family come out and harvest all the pecans. And they could have half and we would take half. And he taught me about riding horses, he made me a real horseman, taught me how, before horse whispering was ever known, taught me how to bond with horses. And he was sort of part of the family in a day when there was lots of segregation. But on my Grandpa's farm, in my Grandpa's mind, there was no segregation. These were all just humans working together. So for years, I considered Elder to be just another relative who was helping to raise me up.

I don't know whatever happened to Elder, but I do know that at one point, when I was older, after I got back from the war, I was up at my Grandpa's, and my Grandpa had already died, and Sarah and Jimmy Fogle had taken over the ranch. And I was there visiting, and all of a sudden there was this thing where somebody was down in the pecan bottom stealing pecans, and everybody armed up and headed down to the pecan bottom to catch all of these interlopers. And we got down there, and it was Elder's family, who were there to help harvest the pecans like they had done every year. Elder wasn't around anymore by that time, he had died. And I stopped what looked like was going to be a shooting war, kind of unbalanced considering that all the black folks down there that were gathering pecans were not armed. And I went over with them and said, "Nobody's doing anything about this, you don't know the real deal. And here's the real deal."

Acme Bricks

I guess I was in the, maybe fifth grade, whatever age that was, and there was going to be a talent show, fifth grade talent show. And my buddy, David Collins -- I had this great idea, a *great* idea, for a comedy sketch. And the comedy sketch was going to be Acme Bricks.

And we got together in each other's garages, and we were rehearsing this, and cracking each other up. I mean, we couldn't stop laughing, it was so damn funny. It was the most hysterical thing that either one of us had ever heard, and we were so enthusiastic about it.

And we got to the fifth grade talent show at Woodview Elementary School out in Spring Branch, and the parents are going to different little skits and sketches and whatever everybody's doing in each room. And we did this Acme Brick sketch. And we had the perfect, the perfect fall-on-the-floor-laughing kind of ending to this thing, that would just leave everybody just crying, while they were laughing, in stitches. And the ending, the hook to the whole thing was, in our mind, "Acme Bricks are the best bricks in town." We just couldn't get over how funny that was.

And so we did this sketch, and everybody's sitting, there were like seven, eight, ten people there, and they were in the little classrooms, and they're all sitting there, adults and children, staring at us as we're going through this hysterical thing, cracking each other up, you know, me and David, and they're all just, like, staring. And we could see that they don't seem to get it, these stupid people. And we finally get to the very end of the sketch, the big hook, and the big tag line, and the big ending is, we stand there, throwing our hands out, saying "Acme Bricks are the best bricks in town!"

And we're expecting this huge applause, people rising up, and just, like, screaming hysterically, and they're all sitting there staring at us. And we're standing there, and they all get up, as we're standing there waiting for the big applause, and they all walk out, slink out, of the room. And I'm thinking, you know, I don't think my course in life is stand-up comedy.

A Paddling to Near Kidney Damage

This was in fifth grade, at Woodview Elementary School, in Spring Branch. And I had gotten in trouble. It wasn't the first time in school I'd gotten in trouble. This time, the trouble was unfair.

I had been in class, and it was one of these situations where there was a substitute teacher. And Claude Blanchard, the principal of the school, had called the substitute teacher out of the class for some reason. And, you know, we were cutting up a little bit. But they were looking in through the window of the door to the classroom, and all of a sudden they barreled in there, and they yanked me out, because they said that I had shot the finger at them, given them the finger. Well, in truth, I had not. I mean, I still remember vividly that no, we were cutting up, but I had not shot the finger at anybody. Not to say that they didn't deserve it, but I was wrongly accused.

And Claude Blanchard came in and yanked me out of the classroom, took me down to the office, and said I would pay for this. And here's what he made me do. He made me pull my pants and my underpants down, and bent me over a chair or something, and he took a paddle to me. And he started whipping me with this paddle. I lost count -- I was counting, because I had never gotten, in school, up until then, more than two or three swats -- I stopped counting at twenty-something. And it kept going and going and going. And it was not just on my butt. It was on my legs and my butt and my back, and he was just out of control.

I somehow, after all of that, made my way home. It happened that my mother was home at the time, and my Aunt Icie and Uncle Benny. They were stunned when they saw what happened. I had bruising from about the back of my knees all the way up to the middle of my back. And they took me to the doctor, and they said there was kidney damage. And my Aunt Icie, who -- none of these people were usually on my side -- but all of a sudden, they were on my side, and they thought something had to be done about all of this.

And they called my father, who was at work at the pharmacy, and he actually said, "Well, I'll be home in like two hours," or something. And I'm listening from the bedroom -- I'm incapacitated, I'm in bed, and I'm in a considerable amount of pain -- but I heard them, and they were animated and talking, "You've got to do something about this, you've got to report this, you've got to do something about this." And I'm thinking, "Well finally, somebody's kind of looking out for me, and maybe justice will be done."

And in the end, my father and mother decided, "No, that would not be a good idea to rock the boat, it might get him in more trouble. And maybe he deserved it." So, yeah. I survived it, I didn't have kidney failure. They did take me to the doctor and I was out of school for a few days. But, you know, there was this notion that something was going to be done, and justice was going to be had, and finally I would get a little justice in this world, and no. They dropped it. They didn't do anything.

And so I just took that for what it was, and moved on, and kind of gutted my way through the rest of that year and sixth grade. And then, after that, I had junior high. But that's a little experience I never forgot, and in retrospect, it wasn't even the beating that I took, it was the fact that my parents -- it became clear to me at that time that, no, my father and mother were never going to rock the boat to take up for me. So I knew who the only person left in the world who was going to take up for me was, and it wasn't them.

Almost Killed at the Grocery Store

So I was 10ish, 11ish, I don't know. My Aunt Sissy was in town from San Antonio, or Kerrville, or wherever they were living at the time. Aunt Sissy was my mother's sister, only sister. They weren't raised together.

But they were in town, and my Aunt Sissy and my mother decided that they wanted to go to the grocery store, Track's Grocery Store, a few blocks away from our house, kind of out in semi-rural, west of Houston, near Addicks Dam. This was when I lived on Timber Oak.

So we went to the grocery store, and they were gonna send me in to get some, like, a couple of six packs of beer and a couple packs of cigarettes. So they pull up in front of the little convenience store, and I walk in.

And I get the stuff, I'm putting it up on the counter. And all of a sudden this drunk woman comes barreling through the front of the store in her car. And boom! Right where I am, at the counter. And it's devastating. I mean, the whole front of the building is crashed through, the glass doors and everything else. And the car winds up on top of where I was standing at the counter. And everybody gets hysterical, everybody's going crazy. And the whole, and things get, I mean, half of, all of the fixtures were destroyed coming in. Counters, cash register, everything. It's chaos.

And what I knew, but nobody else knew, was that I saw the car coming in, saw it crash through the front, I leaped, flew, over the counter, onto the other side of the counter. But the car, everybody thought I was underneath, dead, underneath the car, which is where I had been standing.

I had been knocked senseless, I was kind of out of it, but I was alive. And everybody -- and I kind of come to with everybody screaming and wailing and all of this kind of stuff, and I kind of crawl through the rubble from underneath the other side of the counter and come up, and it's as if everybody has seen a ghost. And then they start screaming even louder! And it's like, I'm standing there and I'm saying, "I'm okay."

And that was another one of those little times when I should not have been, not just okay, I should not have been alive.

Dress Designing

My great-uncle and aunt, the uncle of my mother, Uncle Ben K. Bering -- there was a time when my mother was in dire straits, I don't know which, maybe the Austin State Hospital, or somewhere where she was -- but anyway, I was ten or eleven years old. And Ben K. Bering was a Methodist preacher, hard-shell Methodist preacher, and his wife was my mother's aunt and my great aunt, "Icie" -- her name was actually Alice as well.

But he was ensconced in Galveston in the old Moody Mansion, I think, for the parsonage. But they also had a beach house that he had built by hand almost all by himself on Bolivar Peninsula. And actually this was a beach house that survived just about every single hurricane that ever came along, including Carla, and was finally destroyed in Katrina. But he was long dead by then. But it was a well built place. I give him credit for that.

There was a summer when for about three or four weeks I was going to be staying with them there. Somebody had the bright idea of sending me off for, to spend the "summer" -- which was really about three weeks -- and also my Aunt Sissy's oldest daughter Elizabeth. We were going to spend three or four weeks there, on the beach, at the beach house. We had to endure, of course, daily Bible sessions, but then we got some free time, and we could spend our free time -- well, I should say, my Aunt Sissy was really a good artist, wonderful artist. And Elizabeth, her daughter, had many of those skills. Actually, a number of her children did, including my crazy cousin Butch, who had some artistic talent. All more artistic talent than I had.

But we were spending this time together, and what Elizabeth was spending all of her time on -- and I realize now it was to get away from these crazy people, right? -- but she was designing dresses. She had paper dolls and she would design these dresses for paper dolls. And I kept trying to figure out what she was doing. She was at least five or six years older than I was. And I found it kind of interesting. And I said, "Can I play?" And she said, "Sure."

And we spent those few weeks designing dresses for our paper dolls. And it wasn't like we were -- I mean, we'd go to the beach -- but we weren't spending time at the beach. We were spending most of our time really obsessed with designing dresses for paper dolls! (Laughter)

And actually, that was one of the most enjoyable three weeks creatively that I had ever spent up until that time, and you know, I actually thought along the way, at certain periods of time, "Maybe I could be an artist" or "Maybe I could be a dress designer." And actually sometime in high school, we were

given these aptitude tests. And my aptitude test, like fresh-
man year of high school, was that I had the aptitude to be an
interior designer. Now put that together with my aptitude test
when I was in the Army, which was to be an infantry man.
(Laughter)

But those few weeks there on Bolivar Peninsula with my
cousin Elizabeth were really, really valuable from an artistic
perspective, because it opened up an arena and door into
something I had never seen before, which was, "Oh, you can
actually create something from absolutely nothing." And of
course, the downside of all of that was, we had to spend two
or three hours a day listening to basically preaching of some
really, really evangelical hardcore "Paulistic" Christianity. So it
was a double-edged sword -- it opened my eyes to art, and it
also opened my eyes to the insanity of that kind of Christianity.

Attacked by a Boxer

So I was in the fifth grade. We were living on Timber Oak
Street. And behind our house was a huge pasture. There were
horses out there, and I used to go out and sneak out there and
jump on the horses and ride them. You know, make friends
with them.

But I was cruising around back there one day, it was still
daylight, and all of a sudden here comes this boxer that was
enormous. I mean, you know, standing up on its hind legs, it
was taller than I was. And of course I wasn't very tall at the
time. (Laughter)

But here comes this damn boxer, and I have nowhere to go.
And it comes and attacks me. It jumps on me, and it's starting to bite, and I'm punching and I'm kicking. And I reach over
and finally find some stick or log or something, and I start
pounding on it. And I'm hollering and screaming, but nobody

can hear me. I'm thinking, "I'm gone. This thing's gonna rip my throat out." Because it was one of the meanest dogs I've ever come across in my life, and I've come across a few mean dogs. He had me in his sights, and he was going to kill me and eat me.

And I pounded and pounded and pounded, and finally knocked him silly. And I'm bitten all over the place, including a place on my head, up over my right eye, where the teeth marks were. But finally I beat him off, and off he goes. And he jumps a fence back into the yard of wherever he came from, way down the street. And I was bleeding, and I was scared, and I was angry, and I went chasing after the bastard. (Laughter) And I found him in the yard. And the people were trying to pull him into the house. And I started yelling and cussing at them, and saying, "That dog is gonna be dead! I'm coming after it!" And they're yelling and screaming, saying, "He wouldn't hurt a flea!" (Laughter)

So, at any rate, that was, in the bigger scheme of things later on, in terms of the things that happened in my life, that wasn't the most dramatic or horrifying or dangerous thing, but for that time and that place, it was a pretty dangerous and horrifying and scary situation. But somehow, you know, I skated.

Segregated Bus Station

So I was 11 or 12 at that time -- I was old enough to ride the bus by myself to wherever. And I was going to ride the bus back to Houston from Gonzales. My Grandpa dropped me off at the bus station. And I had the, whatever it cost, three or four dollars at the time, to make the bus trip back to Houston, and my parents were going to pick me up in Houston.

And I got to the bus station and I got inside, and it was kind of weird because I walked in through one of the doors, and there was nobody but black people in there. And the black people were kind of agitated, or concerned, and they said, "You can't be in here." And I said, "Well, no, I'm taking the bus back to Houston." And they said, "No, no, you've got to be in the other section." I said, "What other section?" And they said, "You've got to be in the white section. And that's through that door over there." And I said, "No, I'm going to Houston on the bus, doesn't this bus go to Houston?" And they said, "Yeah, it does, but you can't ride with us because we're in the back of the bus and you're white, you've got to be on the other side."

And I didn't get it. I mean, I sort of halfway got it, but I couldn't believe -- no, no, this is a different time, you know, this, no, this can't be right. And so then some representative of the Kerrville -- it was either the Greyhound or the Kerrville Bus Company -- they came in and said, "Son, you've got to come over here. You're riding in this" And I had never realized until that moment that buses, and bus stations, and I guess every other kind of station, were segregated. And I didn't want to ride, I didn't want do that, I said, "No, I'm here, I'll ride with these folks." And everybody was against me. The black folk were against me. The white folk were against me. And the consensus was, "No, you'll ride where you are supposed to be." And I've never forgotten that.

Chapter 2

Adolescence: Ages 12 to 18

Fish Hook in the Eye

So I was about 12 years old. And my Aunt Sissy and her family, which included crazy cousin Butch, and Elizabeth -- they lived in Kerrville. And occasionally I would head out to Kerrville to see them. I would ride the bus. Actually, one time, I was invited to come up there by my Uncle Owen, who was my crazy cousin Butch's stepfather, and husband of Aunt Sissy, to go deer hunting. I had my 30-30 Winchester saddle rifle and went and got on a city bus in Houston to go to the Greyhound bus station downtown, carrying it in my lap, and nobody ever -- it didn't mean anything to anybody, in those days. Got on the Greyhound bus and went to Kerrville.

So anyway, on one of these trips to Kerrville, my crazy cousin Butch and I decided we were going to go fishing down on the Guadalupe. So we're down fishing, and we've got these little spinning reels, throwing them out into the water. And I'm walking behind my crazy cousin Butch -- this is one of the few times when he didn't do something to me on purpose, that injured me -- but it still injured me. He decided to cast, and he threw back his spinning rod, and cast it, but it came up and caught me in the eye -- I think it was my left eye. I get hooked in my eye by a three-pronged fish hook. Of course, I'm hollering, and my crazy cousin Butch, who generally would not care anything about anything, all of a sudden had a moment of, like, empathy -- "Oh my god! Oh my god!"

And so he goes and gets help and somehow I'm taken with him to the emergency room of the Sid Peterson Hospital, I think it was, at that time. And I'm sitting in the emergency room, I've got this fuckin' fish hook in my eye, and I'm thinking I'm going to be blind forever in my left eye. And I'm sitting there, and I'm sitting there, for almost four hours, because the problem was that the emergency room doctor on call was out deer hunting, and they had to send out search parties to go find the emergency room doctor, and meanwhile, all of these hours, I'm thinking it's just getting worse and worse. I can't really blame my crazy cousin Butch for that, because it was truly an accident, it wasn't one of those many on-purpose kind of attacks.

But anyway, the doc finally drags in, takes a look at it, after four or four-and-a-half hours, and he says, "Okay, well, here's the deal." And the fish hook is still hanging in my eye! And he says, "Here's the deal. I don't think it did any real damage, but I've got to figure out how to get it out of there." So there's discussion with the nurses and the docs and they figure out, "Okay, what we need to do is to go in and get, like, a pair of wire cutters, and clip the part in front of the barbs, and once we do that, we can just pull it out." And so that's what they did -- they clipped it, they pulled it out, bandaged it up, and they said, "We think you might still have some eyesight in that eye, but keep this bandage on, and get to a doctor, if you're not here, get to a doctor in another week or so, and figure out if you've lost the vision in that eye." And I'm thinking, "There's never been a time when I've gotten together with my crazy cousin Butch that something bad didn't happen."

But I finally got back to Houston and went to the doctor -- might have been my old doctor that actually delivered me, Nick Adamo -- and he looked at it and he said, "Yeah, I think you're gonna do okay. You might have a little droopy problem with that eye someday, but I don't think you're gonna lose your vision." And as it turns out, I had 20/20 vision for probably, up until the time I was like 65 years old.

Saving a Child from a Water Moccasin

I was maybe 12 years old. I don't remember. Somewhere around there. We were living on Timber Oak Street out by Addicks Dam in Houston.

So one day, this mother from across the street comes running over, banging on the door, screaming and hollering, and saying, "My baby! My baby!" She said, "There's a snake!!"

So I go over there. My mother followed me, kind of listing. (Laughter) And I get to their house, and they have a sliding glass door leading to a back patio. I look at the door, and the toddler is, I don't know, 18 to 20 months old, and she was sitting out on the patio with a snake on her.

It was a water moccasin. And of course, by that time, I knew the danger of water moccasins. I had dealt with them before. And the mother was hysterical. And other people in the house were trying to deal with the mother.

So I opened the door. And the snake was all over this child. And the child is just sitting there. I went onto the patio and closed the door. And then I got a hoe or a shovel, something. So I walked very slowly toward the child, and told her not to move, and I got close enough to flip the snake off of her, real quick. And then I went after it and killed it. I decimated it.

We didn't know if the child had already been bitten at that point. But she hadn't. She survived. And that was the only contact we had with that family in all the years we lived on Timber Oak. (Laughter)

Sword-Fighting with Butch at the Farm

I was about 12 years old, and my crazy cousin Butch was about 16. We were living at Grandpa's, and it was during the big drought. Things were terrible.

Grandpa had to go off to East Texas -- to, I think it was Jasper -- because there was kinfolk over there. I'm not sure what he was going over there for -- maybe a funeral or something. But he was gonna be gone about four days. So he left us in charge of the place. And it was kind of a big deal. You know, "Oh, boy, he's put the whole thing in our hands. We're in charge!" Right?

So things were going okay. I mean, it wasn't like Butch and I were fighting every minute. I mean, sometimes we were buddies, and sometimes he would go crazy and we were not buddies. But it was just, whatever it was.

But things were going okay. We were pretty proud of everything. But one day, during the course of this four days, some shit started in the house. And Grandpa had a couple of very old swords that belonged to past relatives. They might have been from the Civil War, or some other war. But there were two swords in the house. And I was always fascinated with the swords; I'm kind of a sword/knife guy.

But one day we were messing around in the house, doing something, and we got into, like, a fake fight in the house, with the swords. And one of us said, "We gotta take this outside."

So we're outside. And, you know, the house was, like, 30 or 40 feet away from the mailbox and the road out there. And we got out there, and we were just playing around. But it kept getting more competitive.

Oh, and by the way, we were both in our underwear. The only thing we were wearing was our underwear. But we didn't care, because we were out in the middle of nowhere, and nobody ever came around. I mean, maybe once every two days, somebody would come up or down the road.

But we're out there, clinking around, joking around, and things kept getting a little more serious. Finally, we're out there in the middle of the road, and we're having a real sword fight. And it's life or death kind of stuff.

And we're clinking and clanking and fighting, and all of a sudden, there's this old truck coming down the road. We stop and look, and we went, "Oh my God, it's Gram!" Gram was our great-grandmother -- my Grandpa's mother. So she stops the truck, and we're standing there with these swords in our underwear in the middle of the road. And she gets out and she says, "BENNY!! BUTCH!! What are you doing out here?!?!"

So we have to come up with this elaborate story -- "Oh no, we're just playing," and so on. But, had she not come up there, one of us might have been either severely wounded or dead.

Safe Spot for My Sisters

So, life growing up, for certain periods of time, was not without its challenges. We moved from Chippendale Road out to Spring Branch near Addicks Dam, and we lived in a little kind of urban subdivision -- you know, middle class tract houses -- but in a rural environment. We lived on a street called Timber Oak -- 10926 Timber Oak.

I was maybe in the fourth grade, so maybe 10 years old. And my mother was starting to go downhill faster with each accumulating year. And by the time I was 12, things had gotten pretty bad. I had to become the protector of my two younger sisters because my mother, in her mental illness and drunken rages -- because it was a combination of both for her -- would lash out. And it got to a point to where I would always step in to take the brunt of whatever the lashing out was.

And the lashing out was not just horribly verbally assaulting -- that was something I learned to deal with very early on -- nobody could get through my walls with verbal assaults. But there was always the physical assaults. And it wasn't always directed at me, but I would have to step in to keep my sisters from getting beaten. And it wasn't just hand slaps, it was anything that came to hand -- switches, hair brushes, kitchen implements, boards, whatever it was. And these could have -- sometimes actually were, when I wasn't around -- severe beatings of my sisters. I could take a severe beating -- it didn't matter to me.

But it dawned on me that I was off at school, and I wasn't always at home when they were at home, because Susan might have been in kindergarten, and only there half a day, and we came and went at different times on the school buses. So I decided I was gonna build a safe spot for my sisters. And the weird thing is, and sort of, what I thought, was kind of the ultimate ironic thing, was that it was in my parents' closet.

The master bedroom had this huge, huge walk-in closet. It was at least two or two-and-a-half times the size of a normal walk-in closet. And of course by that time, my mother had become a terrible, terrible housekeeper. And one of the things in their walk-in closet were all these unpacked boxes and stuff from the previous move on Chippendale that never were gonna be opened and dealt with -- at least not by my drunken mother, and of course, my father was gone 12 to 14 hours a day "working" and hiding out from my mother.

So I figured out how to go into that closet and rearrange things to where I created a little tunnel that went through the boxes into a safe space behind the boxes, with boxes on top of that. And I showed my sisters -- when my mother was out of the house for something, had gone to the store or doctor or who knows what -- but I showed them where all this was. And I swore them to absolute secrecy. "You can never, never let anybody know this is here. And you can't ever, ever, *ever* tell Mama. And you can't ever, ever, *ever* let her see you get in there."

So for years, when she was on a rampage, they ran in different -- I showed them how to run in different directions. And showed -- Candy was the oldest, but Susan was the most agile and tough. So Susan's job was to get our mother to follow her while Candy made her way into the safe spot. And Susan was agile enough to be able to duck and dodge and get away from my mother and get into the safe spot. But before she did that, the rule was, she had to open an exterior door and slam it before she made her way to the safe spot.

And it was a pretty elaborate plan. And it worked. It was never discovered, for years -- I don't know, three, four, five years -- maybe not until we moved from that house back over to a different house. And I don't know what went on in that safe space, but I often have wondered, what were the conversations, the whispered conversations, what were the thought processes that were going on in that safe spot during all those years.

Salty and the Cactus Patch

So, during my lifetime on the ol' ranch and chicken farm at the property on Sandy Fork Creek in Gonzales, we had two horses. The first horse was Salty. He was kind of a Palomino. We also had Dan, who was a good horse, a good working horse. But Salty had character. And I'd ride Salty out to be looking for cattle, for where the cattle were, and sometimes looking for where the pregnant cows were, so we could wrangle them up, right? And sometimes I'd just ride him for fun. Salty was a really good horse. Except Salty had one little problem. He would mind you like nobody's business until he got in sight of the barn coming back, and then there was no stopping Salty from heading to the barn. And he could see it, you know, a quarter or half mile away.

And on one of these little jaunts, when I was 12-ish -- I mean, all Salty cared about was getting back to the barn -- Salty all of a sudden sees the barn, or senses the barn, and just takes off like a bat out of hell, and he's not responding to anything that I'm doing. He had a mission, he was on a mission, and it was a mission from God, and there was nothing that was gonna stop him. And as I tried to rein him in, and you know, all these kinds of things, he got irritated with me, and he runs me down a fence line, a barbed-wire fence line, just, like, cutting me on all the left hand side of my body. (Laughter)

And then he gets to this giant, giant patch of prickly pear cactus, which is probably about the size of half of our bedroom. And he got there, and right before he went into the patch, he stopped dead stop, and I go flying over Salty into (laughter) this prickly pear cactus patch, and I thought I was dead. I've got, like, thousands of prickly pear needles in my body. And Salty takes off for the barn.

And somehow, I get out of there, and I look like a prickly pear cactus. And I get back to the farmhouse and my Grandpa and his common-law wife at the time, Jewel -- who was a wonderful woman, she was a nurse, worked in town in Gonzales -- but she spent at least three days pulling cactus out of my body.

And did I ever ride Salty again? Oh, yes. (Laughter) But I knew Salty better by then, and I knew that there were better ways to get him back to the barn than through all the cactus country!

Locked in a Chicken House Overnight

So it was always Butch and me living on my Grandpa's farm. This was when I was about 12 years old, and he was about 16.

And in the mornings, we had to go out and open up the chicken houses. We had to go in and pick up all of the dead chickens, clean every single water trough, these long water troughs, and it all had to be done by hand. And then we had to feed the chickens. And that was hours' worth of work.

And then in the evenings, we had to come and close down the chicken houses. And all the chicken houses had these big shutters that opened up. So we closed the shutters and locked them.

So I'm in one of the big chicken houses. We had a number of chicken houses. But this one had probably twenty-thousand chickens in it. So I'm in there, taking care of something, and Butch is closing up. And then he locks everything up, and locks me in the chicken house. There was no way to get out. The doors are locked, the outside shutters are locked.

So I'm thinking, "Yet again, how stupid could I be to ever trust this guy?" So I'm trying to figure out what to do with myself. And it's getting to be nighttime. And I tried all the doors and shutters, and there's no way to get out. So I know I'm there for the night.

But I'm stewing. I'm not sleeping. I'm trying to figure a way out. And inside this big chicken house was this big feeder. And the way this feeder worked was, they put tons -- they come deliver chicken feed, and there was a big chute on top of the chicken house where the feeder thing would go in and then shoot all this chicken feed down into the bin.

So I crawled up into the bin to explore it. And I started crawling up the chute, and I made my way up to the roof. And I could see that I could get to the roof.

So I went back down and sat there all night long. I'm not waiting for dawn, because you have to open up the chicken houses before daylight. And I knew he had to come out and open up the chicken houses and he would be expecting me to be in there.

So at about 6 in the morning, I had found myself a four-foot length of two-by-four. And I had pulled that up the chute with me, and I'm sitting on the roof, with this two-by-four. And I'm waiting.

As soon as he gets there, right when he's about to open the door, I jump down off the roof and I crack him over the head with this two-by-four.

So he's screaming and hollering. I haul him back to the house, and we get in the truck with Grandpa and drive to Gonzales. And old Doc Siever sews him up. It took about 17 or 18 stitches, but he learned a lesson, which was, hey, fuck with me, I'm gonna come at you.

But things were tense -- if things hadn't been tense between us before then, things became forever tense between us. Especially because all my Grandpa could talk about was that I kicked Butch's ass. And that was the accelerant for how things got way out of whack, real quick, because all Butch lived for was the approval and love of Grandpa. And I was forever after his rival.

Throwing Knives at My Sisters

I have to preface this by saying that, as I was growing up out in Gonzales -- where Indians used to roam, including Apaches and the occasional Comanches, and maybe some other Indian groups, because there were many Indian campsites on our place off of Sandy Fork Creek -- but at some point, I became enamored of becoming an Indian. One of the things that I started doing when I was very young, probably from the time I was six or seven years old -- I first started out with, you know, what every Texas boy does in this world, playing mumbly-peg or something with knives -- where you stand there in front of the other guy, and you take turns throwing pocket knives on either side of their foot to see who can get closer to the foot.

But I had graduated to bigger knives, and I would spend time at Sandy Fork Creek running and moving barefoot, trying to make my feet as tough as an Indian's feet. And I would take a knife with me and I would practice knife throwing -- these were good sized knives, these were hunting knives. And I would practice throwing them at trees, and in the dirt, and everywhere else. That was probably from the time I was like, I don't know, six or seven years old, on. By the time I got to be 12 years old, I was a pretty good knife thrower. I still am, actually.

But my sisters, Candy and Susan -- I was about four years older than Candy and about five or six years older than Susan -- they just worshipped the ground I walked on somehow. And I would use them for knife throwing practice -- and this is back in Houston, not on the farm. But back in Houston, when I wasn't out on the ranch where I could do all this stuff, I would put them up against trees and tell them to, like, spread eagle, and I would throw knives at them. (Laughter) And we're not talking about, you know, little paring knives or anything, we're talking about hunting knives. And they happily -- I mean, they could not have ever imagined that there could have been an accident. And I was so stupid at that age, and thought I was so good, that I couldn't imagine that there could ever have been an accident. And for maybe a year or so, I threw knives at them.

And it was like something off a TV show, you know, when they're throwing the knives, and it sticks beside their head, or between their legs, or under their arms. I never missed! And at some point, I read something or saw something on TV about some professional knife thrower that actually hit somebody, and I thought, "Oh. I guess this could be dangerous." (Laughter) And so that's when I stopped throwing knives at my two sisters. But thankfully, neither of them was ever even nicked by one of my throws.

Blind Marvin

This is a story -- back when I was about 12 years old or so -- which was around 1960ish -- those were not real politically correct days, I will just say. But on Saturdays, when we were out at Sandy Fork Creek, spending the whole week raising chickens, working cattle, doing whatever we could to hard-scrabble our way to survive out there during the Great Drought of the late '50's, around to 1960 -- but at any rate, we would be out there all week working, and on Saturdays, we'd go into Gonzales, Texas.

And the usual drill was, we'd head in, in the old 1953 Chevy Apache pickup truck, and we'd go to the 3-2 Bar, which is now, in the place where, I think it's called, I don't know, the Long-branch, or something like that, in Gonzales. It's been through many incarnations. It was also the bar where, the legend went, John Wesley Hardin, the notorious gunfighter back in the day, who actually wound up being shot and killed in El Paso, but lived in Gonzales for awhile, back in the late 1800's, and he became, somehow, a lawyer -- I guess he read the law or something. But the story went that it was in the 3-2 Bar, or whatever it was called at the time in the 1800's, that some badass cowboy was in the bar, standing next to John Wesley Hardin, and was spittin' tobacco into one of the spittoons that was down at the bottom of the bar. Those spittoons were still there in the 1900's when I was going to the 3-2 bar. But at any rate, in the 1800's, this cowboy spit and missed the spittoon and spit chewing tobacco all over John Wesley Hardin's boots. John Wesley Hardin commenced to pull his pistol and shoot the guy dead. So that was the 3-2 Bar. But it was a little less violent in the times that I was there.

And on Saturdays we would drive into town and spend basically the day at the 3-2 Bar, at least my Grandpa would, with the usual cast of characters. There was Blind Marvin, there was Spastic Sonny, there was Fats, there was my Grandpa Sam, and then one or two other stragglers. Well, Blind Marvin was blind because he'd been in Italy during World War II and gotten shot and had gone blind. Spastic Sonny -- and I know all this is awfully politically incorrect -- but these were how these people were known, and they were happily known that way in those days -- Spastic Sonny was epileptic and spastic. He was a handful sometimes. Sometimes, the younger of us kids, when he was going to get a haircut, would go to watch, just because it was such a challenge for the barber to be cutting his hair. And of course we thought this was just hysterical. But we loved Spastic Sonny, he was a friend. I mean, he was older, he was grown, barely grown.

But Blind Marvin had been around for awhile, and I came to really like Blind Marvin. He was an expert on everything. He just held forth on everything, he was the intellectual of the group. He could tell you the population of any city in the whole world, that you asked. The only problem was, as I found out later, when I was grown -- he just made this shit up. (Laughter) He said one time that the population of New York City, when somebody said, they were testing him, "Okay, Marvin, what's the population of New York City?" And he said, "24,319," or something like that, and they'd all go, "God! How do you know all this stuff?!" Because everybody else around him, including me, and everybody else, we were stupid. We had no idea. But he said it with such certainty, that you know, we believed it.

So one day, during the course of these years -- when I'd get dragged to the beer joint, and I'd be sitting there watching

them all play, you know, 42 and dominoes and Shoot the
Moon and all that kind of stuff -- one day they were talking,
and somebody asked Blind Marvin, "So Marvin, I mean, what
do you miss about not having your sight?" And Blind Marvin
thought about it for a minute, and he said, "You know, I think
the main thing I miss is hunting, most especially squirrel hunting. I used to love to hunt those tree rats." So by the time all
of this kind of unraveled for another hour or two, and it was
time to leave and head back to the place, out on Sandy Fork,
my Grandpa said, "Marvin, you're coming with us." And Marvin said, "What are you talking about?" And my Grandpa said,
"Well, we're gonna go hunting. We're gonna go squirrel hunting."

And so we all piled into, and I'm driving -- and I was 12 years
old -- because my Grandpa was drunk by then and Marvin was
drunk or half drunk. And you know, I'm driving, Marvin's sitting in the middle, and my Grandpa's sitting shotgun, in the
pickup truck. And we're driving along, and this is on the drive
back from Gonzales to the place, and they're talking about
hunting, and Blind Marvin all of a sudden blurts out something
like, "Yeah, and the next thing I miss most about being blind
is not driving, I used to love to drive." And my Grandpa, in his
cups, said, "Pull this rig over!" So I pulled over to the side of the
road, and he said, "Marvin, you're gonna drive for awhile." And
by this time, I mean, I'm not stupid, (Laughter) I know there
are dangers involved here, that's the reason I was driving, because they were drunk, right? And so I said, "I don't think this
is a good idea, Grandpa." And he said, "Son, the man needs to
drive, let him drive." So Blind Marvin got behind the wheel of
the pickup truck, and we drove for about 20 feet before he ran
into a ditch. (Laughter)

And so then I got to be driver again, and we pulled, got the
thing out of the ditch, and we get out to the place. And my
Grandpa goes in and he gets a pistol, a .38 caliber pistol. And

he told Marvin, "Look, I'm giving you the pistol to shoot with because it'll be easier than trying to wrangle a rifle, because I'll be able to tell you where to aim it, to get the squirrels." So we get into the pickup truck and we drive down to the old pecan bottom on Sandy Fork Creek, and I park our truck right in the middle of this pasture. They get out, and my Grandpa is over there, looking up in the trees, waiting for a squirrel to come. And he sees a couple squirrels. So he puts the gun in Blind Marvin's hand, and he says, "Okay, Marvin, just listen to me. Go up with the pistol, now over to your right. No, no, a little over to your left. No, a little over... right, right there!" And so Blind Marvin pulls off a shot or two. Doesn't hit anything, just hits the leaves up in the tree and everything.

But my Grandpa was standing right next to him, and it deafened my Grandpa, he couldn't hear a damn thing after that. And my Grandpa started yelling at Blind Marvin, "No, goddammit, you missed them, Marvin, listen to what I'm telling you, grab that pistol, now up, up, no higher, higher, no over to the left, no more, no to your right, all the way to your right." And Blind Marvin turns all the way around, to where, he's facing the pickup truck now. I'm out of the pickup truck watching this great catastrophe going on, and the next thing I know, my Grandpa says, "Shoot!" And Blind Marvin pulls the trigger. I'm standing at the side mirror on the pickup truck. It hits the side mirror, almost kills me, something from the mirror nicked my ear. And my ear's bleeding. Blind Marvin says, "Did I get it, Sam? Did I get it, Sam?" And my Grandpa grabs the pistol from him and cracks him over the head with the pistol and says, "You damn near killed my grandson!"

So Blind Marvin's knocked out, on the ground. My Grandpa comes over to see if I've been shot. We haul Blind Marvin back to the house -- and, you know he's knocked out but he's okay. But we had him in the bed of the pickup truck. And my Grandpa tells me, while Marvin is still knocked out, he tells me to go out to the barn and kill a rat. So he gives me a feed bag and sends me out to the barn. And I'm bleeding like a stuck pig from my ear. And I find a rat and I kill it, and I put it in the bag and I bring it back.

And meanwhile, he's been tending to Blind Marvin, and Blind Marvin's got a big gash in his head from my Grandpa pistol-whipping him, and Blind Marvin starts coming to a little bit. And my Grandpa says, "Give me the bag." And I give him the bag. And he says, "Here, Marvin, feel this bag." And Marvin's feeling it and he says, "What the hell?" And my Grandpa says, "You got it Marvin. You got that damn squirrel." And it was just this big rat inside that bag. And Marvin was just as happy as a fucking clam. And that's the story of Blind Marvin's big squirrel hunt.

The Best Little Whorehouse in Texas

So this was when I was about 12 years old, you know, living up on the farm with Grandpa and my crazy cousin Butch. It was a Saturday. We worked all week on the ranch and on Saturdays we would go into town and my Grandpa would go to the 3-2 Bar. And when Grandpa was done drinking and it was time to go home, we get to the pickup truck and he says, "Well, I think it's time you boys got bred." I thought he was talking about bread -- I thought we were gonna stop by the grocery store. And Grandpa was three, four sheets to the wind, so Butch was driving that day.

So we're in the pickup truck, and we start driving, and Grandpa starts giving directions, and we don't stop in Gonzales. We get on, you know, Highway 90, and we start heading east. And we get to La Grange, and he gives directions this way and that way and down some long old dirt road, and we wound up at the Chicken Ranch. The Chicken Ranch is famous in terms of having been romanticized and everything in *The Best*

Little Whorehouse in Texas, but I didn't know anything about it at the time.

We got there, and it was just a bunch of little white wooden shacks, basically, kind of all separated and interconnected and whatnot. And Grandpa gets in there, he goes in, and he's in there for a couple of minutes, and he comes back out with Miss Edna, or whoever the madame of the place was. And he says, "Okay, boys, you're going in with her, she's gonna get you all situated."

And I didn't know what in the heck was going on, I had no idea what was going on. I mean, I was starting to get little inklings that this was weird. But we go in and, you know, there's this fancy little room that we're in, in a shack, you know, with red velvet stuff and couches. And these women come in to where we're sitting down, and one of them comes over. And Butch picks one, and I'm not doing anything. And some other woman comes up to me, a really old, old, old woman -- she must have been in her thirties. (Laughter) She seemed old to me. And she said, "You come with me."

So we went -- and there were all these little rooms back in there, little bedrooms -- and we get in this bedroom, and it's starting to dawn on me what this place is, and I'm pretty nervous and not really ready or invested in any of this stuff. And she sits there for a minute and she says, "How old are you?" And I said, "Twelve." And she just shook her head, and she said, "Look, here's what's gonna happen. We're gonna stay in this room for about 30 or 40 minutes, and nothing's gonna happen except we're just gonna sit and talk." And that so relieved me. And she said, "Would you like a Coca-Cola?" And I said, "Yes, ma'am, I would love a Coca-Cola." And so she went down the hall and she got a couple of Cokes and she brought them back. And we sat there talking in kind of low voices for, you know, fifteen or twenty minutes.

After about fifteen minutes, she sticks her head out and checks around, and came back and said, "Well, your brother" -- she thought Butch was my brother -- "your brother has already gone, he's done, he's already gone out to the pickup truck." I said, "Okay, yes ma'am, I can go now?" And she said, "No. We're gonna sit here for another 10 or 15 minutes. Because when you leave here, you're gonna have bragging rights." And I said, "Yes, ma'am." (Laughter)

So we sit there talking, you know, and she's telling me all about her history -- I don't remember anything about it now, except that once, she had gone to UT for awhile, or something like that, that's all I remember of it -- and she came from somewhere, she was telling me her whole life history. But I was so nervous and out of touch with reality that I wasn't paying much attention, I just wanted to get out of there. And so finally she says, "Okay, you can go now. But I'm gonna follow you to the door." So she followed me to the door, and we walked outside on the porch, and she gave me a kiss. And waved at me as I went back to the pickup truck.

And all of that did not escape my Grandpa and my crazy cousin Butch. I got back to the pickup truck -- oh, and she had told me, "Whatever you do, if they ask you anything about what went on, you just say 'I'm not talking about it.'" And I said, "Okay." And so I get back to the truck, and Butch is just fuming furious, because he was in and out of there in seven or eight minutes. (Laughter) And he was about 15 or 16 at the time, right? And we're driving back to Gonzales, and all the way, my Grandpa was just talking about me, and "Boy! Did you see how long he was in there?!" (Laughter) "Wooh! And did you see her coming out to give him a kiss when he left?!" (Laughter) He said, "I know what that was all about!"

And you know, one of them, maybe my Grandpa, said, "What was it like?" And I said, "I promised her we wouldn't talk about it." And that made it even more mysterious to them. So that's how I got bragging rights on my first and only visit to the Best Little Whorehouse in Texas. And after that, of course, my crazy cousin Butch had many reasons to hate me, but that became one of his biggest reasons for a long time afterwards, maybe even until this day, if he's still alive.

Ralph Greer's Spooky House

So, when I was 12 or 13ish, there was a kid I knew at school. Well, first of all, let me back up and say, we lived sort of in the semi-country, a semi-rural area of far west Houston, very close to Addicks Dam. But everything around our little subdivision that I lived in was all rural stuff.

And there was this kid that I rode on the school bus with named Ralph Greer. Ralph was a weird one. He had these dark, dark, dark eyes that looked like he never got any sleep -- one of those kind of things. But I kind of started chatting with him and we kind of made friends. And he lived about a mile-and-a-half, down in the countryside, from where our little subdivision was.

And I got invited over to his house one day. His house was a big old farm house on a number of acres, and he lived with his aunt and his grandmother. And it was a spooky looking place. And the first time I ever went over there, I was only allowed into one little room, it was a little parlor. The rest of the house, they made it clear to me -- the aunt and the grandmother -- that, "You cannot be anywhere but in this room." And I thought that was pretty freaky.

But they were nice, the grandmother and the aunt seemed nice enough, they weren't spooky. Except as time went by, they got a little spookier. But I started spending some time over there. And out on their property, probably about 100 yards from the farm house, there was this tree that I kept eyeing. It looked -- this was a great tree. And I would climb up in the tree sometimes and think about, "This is a strange place, what am I doing here?" And then I thought, "This is a good place to hide out in case anything weird goes on here that I am not quite . . .," because I had a sense that there was something.

So I shimmied up the tree, and got up in some branches, and there waa, like, a few huge limbs that came together in one spot, that made like a little sitting space. And I thought, "Wow, this is very cool." And I started climbing up there and writing.

And then back in the house, when I would get back in the house -- they started quizzing me. "What are you doing in the tree?" I said, "I'm just sitting, writing a little bit." "What are you writing?" "I don't know, like, a little poetry or something." And the grandmother and the aunt looked at each other, and smiled at each other, and they said, "We knew you were writing poetry. We knew you belonged here."

So at one point, even though I was only allowed in this one little parlor, everybody was away from that parlor for a minute at some point in all of this time -- we're talking about a few months -- and I decided to look around. And I went into the next room. And it had shrunken heads, it had skeletons, it had bows and weird arrows, little bitty bows and weird arrows. There was all this stuff in there. It was fascinating, but I thought, "Woah, what's all this about?"

So as time went by, one of them -- aunt or grandmother -- busted me, caught me in that room, looking at all these objects. And they said, "What are you doing?" I said, "Well, this is all just, where does all this come from?" And they said, "We don't know if we can tell you yet." I said, "I won't tell anybody else."

And at one point -- and there's lots of stuff in between -- they decided to kind of explain some of the stuff in there. And they had in there, whoever the patriarch of the family had been, and they had grown up with the patriarch in South America, and that's why there were shrunken heads in there and all this stuff. And they said, "Yes, and do not touch, whatever you do, do not touch the arrow points, because they're all poisonous." I said, "Okaaaay."

But that wasn't even the biggest mystery to me. That, to me, was fascinating. The biggest mystery was that I spent the night over there a few times, but I had to stay down in the parlor, and they all went up the stairs -- Ralph Greer, his grandmother, his aunt. And they told me -- all of them, at separate points -- "Do not ever, ever come upstairs."

And it was pretty freaky, you know? But I still, at night, when I spent the night over there -- and I was by myself, because he was upstairs with them -- and you know, all these things are going through my head, and it was like, "How weird is all of this!" And I was looking around, and there were poison arrows, and there was this and there was that, and I didn't know what to touch and what not to touch. And there were knives, and there were skulls, and there were -- actually, there were a number of skulls. And I'm thinking, "I think I may be in a really bad situation here." And I could hardly sleep.

So one night -- the last night I ever spent there -- I heard people coming down the stairs. And I crept out and I went to my tree place, where nobody else could access, because it was like 30, 35 feet up in the air. And I climbed up in my tree, in my little trough, and I slept there. And the next morning, the aunt was gone, the grandmother was gone, and Ralph Greer was gone. And I boogied out of there like nobody's business. And I never saw any of them again after that. They weren't there anymore. They had disappeared.

Junior High Dance Lessons

When I was in junior high school, I was at Spring Woods Junior High School. And I was in on the cusp of when they were changing over years for high school and junior high school. So,

it used to be that high school started in the tenth grade. But
when I went into junior high, I went in in the seventh grade.
And they switched it around, after that, while I was in the middle of all that, that junior high school would be sixth, seventh, and eighth, and then high school would be ninth, tenth,
eleventh, and twelfth. Nobody cares about any of that, but it
means, for this story, that I was only in junior high school for
two years.

We had — my little group of friends — there were a few
of us who had, you know, little crushes and things on a few
girls. And these girls all, apparently, had mothers and fathers.
(Laughter) So two or three of the mothers got together, because they knew we were all — because they — we would go
over to their houses. And they said, "Look," the mothers said,
"you're not going to take our daughters to any of the junior
high school dances unless you and our daughters go together
and take dance classes at the Oaks Dads' Club," which is kind
of like a YMCA. And not only that, but we couldn't even, like,
you know, continue to associate with them, if we didn't do
this. So it was kind of a real *quid pro quo*. (Laughter)

So reluctantly, we all said okay. Because who would not do
whatever it took to, you know, get a little closer to girls? So we
started these dance lessons. And it was — basically it was ballroom dance. And it was also like a gym and everything, they
had trampolines there.

But we started going through these dance lessons. We were
learning jitterbug, cha cha, waltzes, you know — all the regular
kind of ballroom dances. And we were griping and hollering
about it, but it was kind of fun. But we also were really more interested in the fact that we had little breaks in all of that, and
we could go out and jump on the trampolines. So we would do
that.

At that age, we would go steady for two weeks. We would
trade discs — these little heart-shaped discs that had two

halves, and if you put them together, there was a full heart. And they hung on a necklace. And these little romances would last for a week, maybe two weeks, tops.

I don't remember that any of that wound up resulting in fights. I mean, like, fist fights. That was one of the few normal kind of human cultural activities that I ever took part in, that made some sense. And actually, I kind of wound up enjoying the dancing. And, we got to date the girls. So it all worked out.

Family Vacation to Niagara Falls

I think I was about 12ish, maybe 13, I'm not sure. But my parents, by that time, were pretty well estranged, even though they were still technically living together. And I think they were looking for -- I think in my father's mind, as I kind of have pieced together over the years -- he suggested a big family trip. We'd never had a big family trip. We had little family trips to, you know, Gonzales, or something like that, but we'd never had a big family trip. And it was gonna be like a vacation, which we'd never had.

And the impetus was to see if my mother and father could sustain their marriage. It was like a make-or-break trip. Why they took the kids on this trip, I don't know. Because (laughter) I mean, as an adult, I just wonder, that doesn't sound like a make-or-break trip for, you know, two people trying to connect, right?

But at any rate, the deal was that we were gonna go on this trip, from Houston, to New Orleans, to North Carolina, to Washington, D.C., and Annapolis, to New York City, and up through New York State to Niagara Falls and Canada. And then back to Texas again. We were in a 1959 un-air-conditioned Chevrolet, and both of my parents smoked. It's summer time, by the way, and smoke is pouring back there. It was challenging. And I could tell from the very first few miles this was gonna be a tense trip.

But part of the trip had to do with seeing if -- I guess, in my father's mind, and maybe in my mind, too -- will she be able to make this trip sober at any level? Part of it was to try to sober her up. The trip was probably about a couple of weeks long. It was a long trip. Of course, it was a long drive.

So we get to New Orleans. Oh, and by the way, the reason we're going to North Carolina, and New York City, and Annapolis, is because, when my father was in the United States Navy during World War II, he was going through what was called the Navy V-12 Program, which was an officer, like an officer candidate school. But they would send you to these different places, for officer training but also for more college education credits. One of those places was the University of North Carolina at Chapel Hill; another was in New York at Columbia University; and another place was Annapolis, Maryland. So he was studying at all these different places in World War II. And he was gonna give us the grand tour of every place that he had ever been, because this was his victory lap, kind of -- it occurred to me, during the trip, this was a victory lap to, like, show how accomplished he was. It had nothing to do with my mother, except, was she gonna drink or not.

And when we get to these places, it doesn't seem like we stay very long. Because we've got so much driving to do. And it was almost like, you know, getting to the University of North Carolina at Chapel Hill, and going zip, zip, zip, zip, zip. And then we're off to the next place, Smoky Mountains in Tennessee, or something like that.

But New Orleans was their first stop, and that was supposed to be the most -- that, and New York City, were supposed to be the two, I guess, romance spots. New Orleans was where they went on their honeymoon. And according to my mother -- not on that trip, but in other contexts -- she had never had a drop of liquor in her whole life. And on their honeymoon, they went to New Orleans and my father forced her to drink Hurricanes. And that's when she started drinking.

Anyway, we are working our way all the way up to the east coast, and we get to New York. And of course, in the front seat, there is a lot of bickering. In the back seat, there's a lot -- on both of my sisters' parts -- of just sort of cowering and keeping their heads down. And on my part, it was just like, "This is a really, really fucked up trip."

So finally we get to New York. New Orleans was a bust, she got blind drunk in New Orleans, and it took her until the Smoky Mountains to get sober again. But we got to New York, and they had tickets for the Broadway play *Who's Afraid of Virginia Woolf?* And it was, you know, the big play of the year. I didn't know it then, but it was like the worst possible play that two people in a bad relationship could ever go see, because it's just, the complete disintegration of any kind of relationship you could ever imagine. I didn't see it, they were gonna go see it.

And guess who was gonna babysit the girls while they went to see it? We were in some little fleabag hotel in New York, and I'm thinking, "God, I'm in New York, I'm babysitting, I'm stuck, I can't see anything in New York, we're leaving tomorrow." We were only gonna be there that day and night, and then we were gonna leave! And I'm thinking, "This is just insane!"

So the girls -- I was watching them in the hotel. And they're hungry, and our parents had not made any accommodations for any food. And I set Susan and Candy down, and I said, "Listen, I'm gonna go out and find some food, some hot dogs or something, I know there's gotta be something right around here." And part of that was to get them fed, but the other part of that was, I wanted to see a little bit of New York. So I was gonna walk down and get outside and see a little bit of New

York. And I made them swear that they, A, weren't gonna leave the room, B, that they weren't gonna do anything crazy.

So I head out. And I'm gone maybe 40 minutes. But in that 40 minutes I saw a *lot* of New York. And I thought, "This place is really cool." And I made, like, four square blocks, and you know what it's like in New York -- you can find almost anything in four square blocks, right? So finally I got some hot dogs and stuff and took them back to them, and everything was okay. But I was worried the whole time I was out -- "They're supposed to be in my charge, what happens if something happens, what happens if they fall out a window," all these kind of things. So it was scary in that sense.

So anyway, we continue on the trip, and every place that we stop are places that my father has been before, that he wants to regale us with, you know, how brilliant he was in that spot, or this or that or another, and how he was at Columbia University, and all that stuff. Blah, blah, blah.

Then we head through upstate New York, and the only thing I remember about upstate New York was (laughter) Herkimer County. Because I thought Herkimer County was the funniest word I had ever heard in my entire life. Even to this day, I still think Herkimer County is, like, the weirdest thing. And I wasn't quite wrong. Upstate New York is quite -- it's kind of like the east coast version of *Deliverance*, I mean in the rural areas.

So then we made our way to Niagara Falls. And oh, by the way, I was not traveling without my gun. I was only, like, 12 or 13, but I had a single-shot .22 rifle that I carried everywhere. And it was in the trunk.

But we went to Niagara Falls, and that was scary for me in one way. It was absolutely phenomenal in terms of the falls, but the rapids leading up to the falls were just so, so powerful, and I was in charge of my sisters. I don't even know where my parents were. And I kept thinking, "They're gonna get too close to the edge and fall in." There were no barriers. So I kept yanking them back and yanking them back. And we took the, you know, the little boat down to the mist of the falls, whatever, the little boat that goes up to where you get the mist of the falls.

So after that, we went to Canada. But we got to Canada, and the Canadian immigration people asked, you know, if we had any weapons. And I said, "I got my .22." So they confiscated my .22, but with the promise that they would give it back to me. Well, we were in Canada for a grand total of about 45 minutes. We drove in, and my father said, "Okay, you've seen Canada, now we're going back."

So anyway, after a couple of weeks, we made ourselves -- oh, and D.C. was kind of interesting. But it was very quick. I mean, everything was very quick. It was like, "Okay, there's that, come on, there's that, come on, there's that, come on." So there was no, like -- there was no really experiencing anything, it was just seeing something really briefly, and then moving.

And yeah, we got back to Texas, and within a year after that, my father left. It didn't work. And so that set forth the years where I was basically -- had to be the father/brother of the family. But it was a pretty miserable trip, and the only family vacation we ever took, of any length.

The Cabin at Pine Lake

I think I was around the age of 13 -- it was after the big New York cross-country trip we took in the old 1959 Chevrolet, un-air-conditioned -- it was not long after that trip, and a part of that trip was to try to see if my parents could stay together. After that, after we got back, my father found a cabin around a small 20-acre lake between Conroe, Texas, and Montgomery, Texas. It was called Pine Lake. And he bought this little cabin for a pittance, and it was nothing fancy, but it had kind of a screened-in porch, and it had one little bedroom and then a larger sleeping area, and people could sleep on the porch. He bought it, and everything that was there before was left there -- furniture, cards, games, everything like that. And this was another attempt by my father to try to get my mother into a safer space to where she might be able to stay away from alcohol. It was supposed to be, originally, the first, was like a summer that we spent there. Then after that there were going to be weekends.

Around this lake were all these other little cabins. It was actually a mile and a quarter around the lake, and the lake was fed by a creek that flowed down toward the San Jacinto River. We were there a lot between the age of 13 or 14 and the age of about 16 or 15-and-a-half, which was when my father finally divorced her. But we kept the cabin.

But I started making friends around the lake. And one of those friends was a guy named Jerry Dahlberg, who was on the, whatever the precursor is to the Olympics, he was trying out for the Olympics, he was in the Junior Olympics as a swimmer. And there was a pool there, in addition to the lake, and actually, some of my swimming skills were enhanced by competing with him in this swimming pool.

But there were other people around the lake, and some around our age group. And of course there wasn't anything to do there, except either swim or get together and play games. And so every evening we would all meet up at somebody's cabin and start playing card games or Scrabble or all these different kind of games.

And my mother was pretty well just sort of trapped in the cabin, although she was still figuring out how to get liquor because she could still drive and there was a car there. But I could get away from the cabin. And we played games and it was just a lot of fun. It wasn't super charged. And even my mother, until she crashed into a tree around the lake going about 40 miles an hour, and almost killed herself -- until then, it was pretty much, kind of a benign time, and these parents of the other kids that I was visiting with, were all pretty much sane and normal people. And it was like I was on another anthropological discovery and trek, because I got to watch how normal people interacted. "Oh, everybody's family is not fucked up!" Not to the extent that my little family was fucked up.

And so I also dragged my sisters with me to these things, so that they could learn to play the games, and so we could get them away from whatever was going on in the cabin, which, the first summer there was not too bad, she was kind of on the wagon. But as time went by and we went back and we went back, things kept getting worse and worse and worse, and finally, after about two or three years of that good time -- oh, and there were little romances, you know, flirty kind of things and whatnot -- but, by the time I was about 15 or 16 years old, their marriage had effectively ended, he had moved out, my father, and my mother was just on a, like a meteor heading for a planet of destruction, she was just on that track. But I still to this day have fond memories of that particular time.

Snakeskin Belt-making Business and Raining Moccasins

I was about 13 years old, 12 or 13. Well, first of all, let me just back up and say that I had a long period of my life that I was into leather work. And Tandy Leather Company, which actually later became Texas Instruments, started out as selling leather and tools and mallets for doing leather work, like belts and billfolds and that sort of thing. There's still a Tandy place here in Austin, or was, I guess it's still there, over in Capitol Plaza, over there somewhere.

Anyway, I was into leather work. I would learn how to make belts and billfolds, and just experimenting around. That started when I was probably about 10 years old. But as I kind of morphed along, I found out that I could actually sell some of this stuff. I wouldn't make any huge profits, but I'd make, somebody'd ask me to make a belt for them. And it had their name on the back, and you know, all the flowers and roses, and it was dyed, it was -- they were nice belts.

And then I got this idea, somebody said, "What I'd really like to have would be a snakeskin belt." And I thought, "Okay." I lived out in, what was then, far far west Houston, probably at the city limits, out by Addicks Dam. And there were all these creeks back over, around Addicks Dam, that ran through there -- Bear Creek was one of them. And so I started, every time I was at my Grandpa's, or every time I was in the mood back in Houston, I'd go out snake hunting.

But I didn't want to -- I was always kind of weird about this hunting business. I wanted to try to make it kind of fair, and hunting with guns never seemed fair to me. So I built this -- I had this bow and arrows -- and I rigged up a spinning reel, fishing reel, to it, and notched my arrows, so that I could shoot the arrows, hit the snake, and reel it in. And I was pretty proficient at doing that.

But there was this one kid -- I think it was either Scott Foster or David Collins -- but he begged to go on one of these little hunts with me, along Bear Creek, out in far west Houston. And I said, "Okay." He brought along a .22 rifle, semi-automatic rifle, that held about 20, 22 rounds in it. And I said, "Well, you know, this isn't really the way I like to hunt these things, but come on."

So we're going down the creek bed, and it's pretty dry. There were pockets of some little bit of water, but it wasn't rushing or running, it was pretty stagnant. So we get to this one little spot, and we have to come up, and we decide we're gonna jump down -- I guess I decided -- we're gonna jump down into, onto the dry creek bed at that point. And of course, you know, this is one of these creek beds like all creek beds, it's got trees hanging over it and everything.

And we jump down into, onto the creek bed, and water moccasins start falling out of the fucking trees, after us. I mean, they're everywhere. There's like dozens and dozens of these things. And he freaks out. I mean, they're landing on us, they're hitting our shoulders and everything, and I know that, you know, we're probably dead. But he freaks out and starts firing his weapon in every fucking direction. And I had to, I hit him and knocked him down, because I thought he was going to kill me. I mean, if the snakes didn't get me, it was gonna be him.

And so then I dragged him up on the bank of the creek. And for some reason, that to this very day I can't imagine -- because there were at least, I mean at least, a hundred snakes that had fallen down out of the trees onto us and hitting us, bouncing off and everything -- and even to this day I do not understand why one or the other of us wasn't bitten and why we weren't dead in that little escapade.

But I made it very clear to him after we escaped all of that with our lives that never, ever again was he gonna go snake hunting with me again. It was my solitary pursuit, I should have known better. So he never went hunting with me again. And I wound up getting some snakes, because he had accidentally hit a couple, with his .22. And I grabbed them, cut their heads off and took the skins back.

But then, my snake belt business -- it didn't last long after that, because what I was doing was, I was tanning the snake skins up on the roof of the house. I was tacking them up on the roof of the house. And at one point I had like 15 or 20 of them up there. And, you know, my parents didn't usually interfere with shit, but apparently, the stench of all these rotting snakes had (laughter) so permeated the house that I was forced to not be able to put snake skins up there anymore. And that was pretty much the end of my snake skinning belt-making business. I went back to just doing regular leather work after that.

Mr. Orinderff

I think I was in the eighth grade. Eighth grade was my last grade of junior high school. And for some reason -- probably because I was lazy and hated school -- I decided to sign up for wood shop. So I signed up for wood shop. And my project for the semester was going to be to build a little -- I had it envisioned in my mind -- a little wooden telephone stand, you know, for old-time, the kind of phones we had in those days, which were, you know, just rotary dial phones. But I had it designed so there would be a place on top for the phone, and then a little place underneath it for a telephone book, a little shelf underneath it. And I was gonna make it out of maple or cherry wood, or something, I don't know, but anyway, it was a pretty wood. And I was kind of invested in working on the project.

And so, during the course of the class -- and sometimes I would skip class, I was kind of known for that from about the third grade on. (Laughter) But in this particular class -- oh, and the shop teacher's name was Mr. Orinderff. And he looked like, I don't know, the biggest little wimpy nerd in the world. But at any rate, he seemed very sensitive, very sensitive. But he knew his wood work stuff.

So we're in wood shop one day, and I had used a number of excuses before then to get out of class. Because I was always looking for an excuse to get out of any class. But one day, I'm working on my little project, and I've got a little piece of wood that's about two inches wide, but it needed to be only one inch wide, so I got this saw, and I'm holding the wood, and I'm sawing this thing down, and the saw slips and comes across and slices open my left hand. And it was a deep, deep gash. And

I'm looking at that thing, and I'm thinking, "Huh, damn." And I'm bleeding like a stuck pig.

So I did the right thing. I put my hand behind my back against my shirt to try to staunch the bleeding, and went to Mr. Orinderff up at the front of the class, who was standing in front of the blackboard, and I said, "Mr. Orinderff, I need to go to the nurse." And he said, "You don't need to go to the nurse, I know what you're up to, you're trying to get out of class again." And I said, "No sir, I really need to go to the nurse." And he said, "Why?" And I pulled my hand out, and with my other hand, I opened up the wound, and I said, "Here's why."

And he looked at it, his eyes rolled back, he fell back and fainted against the blackboard and fell to the ground. And I went to the nurse's office and said, "This is gonna be okay, but Mr. Orinderff has fallen in the classroom. (Laughter) Somebody needs to go help him." So they tended to my little wound, and somebody went to retrieve Mr. Ordinerff, but I had to go and get a number of stitches for that. But ever after that, I had control over the rest of the semester of Mr. Orinderff. If I ever told him I needed to leave the classroom for some reason, he did not ask why. He just said, "Go!" (Laughter)

More on Pine Lake

Jerry Dahlberg and I would go out on the lake -- we had a canoe -- we would go out canoeing on the lake. And one day, we were canoeing, and we were getting it back onto land. And he was up at the front of the boat. And apparently he had his foot underneath the keyhole of the boat, and I pushed the boat, and it lacerated his foot, I mean, deeply. It was a deep, deep laceration. And he went berserk. He found this quarter round, like they would put around the base of houses, that was just laying out there, a long, thin stick. And he picked it up like a javelin and threw it at me and severed my ear. (Laughter) Even so, we remained good friends after that, and we both healed up.

And then, my father -- who had sort of what I called a "Johnny Carson" sense of humor, and he kind of reminded me of Johnny Carson, but he hated to hear that, because apparently, I'm guessing, he really was kind of channeling Johnny Carson a little bit sometimes, and so he hated to hear that. But one day -- and we did nothing together -- but one day he wakes me up just before dawn at the lake house, and he says "Come with me," and he's like snickering to himself.

And we go to our rowboat, that we have at our little dock, and we row out into the lake. And there was someone at the lake, this old guy that lived on the lake, that put out trot lines, and in the mornings would come and pull up his trot lines and get his catfish and stuff off of there. But what my father had was this really, really good replica of a human skull. And so we rowed out to the trot lines and pulled up the trot lines, and we put this human skull -- it was plastic, but it looked real -- put it on one of the hooks on the trot line, and then we rowed back and waited for this guy to go out and check his trot lines.

And he's checking his trot lines, and he's pulling up a catfish here and a catfish there, and then he pulls up this skull, and he freaks out and falls over backwards in the boat, and all of a sudden my father just went pale, because he thought that we had caused this guy to have a heart attack and die. But he didn't die, he recovered and got up and finally got himself together and rowed back to the shore. And we kept that secret forever. That was my father's idea of a good time with his son.

Lightnin' Hopkins

I don't know how old I was -- 14, maybe. I spent a lot of time with my dog Fogerty. We were together since before I was ever in my teens. Fogerty and I, we were kind of loners, but we were happy together. We would traipse around the woods at the lake house. And these aren't just some sort of small woods in a city, these are like endless piney woods in East Texas -- Conroe, Montgomery area. And we would traipse, and I'd have my .22 with me, my single shot .22 that I bought at the Western Auto store in Conroe, Texas -- it could only shoot one cartridge at a time -- but I felt well-armed as we were going out, not necessarily hunting, but just adventuring. Me and Fogerty.

And on one of these little adventures, we walked and we walked and we walked, and I'm pretty good at kind of having a sense of where I am, but we walked for hours, hiked for hours through the woods one day, and I didn't know where the hell I was. At some point we came out into some little clearing that happened to be this very sort of remote -- I mean it had a little road going to it, I'm sure -- but it was a little community of black folks that lived way back in the East Texas woods that had been there probably for a century or two.

And we wandered in, and I was the only white kid, and here was Fogerty, and people looked at us and they were weirded out a little bit. And somebody called us over and said, "Looks like you and your dog need some water." And they gave Fogerty some water, they gave me some water.

But I heard some music, like next door or something, and said, "Woah, that's kind of cool." And they said, "Yeah, that's Lightnin'." And I said, "What's Lightnin'?" And they said, "Lightnin' Hopkins." I'd never heard of Lightnin' Hopkins. And we wandered over there, and I listened to Lightnin' Hopkins singing the blues and jamming with some other folks there for about an hour or two.

And Lightnin' and I got to talking, and he said, "How in the hell did you little white boy find your way back here?" And I said, "Well, we just were exploring." And so we talked for awhile, and then somebody there gave us some directions on how to sort of head back in the general direction from where we came. And we went back and we made it back to Pine Lake and I never thought a thing about it.

Until a few years after that, what was I, 17 or 18 years old. All of a sudden, somehow or another, I ran across something that said Lightnin' Hopkins was going to be playing at The Cellar in Houston, in the oldest part of Houston, down in a cellar, kind of the north side of downtown, near I guess Buffalo Bayou. And it was this little club called The Cellar. And I went down there, and there was Lightnin' Hopkins, lighting up the place with some great, great old blues songs. A couple of them I'd heard in the woods, years before that.

And after he was done, and I was about to leave, he came up to me, and he said, "Boy, I think I know you." And I said, "I think we met." And he said, "In the woods, in East Texas." And I said, "Yeah." He said, "Thanks for coming, how'd you like it?" I said, "It was great."

The Chrighton Theater

One of the kids I met in the clearing where I found the little community of black folks was this kid who first made contact with me, I don't know what it was like, I don't know if it was like, "Hey, come over here," I don't know. But he was about the same age as I was, 13 or 14, maybe, I don't know. And we kept in contact. I drew a picture of where we were at Pine Lake, which was probably about four or five miles away from where this was in the piney woods. And one day he showed up at Pine Lake, and I saw him, and we started kind of hanging out together. We'd go out hunting in the woods for squirrels, and looking for crawdads, whatever.

And then one day, when I was 14, we became kind of bonded a little bit, and he said something about there was some picture show, and I don't remember what the picture show was -- we called them picture shows in those days instead of movies -- at the Crighton Movie House in Conroe, Texas. I said, "Well, hell, I can get somebody to just drive us in there, and we can go to the picture show." So we got a ride in, I don't remember who gave us a ride, maybe we hitchhiked, I don't know. But I doubt if we hitchhiked because I don't think people would pick up black hitchhikers at the time.

But we got to the Chrighton, and it was on a Wednesday, because Wednesday was 25 cent day. So we paid our money and went into the picture show, and we were sitting there in the lower section, not in the balcony. And after a few minutes, right before the picture show started, a manager showed up and said, "You can't be doing this." And I said, "Can't be doing what?" And he said, "He's got to go up into the balcony" -- talking about my black friend -- "because that's where the negroes have to sit." And I said, "Oh. Well, okay."

So he goes up there and I follow him up there. And the manager comes back when we're up in the balcony, and he says, "I'm sorry, you can't be up here, you're white, you've got to be down there." And I said, "No, this is not working out right." I don't even remember what the movie was now, but I remember that.

And my friend was saying, "No, no, no, don't make a fuss, just go down there, we'll meet up afterwards." I said, "Not gonna happen." I said, "Either we watch this movie together or we leave together." And so we left. And that was the Chrighton Theater in Conroe, Texas, in the early 1960's.

Thrown Off a Bridge

I'm guessing I was 14. I was in Kerrville visiting my crazy cousin Butch, my Aunt Sissy, Uncle Owen, Sarah, Elizabeth, and all the rest of the family. I think this was the trip where we went down to, there was a place called Five Points, I think, in Kerrville, and there was a pool hall and beer joint there. We'd go there to play pool. I think this was the same trip where my crazy cousin Butch and I got in a fight with about seven or eight pool players and had to fight our way out of there.

But at some point during that trip, we were gonna go -- my crazy cousin Butch had this idea that we were gonna all go jump off the new bridge that went over the Guadalupe River. And I'm not a big fan of heights. I don't mind water. But we're up on this bridge, and there was like three or four of us, and my crazy cousin Butch, who was about four or five years older than I was, was goading me to go first. And I was reluctant. And he kind of pushed me a little bit towards the railing. And I was scared, I wasn't gonna go.

And all of a sudden, the next thing I know is, he has yanked me up and thrown me over the bridge. And it was a 40 or 50 foot, four or five story drop to the river. And there I went. And I have a vague initial recollection, at the moment I was being tossed over the bridge, of "I'm dead." But I hit the water, hit the water feet first. It was jarring. I went down so far under the water, probably, I don't know, 20 feet or more, to where, at that point, the only survival thing was, "Can I hold my breath until I get back up to the surface, because I'm not dead."

And, yeah, I was the sacrificial lamb on that deal. Nobody else went off that fucking bridge. And I just added that to the list of all of the grievances that I had against my crazy cousin Butch. I'm not over them yet. (Laughter) I try to put them in perspective, but the grievance is there.

Stabbed at a Rock Concert

I think this was my last year of junior high school at Spring Woods Junior High School. And you know, I had a few running buddies -- Scott Foster, Gary Holloman, David Collins. I don't know, a few guys. And there was gonna be this big concert, rock concert, at the Houston Coliseum. So we decided we were gonna go to the rock concert. I had never even been to a rock concert. It was all these bands, nobody famous or anything. There were no big bands coming to Houston in those days.

So we go to this concert, and we're at the Coliseum, and it's all packed and jammed, and, you know, there's all these acts going on. So a couple of the guys had gone to get some drinks, you know, soda waters and stuff, and they came back and said, "Come with us! Come with us!" And I said, "I'm watching the..." And, "No, no, you've got to come with us, there's a problem! There's a problem!"

So I go with them, and all of a sudden, one of the guys, I don't remember which one it was, was still kind of in the headlights of about five Hispanic gangbangers. And the first thing that they did -- my friends -- was to yank poor whoever-it-was back and push me out in front. And they're looking over my shoulder, and holding me from the back, and trash talking these gangbangers, saying, "You don't know what you've gotten yourself in for. He's gonna kick your ass! He's gonna take care of you! You are done for! You better get the hell out of here right now!"

And one of them pulls a knife. It wasn't exactly a knife, it was more like an exacto knife. At least that's the way I remember it. It wasn't like some big butcher knife or hunting knife or anything. It was some kind of exacto knife. And now they're all focused on me, and, you know, "So you think you're a badass, huh?! Yeah, we're gonna gut your ass!"

And so the guy comes at me with the knife, and I try to move backwards, but my guys are pushing me forward to get him. And I get stabbed in the stomach. And so that kind of pissed me off. So I started going to town.

And some security guards or somebody came and broke it all up, and they actually had to call an ambulance for the guy who actually stabbed me. But that wasn't viciousness on my part. It was like, I tried to not get involved in this thing, and then there I was. So here I got this -- it was in the gut, it didn't hit a vital organ -- but, you know, I had to get some stitches, and I thought, "I don't think I ever want to go to another rock concert."

Rita LaFerme

This was Gary Holloman's mother. And she was very young. Gary Holloman was maybe 13 or 14. She had had him apparently when she was about 16 or 17. So she was very young. And she was very hot. And her original, previous marriage -- I think she was like on her second or third marriage by the time I ever met her -- but her name at that time was Rita LaFerme.

But the first time I ever met her, I was coming home with Gary Holloman to his place. And it was like an apartment. And she opens the door and kind of peaks out, and she says, "So you're Gary's friend." And I said, "Yeah." She said, "Come on in." And she opened the door, and she's standing there in a see-through negligee and is just as nekkid as the day she was born underneath this negligee. And this is a lot for a 14-year-old kid to take in. But I took it in! (Laughter) Gary didn't even notice, this was just normal to him.

So of course I had, like, this immediate, sort of, you know, adolescent teenage sexuality-inspired crush on this hot chick. And I couldn't get it straight in my mind, because it didn't seem like she was the mother of Gary, it seemed like she was more like his sister, because she'd been so young when she'd had him.

So I start spending a lot of time over there. And she was always, you know, flirty. And one night -- and this was over a period of months, I guess -- but at one point, she called me into her bedroom, where her bathroom was, and she was in the bathroom. And she said, "I need somebody to scrub my back." Gary was off in another part of the house. And I said, "Okay."

So I go in there, and she's naked in the bathtub. And of course, I'm like, you know, this is, like, exquisite torture. I don't know what to do except, you know, play it by ear. And at one point, she said, "Why don't you just spend the night in here tonight with me?" In her bedroom. And I bailed out. I just couldn't figure it all out. I mean, it was just too much for me.

So that went on for a while, but there was never anything that happened.

Meeting David Hefner

David and I have known each other since the time I was about 15 and he was about 16, so he was a little older than I was. He actually was a grade ahead of me. But we despised each other in the beginning. I was at that time working as a clerk or cashier and delivery driver for my father's pharmacy on Airline Drive in Houston. It was a huge pharmacy, it was probably the largest pharmacy in Houston. And it was open 24 hours a day, 365 days a year, so it was, like, the go-to place for people in those days in Houston. And he showed up and I guess interviewed with my father because we needed an extra delivery driver. And he got hired.

David at the time was about six foot one and weighed maybe 130 pounds. I was, you know, not tall, five foot six or seven then, and weighed about 130 pounds. (Laughter) And we were introduced, and I was supposed to teach him the ropes. And I took some immediate dislike to him. And I think the feeling was mutual.

So he did his thing for a while, I did my thing for a while, separately. There was a -- one of the delivery vehicles we had was an old International Scout. It was kind of, sort of like a Jeep on steroids, and that was my favorite vehicle to deliver stuff in, deliver, you know, prescriptions to people, because we did that in those days. And one day, I don't remember the circumstances, but he said something like, "I never get, I don't often get to drive the Scout." And I said, "Well, why don't you come with me and I'll show you kind of the ropes on this."

And we went off delivering. And all of a sudden, I started taking off across fields, and you know, through parks and everything, and we were doing doughnuts, and we were doing all this shit. And, you know, he said, "I want to drive!" And I said, "Give it a shot!" And so we discovered that we were both wild guys. (Laughter) And we sort of started connecting a little bit. And as time went by, we kept getting closer and closer together and becoming really, really good friends.

And I will say, at this point in my life, David Hefner and I are still -- even though we don't have a lot of contact with each other -- he's still probably the best, longest, best friend, sustainably, that I've ever had, both of us, in both directions. We've had our tiffs along the way, but we've squared them all away. And he is now dying of, from the effects of Agent Orange. And he was only in Vietnam for about six months on temporary duty, but it was long enough for him to have gotten exposed to Agent Orange. But at any rate, the adventures that David Hefner and I had, along the way, from the time I was about 15 until he went off to the Army and I went off to the Army, were sort of legendary.

Blue Light Cemetery

So I was about 15, maybe 16. I lived out on the very far west side of the outer reaches of Houston, what was called Addicks Dam. Addicks was a little community outside of Houston.

And there was a cemetery out there called Blue Light Cemetery. It was famous, or infamous, for being one of these, you know, urban legend places, where people driving by on the road would see these blue lights coming from the cemetery. That was the informal name; I don't know what the real name of the cemetery was. But it was a little community cemetery for the old little town that once had been there, that wasn't there anymore, right?

But the story went, you know, that there were -- it was a spooky, spooky place to go, but don't go there. You can see the blue lights as you're going by, but if you go there, there was supposed to be this "caretaker" with a machete or a scythe that would kill you in the cemetery. It was one of those ghosty kind of stories that would just scare people to death.

So Halloween was coming up one year, and I had this brilliant idea, I thought. And I'm talking to my friend crazy Gary Holloman. And I said, "Hey, wouldn't it be cool to go out and camp in the cemetery on Halloween night? And we could set out some Sterno stuff on top of the tombstones to really scare people as they're driving by. Or if anybody comes up, we could make noises or something." Sterno were little cans of a kind of gel that you could light and it would make a little fire.

He was in, and I was really riding high around that time because, about six months before then, I had bought my first car. It was a 1955 Mercury. And this was in 1965ish -- it was at least ten or eleven years old, right? But it was in cherry condition! It was yellow with a green interior, rolled and pleated seat covers, I think it had a green top and a yellow exterior. And it was beautiful, and I loved that car. And I had gotten that car for like $700. And I was riding high, baby!

So we got some sleeping bags, got some Sterno, and we get out there -- we wait until it's, you know, basically almost nighttime. We get out there, we start setting everything up, and we put Sterno cans on top of the tombstones. We find a place back toward the back of the cemetery where we were gonna camp. And I had my car hidden and everything.

And so nighttime comes around, and we start lighting the Sterno. And cars are slowing down, and then they're speeding up and driving off; slowing down, then speeding up and driving off. And we were having a ball. This is, like, this is so cool!

And so, after a while, around 11 or midnight, all of the traffic was gone. Nobody was out there. And nobody came into the cemetery because they were all too scared, because there was this history, or story, about this caretaker of the place who had killed people out there. But we weren't too bothered by that, because we knew that was B.S., right? Or thought it was B.S.

So we start laying in for the night to go to sleep. And then all of a sudden we hear stuff rustling around in the trees, and we hear somebody cough, and we're thinking, "Oh, this is getting a little creepy." And then, in a few minutes, we start hearing babies crying. In the cemetery. And it wasn't just one baby crying, it was a number of babies crying. And Gary Holloman's getting pretty freaked out. And quite frankly, I had some concerns about what was going on myself!

But he was really starting to freak out, and I said, "Listen, stop, stop." He said, "We've got to get out of here, we've got to get out of here!" I said, "Listen. We're here. We said we were gonna spend the night. And if we don't spend the night, we lose all of our credibility. Because that's our goal, to spend the night in Blue Light Cemetery, after we scare people off."

I said, "Look, there's an answer to all of this." I said, "The crying is coming from back behind us." We were in the back of the cemetery but this was even farther in the back of the cemetery. So I said, "Let's go check it out." And he's super freaked out, and I was just kind of trying to figure it all out.

And we get back there, and we hear -- we get to the back fence of the cemetery, and the crying baby stuff is coming from over the fence. And it sounded just like babies! And I was thinking, "What could this be? What could this be?" And then I thought, "Kittens! Maybe it's kittens!"

And so we were gonna look for it. And all of a sudden there was some disturbance back by our campsite. So that freaked us out, and we went running back to the campsite. And the camp-site was all messed up, the tent was torn down and everything like that. And Holloman said, "We've got to get out of here, we've got to get out of here!" And I said, "No, we have to spend the night here!" I said, "Let's just get in the car." And so we got in the car and we locked all the doors. And we spent the night there.

And we woke up the next morning, right around dawn -- be-cause it had to be, you know -- this was my thing, it wasn't his thing. My thing was, "No, by God, we're going to stay here the whole night, and we're gonna deal with whatever comes up." So finally, we wake up, and I said, "Okay, we can leave now." And we crank my car up, we drive out of the cemetery onto the road, we get about 200 feet down the road, and my engine blows up in my car.

So that was the end of my car. And what we never, to this day -- I mean, there's answers for everything -- but all I know, as we sit here in this moment, is that we heard babies or kit-tens or something crying in the graveyard, something or some-body trashed our campsite, and somebody or something or nothing caused my engine to blow up as we were driving away from there.

Antha Mize and Babies in the Freezer

So I'm guessing I was about 15, maybe even 16, at the time. But it was one of those periods of time where my mother was being committed to the Austin State Hospital for her various mental illnesses and alcoholism and whatnot. And my father -- he'd already moved out by that time -- he wanted me to ba-sically stop school and everything and start, just take care of Candy and Susan. And somebody in the family, I'm not sure who, I think it might have been my grandmother, his mother,

said, "You can't do that to that boy. You need to get a housekeeper."

So he hired this old, old, ancient, ancient woman -- I
thought she was about 95 years old at the time -- and her name
was Antha Mize. And she was from Hope, Arkansas. She became the live-in housekeeper. And she made it pretty clear to
me when she got there that she wasn't there really to be my
warden, she was there mainly to take care of the girls, so I could
get on with school and do whatever I was gonna do. And so I
thought, "Okay, cool. I get a little break, finally."

So she was there for about five months, and during the
course of all that, at some point David Hefner and I had headed
out to Gonzales -- I mean, we always were heading out to Gonzales -- but on one of these trips, we decided to do some squirrel hunting, and we killed a few squirrels. I gave a couple of
them to Elder and we dressed and skinned a couple more and
we brought them back to Houston. We were gonna put 'em in
the freezer and, you know, maybe cook 'em up later.

But for some reason, I had the bright idea, when I saw these
little headless squirrels -- I mean, they looked like little humans, skinned and everything -- I thought, "Wouldn't it be
cool to take the doll heads off a couple of Candy and Susan's
dolls and stick 'em on there, and set them up in the freezer,
like they're sitting up." And so we did that. We were so tickled
about that.

And we leave, you know, the house, to go messing around
wherever we were gonna go, and we're just laughing and laughing. But I started getting worried about it. I thought, "Jesus
Christ, she's 95 years old or something like that, I don't know
how old she is, but she's ancient -- what if she opens that
and has a heart attack?" And so we were gone for about an
hour and a half or two hours, and I couldn't do anything, all I
was concerned about was that. Finally I said, "We've got to go

back, we've got to try to get rid of those before she finds them. Maybe she hasn't opened the freezer yet."

And we get back, and we walk in the front door of the house, and it smells so good. Something is cooking up good. And what had happened was, she opened the freezer door, she saw the squirrels, she didn't think a second thing about it, she knew exactly what they were, she took 'em out, she dressed 'em, she put them into a stew and she was cooking this squirrel stew for us. And I tried to apologize for it, and she said, "No, I thought it was pretty funny!" (Laughter)

But that's not the end. That's the end of the squirrel story. But that was when I was like 15ish, 16ish. And she was there for, like, five months and then I never heard from her again. But my grandmother, Granny, my father's mother, the one who had somehow found her somewhere, apparently stayed in contact with her for years and years. And I always wondered, after she left, whatever happened to her or whatever, but I never thought to ask my grandmother.

But sometime after I came back from Vietnam, and this was probably, it was sometime after I got back, I want to say it was like 1974ish, and I was talking to my grandmother, who was, actually, 93 or 94 or 95 at the time, and I said, "You know, I was just remembering this housekeeper Antha Mize, and I wonder what ever happened to her." And she said, "I'm still in contact with her, we write letters back and forth all the time." And so I said, "Can I have her address? I'd like to write her a note and thank her for all that she did during that period of time."

And by that time, Antha Mize really was like about 97 or 98 years old. And so I wrote a letter to her, and I get this nice letter back from her, all kind of wiggly handwriting -- she was old, you know. And basically, in the letter, the main thing I remember about the letter was, she said, "Oh, it's nice to hear from you. I'm back in Hope, Arkansas, now. I've got my garden. Yesterday I was out working in the garden and got bit by a copperhead. But I think I'm doing okay." (Laughter)

I mean, she was a tough old bird, you know? And so I've always had this, both soft spot, and also a little bit of guilty feeling in my heart for Antha Mize, because I used that time she was there to take a break from everything, I really took a break. But she was so cool about it. She had to have been in her 80's then. But especially the squirrel business, which I thought I was gonna be responsible for giving her a heart attack and finding her on the kitchen floor in the house because of the squirrels with the doll heads on them.

Karate at the Movie Theater

So, unfortunately, I lived in a milieu of, where people were always trying to fight. And just as a footnote -- in those days, in Texas, and this is back in the 1960's, almost everybody had guns in their cars. You know, hunting rifles. Never in all of those years -- never in any of these fights that I got in did anybody -- and everybody had access to them -- but nobody -- they might have gotten tire tools and whatever, baseball bats or whatever, out of their trunks -- but never out of their trunks or their gun racks did they ever pull their guns out. It just was not, it just wasn't the way it was then. It's a little different now.

But in this particular situation -- one day, when I was about 15 years old, probably first year of high school or something like that, I don't know. My old buddy Gary Holloman -- he was one of the smartest people I've ever known, he was very smart, and he read a lot, and we bonded -- but he was batshit crazy. But setting that aside for a second, one day I found, there was some little poster on a telephone pole or something, that talked about a free one-hour session at a karate studio. Actually, it wound up being a karate studio that was well-known in Houston at the time, I can't remember the name of it, but it was well-known. And it was a free one-hour training, you know, this was to pull you in, get you to sign up and everything.

So we talk about it and decide we're gonna go to it. And we go to this one-hour training. And in this training, the instructor -- the sensei -- says, "Okay, this is just a brief introduction to karate, but we're going to teach you how to take a knife, gun, or chain away from somebody who attacks you." And they start teaching us how to get in the right karate position, how to say "Hi-yah" and all this kind of stuff. And after that one hour, we were both pretty pumped up.

And the same day we went to that, that night, we were gonna meet our girlfriends -- I don't know even remember who they were -- but we were gonna meet our girlfriends at the Oak Village Movie Theater. And I don't even remember what the movie was, could have been Haley Mills or something, it was in those days.

And so I'm sitting with my date for the evening, and Gary Holloman was sitting behind us, in the next row, with his date. And during the movie, Gary thought it would be kind of funny to be throwing ice over my head onto the guy and girl in the next row in front of us. And so he starts tossing ice over. And I was thinking, "Oh god, no. Crazy Gary Holloman. Stop it, stop it." And I kept kind of turning back and looking at him. But the guy that was getting hit by the ice -- and his girlfriend, in front of us -- started jerking around and staring at me. And at one point, after about four times of this, he turned around and said, "I'm gonna kick your ass." And I said, "Give it your best shot." I said, "Let's take it outside."

And so I'm all pumped up -- I know karate! (Laughter) I am all pumped up. I'm like, "Hey, nothing can get me now, I had a karate lesson!" So I'm walking up the aisle, and I get almost to the exit, to where the curtains are, that divide the theater from the concession area, and right before I get there I turn around, and I'm looking, and I don't see him. All I see is some guy who's about six foot three. And I'm looking around him, and he says, "What the hell are you doing? I thought we were going outside." And I said, "Oh. Okay." But I'm not concerned because I know karate.

And so we go outside behind the theater. And by this time, hordes of people have come out to watch the fight, right? And so we get out there and he's, like, standing there in a traditional boxing, fists-up kind of situation. I go into the karate stance that I learned that afternoon in the one-hour session -- with a loud yell -- "Hi yah!" And the next thing that happens is, this guy -- who's like three feet taller than I am, or two feet, or whatever it was, and has a hand about the size of a small baseball mitt -- reaches out and puts his hand over my outstretched fist. And he commences to start pummeling me. Boom, boom, boom.

And I'm helpless, I'm completely helpless. We covered how to protect against a knife, gun, or a chain, in the karate lesson, but nobody bothered to tell me about somebody, what to do if they were just using their, you know, fists. (Laughter)

So anyway, at some point, I get knocked half senseless and go down. And I get up. And I start all over again. And I get knocked down again. And I get knocked down again. And finally, the guy, whoever he was -- oh, and by the way, he was about 19 years old, I was about 15 years old -- finally, he's down on top of me, whispering in my ear, "Please don't get up again. Please do not get up again." And by that time, all this crowd was coming in and saying, "He's had enough, he's had enough." I think, I believe that that was the worst and most instructive ass-whipping I ever got in my life. Because after that, I *did* learn martial arts. (Laughter)

Trying to Get Out of the Psych Ward

Well of course my mother was committed voluntarily or involuntarily many times to various mental facilities, mental hospitals, including the Austin State Hospital. But there was a time, and I think I was about 15ish, because I was driving, and she had been committed involuntarily for some period of time to the Methodist Hospital psychiatric ward. And I don't know why, I don't know if somebody prevailed upon me or whatever, but I was asked to, you know, encouraged or inveigled, to go visit her.

I put it off and put it off, I don't know how long, and finally, probably out of guilt or whatever, I decided okay, I'm gonna go. So I get to the psychiatric ward, they let me in, I have this short visit with my mother, 20 or 30 minutes to see how she was doing. Quite frankly, I think the main thing I wanted to see was, was any of this working? Was she still just batshit crazy? Had she sobered up? Because it was always a combination of both of those things.

So we visited for a bit, and it's time for me to leave, and I start walking out and somebody stops me. Because it's a secure area. Somebody stops me from going out and they said, "Woah, where are you going?" And this psychiatric ward held people from teenagers on up. And I said, "Well, I'm leaving." And they said, "No, you can't just do that."

And I said, "I was just visiting here." And they said, "We hear that a lot." And all of a sudden they're talking to me as if, you know, and they're saying, "How are you feeling?" And they said, "Well, we're gonna have to have you talk to a doctor before you leave." And I said, "Well, okay."

So I'm sitting in some little side room with this psychiatrist, and the psychiatrist is asking me all these questions. And it was obvious to me, even at 15 years old -- because this wasn't my first trip to a psych ward, you know, because of my mother,

I'd been in other ones -- and I said, "Wait a minute, you think
I'm crazy and I belong here, right?" And he said, "Well, do you?
Are you?"

And I said, "Well, here's the trap, isn't it. If I say no, I'm not
crazy, you're gonna think I'm crazy. And if I say yes, I'm crazy,
you're gonna think I'm crazy. So you tell me, because it's not
my job. You figure out whether I'm crazy or not. And if I'm not
crazy, open these doors for me and let me go. And if you think
I am crazy and you don't let me out, when I get out, this hospital is gonna belong to me." (Laughter) At 15, I said that. My
Uncle Jay, the lawyer, had given me some little counsel along
the way. And after -- it took me about 45 minutes to an hour
to get a clean release from that psychiatric ward.

My Mother and the Lawnmower Accident

I was about 15ish. We were back on the north side of Houston,
on Bluewater Street, in what was called Candlelight Woods. My
mother had an alcohol problem, and a drug problem, and a life
problem. She was spiraling down really, really fast.

It was a nice house. My father did well. He bought a nice
house and then he marched out of it as soon as he bought it,
and left me in charge of my mother and Candy and Susan. And
he was gone.

So one day, my mother decided she was gonna go out and
mow the backyard. And she gets out there, and she runs the
lawnmower over her foot, which pretty much almost severed
her entire foot.

My sisters were screaming. I had just come home from
school or wherever, and they're screaming and hysterical. I go
out to the backyard, I drag my mother in, and I put her in the
bathtub, and she's bleeding out. I put a tourniquet on her, do
the best I can to stop the bleeding -- and the girls are hysterical, I mean, truly hysterical. I'm trying to keep them calm. I'm

trying to tell my mother, who's yelling, "I'm dying! I'm dying!" that, no, you're not dying, we're gonna get you taken care of.

I call 911, I get an ambulance out there, and they take her to the hospital. So it was a wild and woolly day. She was drunkenly trying to mow the damn yard. And she was blind drunk. And she didn't even know what was happening.

Got her to the hospital. They sewed her up, they put her more or less back together. Her foot was probably never quite the same, but she didn't lose it.

So, yeah, that was just, I guess I have to say, a typical untypical day in the growing up with my mother.

Fogerty's Death

My dog Fogerty, that I had from the time I was five, six years old -- and he and I were, we did everything together, it was like Lassie and whatever Lassie's kid was. The only time we were ever separated was when I had to go to school, but other than that, we did everything together, went everywhere together, to the woods, any time I would go anywhere.

And I was about 15 or 16 years old, and all of a sudden he disappeared. He ran away, is what the story was. But I didn't believe he would ever run away. So I kept looking for him, I looked for him for two or three days.

And about five or six days after that, I had been on a date on the other side of town, and I was coming back to the house, where we lived in the Candlelight Woods. I had him a lot of the time that we were still at the Chippendale address, and all the time we lived out in the country near Addicks Dam, and then back over onto the north side of town. He was my best friend. The family was a total mess, but he was my one constant center in that family situation.

So I'm driving home from a date one night, when I was about 15, 16, and I'm going down this two-lane road, probably

about a mile away from my house, and it's night, and I caught
something in the light, like a reflection or something, and I saw
some form over there, in a ditch beside the road. So I stopped,
I went back to look, and it was Fogerty. And he had a rope tied
around his neck. And you could see where the rope had broken at some point. So somebody who had a grudge against me,
I'm guessing, lassoed him, tied him behind a car, and drug him
until he died.

And the girls, Candy and Susan, were really attached to him,
too. I had a poncho in the car, in the trunk. I put him in the
poncho, and I took him to the woods -- it's now part of a park
over there -- and I had a shovel in the trunk, and I buried him.
And I never, ever told my sisters what had really happened to
him. But that was the end of Fogerty. They tried to replace him
with another dog, but it never took.

Crazy Dee Dunkerly

Dee's younger sister was a friend of mine in high school, actually I think from the eighth grade. And crazy Gary Holloman
was the boyfriend of Crazy Dee's sister. And Crazy Dee and her
sister lived in a pretty dysfunctional family, which was always
kind of interesting to me, because they had a very nice upper-
middle-class home, with a mother who was a complete mental
wreck and a father who was somehow a bigwig in the oil industry but nutty as a fruitcake.

But I met Crazy Dee through her sister, and Crazy Dee was
about -- when I was, I don't know, let's say, 15, she was 17, she
was a year and a half or so older than I was. And boy, I fell stone
entranced with her. She was smart and hot -- not in the con-
ventional sense of hot, but in the sort of -- I don't know what
you call it, not necessarily physical, although she was cute and
everything like that -- but there was something I saw in her,
that was, "this is somebody with a brain." And I was always at-

tracted to brains. And other things, but brains even maybe primarily.

So we kind of got to, you know, flirting around and so on. She had some boyfriend who was, the best I could tell, he was sort of a bisexual. But Crazy Dee was crazy about me, and I was crazy about her, and we started a relationship. But it wasn't like -- let's put it this way -- it wasn't like a sexual relationship, it was like the promises of a potential sexual relationship somewhere down the road -- apparently, a lot farther off in her mind than it was in my mind. (Laughter) But, so what.

One of the things about Crazy Dee that I discovered was that she really, really liked to tease. But she stopped stuff. And whenever she got into a mess, she would try to get me to get her out of the mess. But she also liked to get me into fights. She loved to see two men fighting, I mean, not arguing, I'm talking about fistfights. And as an example of one of those times, we were in some little, you know, cafe or restaurant -- it had booths -- and let's say it was something like a Jim's Restaurant, or something. And we were sitting in this booth, and she had ordered spaghetti and meatballs. I don't know what I ordered. But behind her was another couple, and during the dinner, she picked up her whole plate of spaghetti and meatballs, turned around, and dumped it on the head of the guy that was sitting behind her. And when he of course turned around, like, "what the holy hell," she said to him, "He told me to do it," pointing at me.

And so the fight was on. And we fought our way up and down the aisles in that deal, and I felt terrible about it. I mean, I felt terrible because I thought, "this woman is just crazy as a bedbug," but she never came across crazy, except in certain moments, right? And so, unfortunately, I think unfortunately, I subdued him. And I think, I may not be remembering this correctly -- if I didn't say it, I meant to say it -- which was, when he was completely disabled, I whispered, or hoped I whispered

in his ear, "Listen, this wasn't me. I didn't want this to happen.
I am so sorry." But he was injured. So it was a big mess. So that
was one little tiny episode of many, many different episodes.

And one of the things that never happened with us -- and
we were somewhat of a pair, or connected, semi-romantically,
for probably, from the time I was 15 to 17 -- and never once
was there ever any full-on, you know, consummation of the relationship, as we say in the trade. But there was one time when
she promised it. And I took her to Pine Lake, where we had
the cabin. And we got there, and the promise was, tonight's the
night! And when we get there, all of a sudden, we're getting out
of the car, I'm heading towards the cabin, and she said, "Woah,
woah, wait a minute. Open the trunk." And she had brought
in the trunk her little brother Beau. He was in the trunk the
whole time. And she brought him out to be her reason for not
being able to consummate the relationship. And at that point,
I started having thoughts about, "you know, maybe this is not
the girl for me."

Hamilton Pool on Christmas Eve

This was another time when I was about 16 and David Hefner
was about 17, I guess. Somebody, I don't even remember who,
but we had about four or five buds at the time; quite frankly,
I don't even remember which ones the other buds were. But
somebody had told one of us, I think it was me, about Hamilton Pool, which was "up around Austin somewhere," they said.
And it was all private property, but it was this great, great kind
of little pool on a creek that went into the river, and there was
this waterfall. One of the group knew about it, and we said,
"Well, hell, let's go!"

And it was December, it was actually Christmas Eve, and we
headed out from Houston, there were like four or five of us. We
drove, and somebody knew the directions to get there, I guess

they had been there before, somehow. And we got to Hamilton Pool. But it wasn't like Hamilton Pool today. I mean, there was no road down to Hamilton Pool. There was private land, and you had to go to this cliff, and there was this old bucket contraption, that, from the top of the cliff, you could lower yourself down in these buckets into what we know as Hamilton Pool. And we were gonna camp out there for the night. It was Christmas Eve, and we thought, nobody's coming looking for trespassers on Christmas Eve, right?

And so we make our way there and somehow found it, and we go through this huge, huge project of lowering these buckets with each one of us in, down the cliff, all the way down to the bottom of Hamilton Pool, then pulling it back up, and lowering the next one. And you know, there's caves up underneath the pool, so we were gonna camp out there. And our goal was to campout on Christmas Eve and say we had done it. That was basically, I guess, (laughter) that was about as much thought process as we put into it. Can we get there without getting caught? Can we get there and spend the night? And can we have a little adventure?

And so we wake up on Christmas morning, in our sleeping bags, and we'd built a little fire and everything, up underneath the cliffs, in the crevices, and we wake up on Christmas morning, and somebody, I don't know who, it could have been me, possibly, said, "Well, you know, we can't leave here without getting in Hamilton Pool," I mean, into the water. And so we decided to all strip naked and line up, and I guess since it was my idea, I was gonna have to go in first. So it was me, and then David Hefner, and I think three other guys. So I'm thinking, "I don't think was a great idea, but it was kind of my idea." So I leap into the water off of one of the rocks. And I hit that water, and it was like twenty-five million volts of electricity coursing through me. I thought I was gonna die on the spot from the shock of it all. But I was able to gather myself a little bit --

I'm still facing outward, away from them -- and I'm thinking, "Oh my fucking god, if I start yelling and screaming like I want to and frantically making my way back, nobody else is gonna come in."

So I gather myself for a second and I turn around, and David's second in line, because the other guys were all kind of timid, right? But David wasn't timid, and I wasn't timid. I turned around and I said, "Hey, it's really warm! Come on in!" I'm already experiencing hypothermia, right? And so, David comes jumping into the water. And he hits the water, and I'm, like, frantically trying to make my way back, but I see him when he hits the water, and I see his expression, and I know that expression because it was my expression! And he looks at me, glaring, you know, like, daggers, and then, I could see in his eyes, he got it. And he turned around and said, "Woah, he was right! It's great! Come on in!" And he and I are, like, going crazy, trying to swim back. And every single one of them came in.

And we finally get back -- and it seemed like it took forever, I mean we were, like, almost paralyzed -- and we make our way back to the, get up and crawl up under the rocks, and we throw more wood on the fire, and everybody who went in did the same thing. They figured out what the hell was going on, and so every single person there, all five people, four or five people, made it into the water, made it back. And for *at least* three-and-a-half or four hours, we sat shivering next to this fire, that wasn't really big enough, but just trying to seek enough warmth to keep us alive. And how none of us succumbed to hypothermia on that little escapade, I don't know.

And then of course, because it was private land then, and because we had done what we wanted to do, we spent Christmas Eve, snowing -- it was snowing! I don't know if I mentioned that, but it was snowing all night long, that's how cold it was! -- and we finally, even though we weren't completely thawed out, were able to -- and you had to manually pull these things to get the buckets back up to the top -- and we finally made it back up to the top on Christmas Day and we finally all made it out alive. And yeah, then I guess we made our way back to Houston. But that was our little secret trip to Hamilton Pool, which is now, of course, a public park, and you can get to it without having to climb down a cliff in a large bucket.

The Demolay

When I was about 16, there was somebody, and I don't remember who or why or how, but somebody said, "Hey, we'd like to invite you to become a member of the Demolay." And this is the sort of junior order of the Masonic lodges.

I knew that my Grandpa was like a thirty-second or thirty-three degree Mason, and that was an important part of his life. And I knew that my screwy Uncle Benny was a Mason. I didn't really know what it was all about, but I thought — I said, "Okay, well what do I have to do?" And they said, "Well, you have to go through an application process and then an initiation," and so on. And I said, "Okay."

But I thought, even dealing with whoever I was dealing with, I thought these were pretty goofy people. And this is not to say that Masons are necessarily goofy, but there's an aspect of goofiness to it. And the guy that sort of recruited me — you know, they walked me through what I needed to do to get accepted. I did that. And then they walked me through the "initiation," which of course, as you might imagine, you know, this was a hyper semi-religious kind of — I mean, it's not a religion, but the ceremonies were all of this "do this, do that." And I went through all of this ceremony, where you've got to go from one point on the compass to the next point on the compass, and there's all this stuff that you had to recite and do and everything. I'm not even sure I did it right, but they were happy to have me.

So I became a Demolay, which is like a junior Mason. The teen version of a Mason. And I went to a few of their, two or three of their little meetings and conclaves and everything, and quite frankly, to me, it all seemed like kind of bullshit mumbo jumbo-y, hoodoo voodoo stuff. So I was done with it. So that was when I was about 17, I guess, when I said I was done with it.

So the funny part of all of that is that I was 20 years old, and in Vietnam in the Army, and at some point, I get this letter from the Demolay saying that, "You are on the Rifle Team for the Demolay, and there's going to be a rifle competition," and it was like in a month or two from the time I got this letter. And they said, "We want you to be there." I never signed up for any Rifle Team, I don't know what that was all about, but I looked at this thing, and I'm just laughing. Because it didn't make any sense. (Laughter)

So I sent them back a letter, and I said, "Just wanted to let you know that I am in Vietnam, I'm not available for the Rifle Team competition in Houston, and by the way, I resign from Demolay. Please make sure this gets on the record."

That was my Demolay story.

Phyllis

So I was at the age of about 16. And I had a friend, I think his name was David De La Moné. And his younger sister, who was about -- and he was about 17 -- his younger sister was 15. Her name was Phyllis De La Moné. And he was part of the little group that worked with us when we were building the rodeo arena in Spring Branch, the first rodeo arena, you know, ever, in Houston, other than the big rodeo arena, but a small amateur rodeo arena. And I met her. And boy, the sparks were immediate. I mean, it was like, eyes, eyes, eyes. And I was smitten. And I think she was smitten.

And there was going to be, for the Houston -- what was then called the Houston Fatstock Show and Rodeo -- part of that was that there were trail rides that would come in from all different places in Texas to Houston. And these were like old-timey trail rides, horses, you know, covered wagons, chuck wagons, that sort of thing. And so we were all on the trail ride together from San Antonio -- I forget which trail ride it was -- but we were coming from San Antonio to Houston. And we made that trail ride together.

And you know, I mean, it took days and days and days. And there was camping, and we kept getting closer and closer together. I mean, nothing serious, but we sort of -- she was like the sweetest person up until then I had ever, ever met. And I was especially smitten by the fact that she did not seem crazy. Because I seemed to have either attracted crazy people or been attracted to crazy people, I don't know.

But we got to Houston, and all the trail riders, from all these different trails, camped out in Houston's Memorial Park. And so we spent the night together, in the same sleeping bag, with each other. Nothing happened. It was just closeness.

And within three months of that time -- and what I didn't know at the time, she had been diagnosed with some rapid form of, I forget, leukemia or bone cancer or something -- and within three months after that, she was dead. And that was hard. Yeah.

And to make matters worse, by the time she had her funeral, I showed up at her funeral completely, completely blotto smashed, and apparently made a huge scene and I had to be dragged away from it. (Pause) I felt bad about that. (Brushing away tears) But I've never forgotten her, and she still lives, right in my heart.

Little Pecan Island

This was when Crazy Dee Dunkerly and I were still sort of an on-again, off-again thing. Of course, we'd gone on for a year or more, and there was never any, like, consummation of anything. There was, you know, fooling around. But at any rate, that summer, I was working for David Hefner's father as a welder's helper. And in that same little industrial complex, was this guy named, I think it was Bob Parvin. And he was sort of a wheeler dealer, hustler, into this, into that, kind of guy. You know? So he had asked us, David and I, if we wanted to take a truck and a big trailer to Lake Charles, Louisiana, to pick up -- he had bought the fixtures in a thread or sewing shop or store, that sold, you know, threads and fabrics and stuff. But he didn't buy the threads and fabrics, he just bought the fixtures for that store, because it had gone out of business. And he wanted to know if we would sometime -- it didn't have to be immediate, it could be sometime during the summer -- go down and gather up all the fixtures and bring them back to his place in Houston. And we said, "Yeah, okay, we'll think about it." You know, he was gonna pay us for doing it.

So at any rate, maybe a few days after that, back at our place, I think we were living in an apartment at that time, David and I and crazy cousin Butch. Anyway, I got a call, and it was Crazy Dee Dunkerly, all hysterical. And her father was a sort of bigwig in the oil industry somehow. I say bigwig, I mean, I don't think he was the biggest kind of wig, but anyway, they were well off. And she was crying and she was almost hysterical and she was saying, "They brought us to this place in Louisiana, it's on an island somewhere, I have no idea where we are, but everybody's drunk, and people are trying to hit on us, and they're getting all completely crazy, and my father's threatening to kill us." She said, "Can you come? Can you help?" And I said, "Well, I don't even know where you are. Is there a name of this place?" And she said, "Well, the only thing I heard was that it was Little Pecan Island." And I said, "Well, okay, can you give me a number where I can call you?" "No, no, no, no! I just snuck in here on the phone, there's no way to do that. But please help!" And boom, that was the end of the conversation.

So I'm thinking about it, and I'm thinking this is the craziest thing in the world. And then I'm thinking, "Well, wait a minute. David and I are supposed to go to Louisiana." And so I got out a map and looked at everything, and I saw where Lake Charles was, but I couldn't find anything about where Little Pecan Island was in the middle of the swamps of Louisiana. So I called David up, and I said, "Hey, why don't we do this tomorrow? Why don't we head out tomorrow?" And he said, "Why?" And I said, "Well, you know, I'll explain it to you when we get on the road."

And so we get on the road, and we're headed to Lake Charles, Louisiana, in a big pickup truck, with a big open trailer in the back that we're gonna load stuff up on. So we get to Lake Charles, we get to the fabric shop or whatever it was, we load up all the fixtures that were there. And then somebody -- I forget if it was like a cop or the owner of the shop, or something -- kind of came up to us while we were in the parking lot loading all this stuff up, you know, thinking maybe we were stealing it, and we got that all squared away. So I asked the guy, and I think his name was Boudreaux, something Boudreaux, I said, "So, have you ever heard of a place called Little Pecan Island?" And he said, and he's got this thick, deep, Cajun accent, and oh yeah, he knew all about it, he'd been there before, he knew where it was. It was near Big Pecan Island. (Laughter) And I said, "Well, that makes sense."

And I said, "So, how do we get there?" And he kind of laughed and he said, "Well, it's kind of complicated. The only thing I can tell you is, you go down to, you know, Evangeline Country, and you try to find such-and-such" -- he gave some

name, I don't know, some cousin of his, he said -- "who has
like a boat dock and takes people out fishing and stuff, and
he knows exactly where it is." He described it as this thing
with, like a red thing with a boat on top of the shed, or something. And so we make our way down to wherever that was,
near where, through the town where the Longfellow tree, the
tree that inspired Longfellow's poem, was. And we ask around,
and we get directions here and there.

Finally, we made it down this old dirt road that went out
towards the swamps, and we see the building with the boat
on top. And we stop in there, and the guy comes out, and we
start talking to him, saying, you know, "We're trying to get out
to Little Pecan Island." "Wha you wan' go Lil' 'can Isle for?"
(Laughter) And it's like, "What?" "Lil 'can Isle?" And we said,
"Well, got a friend out there, gonna go visit a friend, they're
having a little, some sort of retreat out there." And we only
had maybe, between the two of us, David and I probably had
maybe ten or fifteen dollars. And he said he could take us --
I'm cutting out all the coon-ass brogue -- but he said he could
take us and it was gonna cost like, you know, ten dollars. And I
said, "Well is that out and back?" And he said, "No, that's just
out." And I said, "Okay. So that would be twenty dollars. How
about I give you" -- and I forget what it was I said, like maybe
eight dollars, ten dollars, whatever, for the whole deal. And he
said, "No" and he starts walking back into the house. And I
said, "Fine. Great. Bye." and started walking to the truck, and
he comes back out and says, "Okay."

And so we go down -- there's two kind of main boats in the
swamps of Louisiana. One of them is pirogues -- they're sort
of like canoe-ish kind of things. And then there's these mud
boats. And these mud boats are kind of like just little row-
boats but they've got a little electric motor on the back. And
so we get out, and we're going and going and going, we're going
through these swamps, and . . .

Well first of all, we have to drive down to get to where the boats are. And it's along this long, long levee that must have been about three, maybe three or four miles long. And we're driving down this levee and following this guy, and the whole top of the levee is squirming. And we realize as we're driving down this levee that these are hundreds of thousands of water moccasins, doing whatever water moccasins are doing during that period of time. It must have been play time. And it was just crunch, crunch, crunch, crunch, crunch. And they were being thrown up, you know, underneath the car, and up underneath the wheel wells, and some would fly up on the windshield, and we had to roll up the windows.

And so finally we get out to the end of this levee and we get in the mud boat. And it's probably, by that time it was maybe 2:00 in the afternoon or something, but it was dark. I mean, the swamps are dark. You know, there's lots of overhanging -- it's just dark. And so we get out -- and it seemed like we were going for a long, long time. And I was getting kind of squinky about the whole thing, so was David, thinking we were being taken for some ride or something, we were a little, you know, we kept saying, "How much longer?" you know. And he'd say, "Oh, we're almost there." And then like thirty minutes later, we're still going. And thirty minutes later, still going. Well finally, he points out -- and we kind of broke out of some of the mangrove swamps and stuff, and we're in some kind of open water -- and he points out there and says, "Little Pecan Island!"

There was a boat dock there, and he said the boat dock was on the back side of the island. So we went around to the back side of the island, he went to the boat dock, we got off, we left, and then he said, "I ain't coming back." And so he's gone, with our ten bucks or whatever it was, and we're there on the island stuck. So we go into, like, full "skulking sneaking" mode. And it's not a huge island. It was probably about the size of Red Bud Isle -- no, maybe twice that size, just to give you perspective --

but we saw some buildings in the distance. We went over and started looking around, you know, sneaking around and looking, and finally --

Oh, and the other thing that Dee Dunkerly had said was that there was this creepy kid that kept trying to, you know, like a peeping tom, and was trying to do all this stuff to them, and everything like that. So we're moving around, and finally I look in this one window of this cabin kind of thing, and there she is with her sister. And I'm looking in the window, and she glances over that direction and starts screaming. And they drag us in, and we say, "What's going on?" And the first thing that she said was, "You guys gotta go, you gotta go, they're gonna kill you, they're gonna kill you! If anybody -- this is crazy, this is crazy!" And I'm like, "Well, hey, you wanted a couple of knights in shining armor, they're here."

And so she said "this is terrible, this is terrible, I shouldn't have called you, I shouldn't have called." And so then, Peeping Tom came up to the window, and he saw us, and she saw him. And he goes running off, because he's going to ring the emergency bells. And so then she's going really, really crazy. So there's -- we didn't know what to do -- but her sister Lynn said, "You guys have to get off the island, they're gonna kill you, they're really gonna kill you. They've got people out here that are armed and have threatened to kill anybody that comes around." And she had this idea -- there was this little shed where there was a little short-wave radio kind of thing, and she said, "There's a boat here on the island, a motorboat, a little cabin cruiser kind of thing, and we can call him on that, because he's always listening, if anybody needs a ride."

So they -- and we concocted this story. I always regretted this story, especially after having gone later to Vietnam. But the story we concocted on the fly was that we had just gotten word that my brother had been killed in Vietnam, and we had to get back, it was an emergency. Because Lynn and Crazy Dee said it has to be some kind of emergency. And we tried to get them to go with us, but they wouldn't go with us, they were too afraid of their father, and you know, the people on the island. But they said they were gonna be okay.

So we get on the boat with this other coon-ass Cajun that is -- and his son was also on the boat. Actually, I think his son was the Peeping Tom kid. And so we're on the boat, and David and I are sitting kind of in the back of the boat, and the captain of the boat is up front, and he's gunning it, and he's going like crazy. And he and his son were up there talking. And they had figured out something was really squinky about all of this. And they didn't know what. But David and I were back there, with David consoling me, as I'm, like, crying. And it was too crazy for words. I mean, nobody could have made this stuff up.

But we finally get to about thirty or forty yards from the place where our truck was parked, where the boat dock was, and that was after -- but now it's getting dark, and it's just about dark. And all of a sudden, forty yards, thirty yards away from the dock, the captain cuts the engine, and the boat's just sitting there. And he comes back, and he knows something's wrong. And he says, "Been thinking about it. How would you know, out on the island - there was no way to know that something had happened. I think you're messing with us. And I ain't doing this for free. I want fifty dollars." Or whatever it was. And we said, "Well, we don't have fifty dollars." And he said, "Well then you're leaving the boat." And I said, "Well, we're not leaving the boat." And then he picks up a gun, and he says, "I'll kill you." So David looks at me, and I look at David, and we were thinking the same thing, and we fly over the edge of the boat and we're in the water. And this guy's popping caps at us. And we're bumping up against snakes all over the place because they're everywhere. And he's firing his weapon, pop, pop, pop, pop, pop. And we're thinking we're dead. But it's gotten dark

enough now to where he can't even see where we are. So we
keep making our way towards the dock.

We get to the dock, we climb up on the dock -- neither one
of us got hit by a bullet or bitten by a snake -- and we get
up to the truck, we get in the truck, we haul ass back down
the levee, and it's nighttime now, and all we hear is crunch,
crunch, crunch, crunch, crunch, running over all these damn
water moccasins. And we got out of there, and we hadn't even
said a word to each other since right before we jumped off the
boat. And we finally get back to a highway, and we're getting
ready to head back to Texas, David said something like, "So
why did we go out there?" (Laughter)

Riding Logs in a Raging River

The San Jacinto River is a big river, one of the biggest in Texas.
And when I was 16 years old, there was a huge, huge flood on
the San Jacinto River. And me, and David Hefner, and Scott
Foster, and a couple of other guys -- we decided -- okay, I con-
fess, I suggested -- "Hey, let's go see this flooding river." It was
up around Conroe or somewhere in that area.

So we all pack up and go to see this flooding river. And boy,
is it flooding! It is just phenomenal. I mean, we had seen this
river before, we had been in this river before. It was just a lazy
river as a general rule. But this thing was going crazy! It was
flooding squared.

And I don't know who it was that came up with this idea,
I sadly suspect maybe it was me, but I'm not quite sure, but
we decided, "Hey, let's get in the river and find some logs and
shoot down this flooding river." And so we decided to do that,
but we decided, for whatever reason, I don't even remember
now, except that we didn't want to mess our clothes up -- "let's
strip naked and do this."

So we all strip naked. There were four or five of us. And we launch ourselves off the banks into this flooding river. And we're struggling for survival from the first seconds that we were in there.

I was yelling, "Find logs! Find a tree!" Because everything was going down this river. And so everybody was trying to glom onto stuff. And we are being battered and threatened for at least five miles, down this raging, raging river.

And finally, it eases up just a tiny bit, and I'm hollering, "Get out! Get to the banks! Get out!" So somehow, each of us, helping each other, were able to get ourselves out of the river and on to the banks. And we are stark naked, of course, and we're five miles away from where our cars were. We weren't thinking. We were teenagers. Teenagers don't often think through things completely. (Laughter)

So we started walking up the banks of the river, and all of a sudden we're at some park on the river. And we're completely naked, and there are parents and children and people having picnics in this park. And so we scurried back down, not into the river, but near the river, and we said, "We've got to get clothed."

So we were finding everything from palmetto bushes to wrap around us, to moss -- you know, tree moss -- and everything (laughter) to get back to where our cars were, five miles away. And lucky and happy that we're all actually still alive. We go walking through this park, and all these people are, like, staring (laughter) at these idiots who are dressed in tree moss around their loins, and palmetto bushes as little spurts. And we're barefooted, so we had to find tree bark to tie onto our feet so we could make this trek.

So we made this trek, finally, finally, five miles back to where our cars were. And yeah, somehow made it through that, made it out of that, changed into our clothes, and made it back to Houston.

Drugs from the Night Pharmacist

When I was maybe 16, and David Hefner was maybe 17, we were in the Delivery Boys' Union -- our own little two-man union, that we started up. We were both delivering for Cunningham Pharmacy Number Three. It was open 24 hours a day -- it was a huge pharmacy.

And we decided one night that we were gonna head to Mexico, because we had a couple of days off. So the night pharmacist says, "Wait a minute, you guys are heading out tonight?" It was after we got off work, like 10:00 at night or something. "And you're driving to Mexico? Aren't y'all exhausted?" We said, "Yeah, but we'll be fine."

"No, no, let me give you a little something." So he gives us a little bottle of pills. And he says, "Take a couple of these to start out with." And we did. And we launched off for our big trip to Mexico. And he had said, "Take two now and one every" so many hours. And there were only about four pills for each one of us in the bottle. So we took a couple, and we're off, heading towards Mexico. And somewhere along the line, we took another one.

I don't know if we ever made it to Mexico. What I do know is, two and a half days later, we wound up on the edge of a levy in Louisiana, with three or four bullet holes in our car. It was like fifty feet high, and the whole front of the car was over the end of the levy. And we had to very, very carefully crawl backwards and out the back window, and then the car went boom. It fell into the levy. We lost the car. It wasn't my car, it was David's sister's car.

But apparently, we had been solidly awake but completely out of it for two or two-and-a-half days. But we survived. And we have no idea and no memory -- and we've talked about it, David and I have talked about it *ad nauseum* -- Where did we get shot at? We didn't know. And how come we never made it to Mexico and wound up in Louisiana, of all places? We didn't know.

Whatever that night pharmacist gave us was something I would never want to experience again.

Staring Down a Rifle at a Poker Game

So, when I was about 16 to 17, and David was about a year older -- and we each had our kind of, had our sets of other friends. We went to different high schools. He went to Sam Houston High School in Houston, and I was at, at that time, I think I was at Waltrip High School, where I really had not too many friends there, all my friends were out in Spring Branch, and I still went out to see them. But David had a few renegade friends. One of them's name was James Sermon. And then there was another one. But they were about 20 years old, 20, 21. And they had an apartment. And they had poker games and they had plenty of booze and beer.

And David was telling me about that, and saying, "We really ought to go over there and play poker, you know, drink beer." And so I said, "Okay." But I said, "You know, I don't really like these guys very much." Because I'd met them before. And he said, "Aw, they're okay, they're okay." And I said, "No, they're not okay. You know, one of the things that they're proudest of is that they were talking about cruising down these roads and looking for black people and shooting at them, and trying to run them over and stuff." I said, "I don't think I like these people." And he said, "No, no, no, they're just big talkers." So I said, "Well, okay, we'll go over and play poker."

And so we were at their apartment, with James Sermon and the other guy, and we're playing poker and drinking beer or whatever, and there's like a loud bang/knock on the door. And somebody, I was closest to the door, and somebody said, "See who that is." So I go over and I open the door, and there's a guy standing out in front of me with a large caliber rifle pointing right at me. And as soon as I saw the rifle, I flew off to the side, and I look up, and the rifle's going this way, to the left, to the right, and all of a sudden, boom. He shoots the guy who had the apartment, which, I don't remember if that was James Sermon or the other guy. Killed him dead.

And it turns out -- and all the rest of us, jumped up, grabbed the guy, wrestled him to the ground, and held him until the police got there -- but it turned out that the deal was that whoever it was that he was shooting at, he was shooting at him because he had parked in the shooter's parking spot.

But I will tell you that he was looking to shoot the first person he could see, and the first person he saw was me. But since I flew off to the side, he pulled the trigger and it hit the guy who actually had the apartment. And that was hours' worth of dealing with the police and everything. But after it was all over, I told David, "You know, I told you I didn't like these guys!" And he said, "You know, I think you were right. I'm going to listen to you more."

Almost Arrested for Theft

David Hefner and I had a little business that we started up, when I was around 16 and he was around 17, which was basically lake-lot and small-acreage clearing. We had little cards made up and we put them up different places. We started getting some business! We had a number of things. It was like, "Woah! We didn't see this coming!" And so there was a lot in, somewhere around Conroe, one of the small lots that people had bought that, you know, wanted the brush cleared out and wanted the trees saved, and that sort of thing. And we took that task on.

Now remember in those days, this was back in '65 or '66, there was no such thing as cell phones. And so we had, before we left on that little jaunt out there, we had gotten -- this is kind of a two-prong deal. The night before we left, Crazy Dee Dunkerly had reached out to me and said she was in big, serious trouble. She was at a party, and things were going south, and people were threatening her, had threatened to rape her, and we needed to come over there.

So of course David and I went over there. And we got there, and it was at some high school guy's house, and it was like, you know, 80 or 100 people, I don't know, a whole menagerie of people. And whoever's house it was came out and started giving David and me some shit. I said, "We're taking Dee with us." "No, you're not." And we said, "You don't want to go there, guys." And they wanted to go there.

And so they went there. And this wasn't 70 or 80 guys, this was five, maybe six, guys. But they attacked us. And we are fighting -- this was in the front yard -- and we are fighting to save our lives, right? We're just going at it like nobody's business. And as it turns out, we prevailed. And Dee came running out of the house. And, you know, we snatched her up, we put her in the car, we drove her home, and dropped her off. Because we had to head out of town, we had delayed heading out of town, right?

So we get to around, somewhere around Conroe, and we open the trunk to get all of our tools -- this is my car, this was a 1959 Chevrolet -- so we open the trunk of my car to get the tools, chainsaws and axes and whatnot out of there, and I look in the trunk, and it's filled with silver services, jewelry, all this shit. And I thought, "What the fuck?" to put it mildly. And I put two and two together pretty quick. And what had happened was, while she had gotten David and me involved in this big fight outside, she had ransacked the house and put the stuff in my trunk! And we had no idea until we got there. And so we got there on this job, and I thought, "Oh my god."

And so we drive to a pay phone in Conroe, and I call her, and she says, "Thank god you called! You've got to get back here, you've got to get back here now, because the parents of this guy" -- they were away for the night, it was one of those kind of deals -- the parents had called and said, "Look, if you'll bring everything back, everything will be okay and there won't be any problems." So she said, "So you've got to get back here with all that stuff!" And of course we didn't know the stuff was there until about 30 minutes before then, right?

So we haul ass back to Houston, and we start pulling up to where the house was, but the police were all there, and they're hauling Crazy Dee out to the police car. And what had happened was that it was a set-up. The parents had called the police, the police said "Get her back here, give her some excuse," and the minute she showed up at the house, they arrested her and took her to jail.

And so I said to David, "Well, I've got to go down and try to get her out of jail. I've got to explain all this stuff that's going on." And David didn't want to have anything to do with that, and I don't blame him. He'd pretty much had enough of that kind of stuff.

So I get to the Houston Police Department jail, and I go in, and they bring me in, and they -- they don't arrest me, but they're questioning me. And they said that they had Dee in another room, and they're going on and on and on, giving me the third degree, like, "We know it was all your plan. She said it was your plan. And if you don't take responsibility for it, you're just a pussy, letting the girl take all the," you know, all that kind of stuff.

And I was just honest with them. I said, "Nope. It wasn't my plan. I don't know what happened. All I know is that all this stuff was in my trunk, I have no idea who put it there." Because we never saw Dee put it there. And I just stuck with my story the whole time. And they kept saying, "We're gonna arrest both of you. You're both gonna be in jail until one of you talks. And if you're such a chickenshit that you can't cop to what you really did, and you're gonna let her take the fall for all of this." I said, "I'm not letting anybody take the fall for anything. I'm just telling you what I know about this situation."

And after about four hours, they cut me loose, because I said, I asked them, finally, "Am I under arrest?" "No." "Am I free to go?" They said, "Well, we can't stop you." And so I left. And she took a fall for it, because it was her rat killing. And I was done with her, I mean, done with her. And so, yeah, that was when -- I'm not quite sure, even though I was later a cop -- I'm not quite sure whether I was actually just detained and interrogated, or whether I was actually under arrest until I finally snapped to the fact, as a young teenager, that, "Nobody's put me in handcuffs yet." And, "either charge me or cut me loose." And they cut me loose. And that was pretty much, that was the end of the Ben and Crazy Dee Dunkerly relationship.

Last Rodeo

I started rodeoing when I was about 14, and I started out -- we built a rodeo arena in Houston, out in Spring Branch. Turned out to be a pretty good little rodeo arena. And then I started riding rodeos all around Texas -- amateur, I was an amateur rodeo rider -- ride rodeos at, you know, Circle 8, and Hallettsville, all around South Texas.

And when I was about 17, I was gonna be riding a rodeo up out of Kerrville at a place called Crider's, which is still there, I think, it still has a rodeo arena, and it was up a few miles west of Kerrville in Ingram. And I was a bull rider. I rode bulls. And at the rodeo, at one point, the announcer, on the loudspeaker, was announcing the riders coming up next for the bareback bronc event, and my name was called out. And I went up and talked to the people, and they said, "Well, it's too late to do anything about it now. I don't know what the mistake was, but either you ride or you forfeit. Because the bull riding event is full now."

So I thought I was just gonna have to forfeit it. And some other cowboy came up to me, older guy, and said, "Well, I got a bareback riggin' in the back of my truck, if you want to use it." Because the riggings for bareback bronc riding are very different from bull riggings. And also the spurs are different. In bareback bronc riding, the spurs are not locked, they are free-wheeling, because part of the event is spurring the horse. And in bull riding, the spurs are locked, they don't twirl, you use them to dig in and try to hold on for dear life. Because bull riding is a pretty dangerous event. So some other cowbody said, "Well, I've got a pair of bronc spurs you could use." And I said, "What the hell."

So I got the rigging on, I got the spurs on, I get up in the chute, and I'm sitting in the chute, and I don't remember the name of the horse, but in my mind, the horse's name wound up being Diablo. (Laughter) And I'm sitting in the chute, and Diablo is just, you know, he's thrashing in the chute, and I'm getting thrown up against the sides of the chute, and I'm thinking, "Well, I'm going to have to tame this little rascal."

So when the chute opens, we're out of the chute, and probably maybe two or three bucks out of the chute, the old rigging that this guy had given me broke. And all of a sudden, I found myself sitting about 14 feet in the air, with my feet up above my head, because that's the way you spurred, you know. And Diablo is gone.

And I come down and land on my butt and break my coccyx, break my tailbone. Probably one of the most painful and long conditions I've ever had. It took about, I was pretty laid up, for about four or four-and-a-half months after that. And I thought, "You know, I think the universe is sending me a message. I think I'm done with rodeoing." And so that was my last rodeo.

Clearing the Catholic Cemetery

So during the time that David Hefner and I were doing our surprisingly profitable summer land clearing business -- Lake Lot and Small Acreage Clearing -- we had little cards, somewhere there's a card in all of my stuff. We had little business cards.

And one day we got a call, and it was this old Catholic cemetery in far east Houston that had not been tended to for 30 or 40 years. And they wanted us to come and clear out and make the cemetery good again, you know. We talked to the guy that was in charge of all that for the Catholic Church out there -- I don't remember the name of the Catholic Church, but it can easily be found because, it turns out, there were a number of very famous Texans buried there, including Dick Dowling, who was the hero of Sabine Pass during the Civil War, who had kept the Yankees from entering Texas by sea. So whatever Catholic -- wherever he's buried is where the Catholic Church was.

And we went out to take a look at it, and it was a massive cemetery -- or, it seemed massive, it was huge, it was a huge cemetery. Not as big as the Texas State Cemetery, but still a big cemetery. And we're looking at all of this, and it is just a holy mess. You can't see any tombstones. I mean, you can walk through it and find tombstones, but it was overgrown way above the tombstones -- trees and bushes and everything else were growing through there.

And David and I thought about it and thought about it, and said, "Well, we need a tractor. A brush hog, to do the -- we've got to do the major clearing, where we're not gonna hit tombstones, with that, but then we've got to tend around all the little tombstones." But we had to identify all the tombstones, every single one of them, we had to put little flags up, so that when we're using the tractor going through there, we wouldn't hit any tombstones. We got most of it right. (Laughter) We did hit a few tombstones, but that's, you know, that's just the way it was.

But we didn't have a tractor. So I figured out that, about a mile or two away from this cemetery, there was a rental place that rented tractors. So we got us a tractor. We drive two miles down the streets of east Houston in our tractor, and we get out there. And we were out there for probably --- it probably took a good week. And we're working, and we're working hard, and we're trying to identify every tombstone, we're trying to be respectful of all these people.

But as we were going through this, you know, David's doing one thing -- I mean, you know, he's marking tombstones right? And he's getting mad at me, because I'm spending all this time studying the tombstones! And I'm saying, "Look at this! This is Dick Dowling! Do you know who Dick Dowling was?!" You know, "No, who was he?" And there were all these people that I was finding, historical people, because I was kind of a history nut even then.

So we work and work and work on this, and one of the main things I remember about that is, that as we were working out there, the Beatles song *Eleanor Rigby* came out. And we had it playing on a radio, I don't know, a transistor or the car radio or something. And I always associated that experience with a more profound experience with *Eleanor Rigby* because, you know, it was all about living and dying in a cemetery, and the headstones, you know, and all this kind of stuff.

So we did that job, and we got paid very, very well for that job. Even though we confessed to the Catholic priest who was in charge of it that we damaged some tombstones accidentally. But they still paid us and everything. And that was -- now that I think about it -- that was about a year before, a year-and-a-half before I went into the Army and to Vietnam. David went into the Army about a year before I did.

But while I was in Vietnam, I got a letter forwarded to me from Houston to Vietnam, to my A.P.O. -- Army Post Office Box -- in Vietnam, and it was the Catholic Church wanting to know if we could come back and -- they didn't know where we were -- if we could come and redo the graveyard and maintain it on a regular basis. And I had to send them back a letter saying, "I'm sorry, we're both in the Army and we're overseas and we won't be able to do that anymore."

But the takeaway from that was not just all of the famous people that were buried out there, and what a difficult job it was, but how it was infused and imbued with, forever in my mind, the story and the song of *Eleanor Rigby*.

The Columbus Prom

David Hefner and I would launch off on little road trips sometimes. We both skipped school. And we'd take off, sometimes it was in a car I had access to, sometimes a car he had access to. And on one of these road trips, we, for some odd reason, wound up in La Grange, Texas. Now, La Grange, Texas, is famous for having the best little whorehouse in Texas, but that's not why we were there. We were there because somebody had, we had gone through there and stopped for a chicken-fried steak, because we were always on the lookout for the best chicken-fried steak places in Texas. That was part of our, you know, *raison d'etre*.

And we met a couple of girls at some cafe, and we started, you know, kind of getting to know each other and whatnot. And they were gonna be graduating from high school -- I guess this was about the time we were, I was probably a senior at that time and he had probably just graduated from high school. But they wanted us to be their dates for the senior prom, which was not in La Grange, they went to school in Columbus, Texas. And we said, "Yeah, sure, we'll do this."

But the more we talked about it -- and we didn't really have much of a connection with these girls, and we didn't like either one very much really, as we talked about it -- we weren't, like -- this wasn't like love stuff or anything. But we thought, maybe, you know, there's a chance of some who-knows-what. So we said, "Yeah, we'll take you to the prom."

So we thought about it and thought about it, and we thought that, "we really don't want to make this a lifetime relationship with them, let's kind of fuck it up a little bit." So we both rented tuxedos for the prom, but these were not your standard prom tuxedos. Mine was a madras plaid tuxedo and his was something like, I don't know, pink and blue and red stripes, or something like that. Because we thought we really don't want to get too attached to these girls.

And so we get up there for the prom, and it turns out that the prom was being held in the gym of the Columbus high school. And we were, like, the hit of the prom. Nobody had any kind of -- they were all wearing, you know, jeans and sports coats, and here we were standing out like a couple of goofballs from Houston, Texas, right? But we were the hit of the ball. And these girls fell in love with us, or so we thought.

And then we were gonna take them to dinner because, you know, prom night, you take the dates to dinner. And we said, "Well, where can we go to dinner?" And they said, "Well, we'd like to go to the cafe at the Shell service station on I-10. That's where we want to go." So we said, "Okay!" That was something we could afford! And I think they were factoring that in, they knew we were not rich guys. So we go to the Shell service station cafe on I-10 and have whatever, hamburgers, or whatever they had.

So then afterwards, they said, "My parents are away for the night, would you like to spend the night?" And David Hefner and I thought, "Score!" (Laughter) And so we, yes, we take them back to one of the girl's parents' house, and they bring us some drinks to drink, and little did we know, they had spiked these drinks, because they were not gonna lose their virginity that night. But they were into it, you know. And the next thing we know, we've had a couple of drinks of whatever the drinks were they were bringing us, and we both passed out.

And the next morning, we said our goodbyes, and didn't know what happened. It took us a while to figure out, we didn't figure it out immediately, we figured it out kind of driving back from Columbus to Houston. "These girls slipped us a mickey!" But they were incessant, they apparently had fallen in love with both of us, and so they kept calling the pharmacy all the time.

And there was a woman -- the pharmacy was attached to a hospital -- and there was a woman, an older nurse, who we had helped out carrying pianos, or moving her house or something somewhere. And at one point they were just calling, calling, calling, and David and I got together and said, "We need to end this. But we don't want to hurt their feelings or anything, tell them we hate them, or whatever."

And so we concocted this notion, that we gave them the telephone number to call and it was this nurse who was going to tell them, "Oh, I'm sorry, they both died in a car crash." And that's what she told them. And we thought, "We're done, this is all over." But they were so distraught, they came to Houston for the funeral services or whatever, and it all kind of blew up. And I think, after that, I'm pretty sure, that despite our efforts to let them down easily, they pretty much hated our guts for the rest of our lives.

Mrs. Robinson and a Broken Nose

For some reason, I don't remember how this happened, but I think I had gotten a call from Rita LaFerme. She said, "Can you come over? I'm living now off of Airport Boulevard near the Houston Hobby Airport." I was between 16 and 17 at this time. I said, "Well, I don't know." I said, "I've got my buddies with me, I've got my cousin Butch and his brother-in-law," who was named James Wachter. I said, "I'm really kind of tied up right now." And she said, "Well, I've got some liquor and beer over here if you want to come. I just thought it would be nice to see you again, I haven't seen you in a few months."

So we head over there. Because I still had this little thing for her. And we get there, and we're all sitting out in her little TV area, and she said, "Well, I'm going to bed. You guys just stay out here and do what you're going to do." And so they're sitting out there drinking, and they're getting just shitfaced, and she comes over and says, "Come and see me in a minute." So they're drinking, and I'm thinking, "Oh, who knows?"

So I kind of scoot around from that and go in to see her. And she's lying on the bed, and she says, "It's time." And she kind of pulls me to her on the bed and kisses me. And I'm still fumbling around, crazy stuff, you know, and so I'm kind of rubbing her, touching her, and all of a sudden she goes batshit crazy. Because apparently I had touched her belly, where she had stretch marks or something, and she was very, apparently very sensitive about her stomach. And she just threw a holy fucking fit, and said, "Get out! Get out! I can't believe you touched --" You know, on and on. And I'm thinking, "Okay, well, obviously crazy people are attracted to me."

So I go out, and James Wachter has his own car or truck there, and he heads out. Both of them are just, almost blind drunk by then. And Butch and I are driving back towards the Gulf Freeway from there. And I'm in this little International Scout, which was the previous little delivery vehicle for the drugstore that I had absconded with somehow. And we're driving down the street, and he starts all this trash talk. And all of sudden he wants to fight, and he starts swinging at me in the car. And I jam the brakes on at this light on the corner of whatever street that was and the service road for the Gulf Freeway, and I reach across him and I open the door, his passenger door, and I shove him out onto the ground. I close the door, and I drive off. And it's like, "I'm not dealing with this guy ever again."

And we were roommates at the time, we had this apartment over off of T.C. Jester Boulevard in Houston. So I went home. And I'm trying to process this night. (Laughter) Almost got laid, but, and it was like Mrs. Robinson. Although I'd never heard of Mrs. Robinson at the time, but I always later thought of her as Mrs. Robinson. And I went home, I went to bed, I went to sleep.

And the next morning I wake up, and I'm thinking he probably had found his way back somehow. No, he wasn't there. David Hefner, or I don't know, somebody who was there with us, said, "Where's your cousin?" I said, "I thought he'd be back by now." They said, "Well, what happened?" And I told them. And they said, "Damn, don't you think you ought to go check on him?" And I said, "Well, I guess so."

So I get back in the old International Scout and I drive way across town from, you know, T.C. Jester Boulevard on kind of the central-west side of town to the east side of town near Hobby Airport. And I'm driving along, and I'm thinking, "this is just a lost cause, I have no idea where he's gonna be." But no, I see him sitting on top of a fire hydrant on the service road of the Gulf Freeway. And I thought, "God, has he been sitting there all night long?" And yes, indeed, he had been sitting there all night long. And yes, indeed, he had been sitting there all night long thinking of how he was going to kill me when he found me.

So anyway, I pull up near the, on the service road and stop and get out. And I basically say, "Look, are you sober? Is it okay to come home now?" And he starts walking towards me, you know, just kind of normal, and he gets about a foot-and-a-half away, and all of a sudden, he sucker punches me so hard that not only did it knock me out but it broke my nose. And I'm bleeding like a stuck pig. And he throws me in the International Scout and drives back to our apartment.

And he's feeling, actually, by that time -- for some reason, it's probably the only time I ever saw him show some bit of being sorry for something. And, I mean, he was scared, he was scared that he'd hurt me really, really bad. And the truth of the matter is, he had. And it took about three or four months for all of that to heal up. And I did not speak a word -- we were living in the same place -- but we were not speaking a word to each other, and it was very tense, all of that time.

And it was at that point, when I decided, "Nope. These people are -- somehow I am thrown into groups of crazy people, and maybe that makes me crazy, but I'm getting out." So I left, and it was probably at that moment when I started my own singular life of never having roommates again -- I mean, except for forced ones in the Army -- but in terms of, I cut all ties with my crazy cousin Butch and his crazy brother-in-law. But not with David Hefner.

Hope, Texas

So David Hefner and I had been out somewhere, who knows where, in west Texas, I don't know, I have no recollection of it, but I know that we were headed back to Houston. And David was saying, you know, "We're in no condition to keep driving." And I said, "Well, we don't have any money." He said, "No, my sister and brother-in-law, Vava and Warren, live in Hope, Texas." Which is not, as I recall, is not too far out of, kind of, in the general vicinity of Gonzales, probably within, I don't know, a 40 mile radius. He said, "Let's head there. At the very least, they'll feed us." But we were, I think it's fair to say, we were both pretty inebriated.

And we roll up there at their place in Hope, Texas, and they welcome us in. And they feed us. And they give us a place to sleep. But they insisted that tomorrow -- it was a Saturday night -- Sunday, David told me, his sister had talked to him, and we had to attend the church service, where Warren was the preacher, at the little Hope Baptist Church. And after some discussion, I said, "Okay, whatever."

So anyway, the next morning, we are hung way over. And we make our way to the church. And quite frankly, the church was -- probably had -- I mean, it was very, very tiny. There were probably enough pews, like four or five or six pews, probably enough for about 30, perhaps 35 people maximum. And we sat in a place a number of rows back from the pulpit, kind of off to ourselves.

I won't say the place was packed, but there were probably 25 or 30 people there, in the church. And it's excruciating. The sermon was excruciating. It was all, the whole sermon was toward saving the sinners, saving the sinners. And then they had a person who sang, an old lady, and this was probably the worst singing I've ever heard in my entire life. It was so bad, but so funny, that David and I were actually pinching ourselves, hard, to keep from laughing, it was so bad. And even so, I'm sure we snickered.

And then at the end of the service, this is the time in a service, in most of these Christian services, where they start calling people up to come and get saved, you know. But one of the things that was pretty obvious to me was that there were only two people in that church that had never been saved and baptized. And so Warren goes through this whole long thing about coming to Jesus and getting saved, and absolved for all your sins, and so on, and we're just sitting there kind of looking down, you know, trying to be inconspicuous. And the old woman sang another song, and then he started all over again. And they went through this about four or five times waiting for people to come up to get saved -- waiting for us.

And finally, at sort of the end of the deal, Warren is standing over us, in the pew, begging us to come and get saved for our sins. And David sat there, and I said, "I'm done." I got up and I walked out of the place. And David let him have his say, and David said, to Warren, "It's too late." And he got up and walked out. And we went out, we got in our car, and we drove away from Hope, and never ever went back again. That was the first and only time that I ever met his sister and brother-in-law.

A Bathroom Fight and Kicked Out of School

After we moved out to Spring Branch, near Addicks Dam, I went to Woodview Elementary and Spring Woods Junior High. When I started high school -- they were building a new high school out there, but it wasn't built yet, so I was shipped over across I-10 to Memorial High School for one year. Then we moved back to the north side of Houston, and so I went to Waltrip High School for my sophomore and junior years. It was a pathetic school. I hated the people. All my friends were in Spring Branch.

So as soon as I started driving -- I got a license when I was 15 -- I would start skipping a lot of school to go back over to visit with my friends in Spring Branch. So, at the beginning of my senior year, I decided I wanted to graduate from Spring Woods High School, which had been built by that time. I had been on the football team during junior high, and in ninth grade, and I knew a bunch of people who had been on the football team. I was a halfback. We had terrible seasons, but we were a credible team.

So I enrolled at Spring Woods and gave them my old address and my old telephone number. And I went to school there, and everything was fine! Everything was good. I was, like, "Yes! I took control of something and I'm gonna graduate from Spring Woods with all my buddies!"

A few weeks or a couple of months into the first semester, I was in the bathroom. The seniors were all in the very back of the bathroom, then the juniors, then the sophomores, then the freshmen. That's how the bathroom was divided up. And the seniors were back there smoking and joking and everything.

Well, the coach of the football team had sent the seniors on the football team in to clear out the bathroom and the smokers. So they get to the freshmen, and they scamper out, and the sophomores finally leave. The juniors are pushing and shoving a little bit, but they get out. So it's just left with the seniors in the back against the seniors of the football team.

And these football players were all guys that I had known forever, growing up with and playing little league football with, and junior high football with, and high school football with, in the ninth grade. And they came in like Nazis and started laying into the smokers. I wasn't smoking, but I said, "This is bullshit." So I weighed into the whole thing, and it became this huge fight. Because the senior football players had gotten it in their heads that they were so rough and tough -- they didn't realize how rough and tough the non-football players were. So it turned into this huge, massive fight. I came out okay, but two or three of, what I thought were friends of mine before, that came at me, had gotten hurt.

So I was dragged down to the office -- there were, like, two or three of us that were identified. And they said they were gonna kick me out of school for three days or whatever it was and they needed to call my parents. And they looked up my stuff, and they called the telephone number that I had listed, from my old address, and people answered and said, "No, we don't know him at all."

Pretty soon it became apparent to them that I didn't belong in their school anymore. So within 45 minutes of having been busted and taken to the office, I was kicked out permanently from Spring Woods High School and then had to go back to Waltrip High School, where I finally graduated from. But I never forgot, the guys that I once thought were friends, that had become Nazi drink-the-Kool-aid enemies, and to this very day, there are some of those people that are still on my shit list.

Pole Vaulting and a Concussion

Probably, I'm guessing, in retrospect, this was the worst injury that I ever had growing up -- and this was a relatively benign activity.

In my senior year of high school, I stopped playing football. I'd played football all the way from the time I was, like, nine years old all the way up to the time I was a senior in high school. But I was done with football.

And I thought -- and the track coach had said, had been on me for a couple of years to come out for track, you know, because I was a fast runner. But I was tired of running, I was tired of all this, but what I kind of got glommed onto was pole vaulting. I was watching the pole vaulters and I thought, "That's what I want to do." And so I became a pole vaulter. And I became a pretty good pole vaulter. Not great.

And in those days, they didn't have, like, plexiglass poles that would bend halfway. We had aluminum poles or bamboo poles. They were phasing out bamboo poles because too many of the bamboo poles had broken and impaled people who were pole vaulting. And the aluminum poles were so rigid that there just wasn't much give to them at all. But those were the days that I was pole vaulting.

And on one of these times, after a practice -- I loved practicing and I loved pole vaulting because it was just me against it, you know? I finished practice one day -- and I was a senior in high school at this time -- and was heading back to the locker room and showers and everything, to change clothes and go home. And at that time, I had a car, it was a 1959 Chevrolet.

But at any rate, I got to the outside of the locker room, and outside of the locker room was this high, sort of jump-up-and-catch-it pull-up bar. And this was all on asphalt out there, it was over asphalt. And I was feeling frisky and everything, and I spun myself up on top of the bar. And I'm sitting up on top of the bar, and I thought, "Okay, I'm gonna do a backwards flip off the bar." And I'd done it a million times. This was not the first time. But I was super sweaty. And I came down, and I was so sweaty, I went straight down, head first, onto the asphalt concrete.

And the only thing I remember after that was some spitting out of asphalt from my mouth and not being able to focus on anything. And then the next thing I knew, I was somehow in the locker room and people were meandering around, and I couldn't understand anything anybody was saying. And I think people were talking at me, probably saying, "Are you okay?" or something, and I was completely out of it.

And somehow I managed to get dressed and changed, and the next thing I know, I am in my front yard at my house, in the front yard, lying unconscious. And my car -- that I drove home somehow -- was halfway up on the curb and halfway up on the driveway.

And I obviously had a serious, serious concussion. But it never dawned on me, and I didn't have parents around who would say, "God, we've got to get you to the hospital, or a doctor, or something." And so I just crawled into the house and was out of it for two or three or four days. I don't remember anything about that time, I have no clue what happened during those days. And I never even got it diagnosed, never went

to the hospital, never went to the doctor. And I just waited until I kind of came back a little bit.

And the ironic thing was, that had I gone to the hospital or
the doctor or anything like that, it probably would have kept
me from getting drafted and sent to Vietnam. I mean, it was
that serious of an injury. And of course, I mean, you can probably see the results of all of that, right before your eyes. (Laughter)

Gang Fight at the Mighty Burger

This was around 1967, the year I graduated from high school.
From the time I was about 15 or 16, I was living in an apartment, shared by David Hefner, me, and my crazy cousin Butch,
and sometimes one or two other people who would come in
and out. One of them was crazy cousin Butch's brother-in-law,
James Wachter, who I think is in prison now.

So one night David and I decided we wanted to go to the
Mighty Burger, which was over close to my high school, Waltrip High School. I didn't have a lot of friends at Waltrip High
School. I had some, let's say, run-ins with some people there. I
was sort of -- let me put it this way. From the time I was about
in the, oh, I don't know, whatever grade, I was kind of known
by some people as a hard-ass and not somebody that would
ever back down from any kind of bully, even if it was a bully
going after somebody else that I didn't even know. I didn't like
bullies and I didn't like assholes. So I had this kind of reputation. And of course nobody knew David Hefner or my crazy
cousin Butch.

But David and I had decided to go get a Mighty Burger and
some fries. And we went through the drive-through at the
Mighty Burger. And all of a sudden there was this, somebody
who had it in for me that went to high school with me -- I don't
remember his name, I can't remember -- but he came up to the

car -- and I think I was driving -- and he came up and started talking trash to me. I kind of blew it off, and said, "You're not worth even messing with." And at that point, he and two or three or four other guys, who were standing behind him, all threw drinks -- you know, soft drinks -- in through my window, into the car, hit me and David. And I looked at him and I said, "You know, you got a bunch of people with you. Hang in there for a few minutes, I'll be back." And I drove off.

And we went back to the apartment and got crazy cousin Butch. Crazy cousin Butch, I will give him credit for this. I mean, he was a psychopath, he was a sociopath, and he was a force of nature, and he was a good fighter. I knew this because I'd had many years of experience being on one end or the other of fights with crazy cousin Butch. Actually, I had many years of experience of having to sort of defend myself. But we told crazy cousin Butch what was going on, crazy cousin Butch -- the minute I said "fight," he was in. And he had already come back from the Army by that time.

So we get in the car and we drive back to the Mighty Burger. And there were -- while we were gone, the four or five guys had gathered together all of their forces. There were somewhere, depending on the police reports, somewhere between 18 and 22 people on their side. And we parked, we got out, and even crazy cousin Butch was a little worried about this situation, because he said, "There's a whole fucking lot of them." And I said, "Yeah." And they said, "How are we gonna do this?" And I said, "We all back up against each other, we make a triangle, and we go after it."

And David and Butch liked that idea. So here we were, three guys, and here they came. And this fight went on for a good fifteen or twenty minutes. And bad guys were going to their trunks and getting, you know, tire chains and crowbars. And by the time the cops got there, about twenty minutes later, there

were maybe four or five of the 18 to 22 people left standing --
three of those four or five were Butch, myself, and David.

And the ambulances came, and they hauled off a number
of people to the hospital. And the police were there to arrest
us, because the first person they talked to was one of the bad
guys. And they got to us, and we explained what the situation was -- I explained what the situation was -- and they said,
"Okay. Well, we're not gonna -- you've done about as much
possible damage as you can do to these people. We're not arresting whatever's left of them, and we're not arresting you.
But, Jesus, how did you do this?" (Laughter)

And so that was our big fight at the Mighty Burger, and it
was probably the biggest -- it certainly was the biggest gang
fight at that time that I had ever been in.

Trip to Fort Monmouth

Back when I was 17, maybe almost 18, David Hefner had already gone into the Army. He was stationed at Fort Monmouth,
New Jersey. Fort Monmouth was one of the most unique Army
sites I ever visited because most Army forts are these huge
massive complexes, but that was probably 10 acres of military
stuff.

But we made arrangements for me to come up there -- well,
I said I would come up, I wanted to come up and see him. But
I didn't have any way to get up there, and I had no money to
speak of, only pocket change kind of money. And one of the
people who worked for my father as a clerk at the drugstore --
and I liked her a lot, we chatted about, and I told her about this
big plan of mine, and she said, "Well, you know, my nephew
just got back from Vietnam." And this would have been about,
maybe '66, I'm thinking. Maybe '67. But at any rate, she said,
"He just got back, and he's heading to New Jersey for his next
duty station, and he's got a car and he's gonna be driving. Let

me see if you can hitch a ride with him to New Jersey." And I said, "Great!"

So I never met him until we met up to get on the road to the trip. And he had this jazzed-up, super-charged vehicle that he'd bought when he came back from Vietnam, that was a monster of a car. You know, like an engine monster of a car. I don't remember what it was now. It seems like it was a Pontiac or something. Anyway, we say hello to each other, get in the car. We meet up at the drug store on Airline Drive, which was where one of the pharmacies was. And we get on the road.

And we're heading out, and we're going along, and after about 30 miles -- I mean, he -- I can see -- I could tell from the beginning that there was something off. But it kept getting worse. I mean he was a total, total meltdown wreck from where he had just come from. And he was jerky herky, and, you know, hyper, crazed, and probably about 30 miles out of Houston, I told him to pull over. And I said, "Here's the deal. I feel for you. But you're in no condition to be driving. And either I'm going to get out of the car here, or I'm gonna drive the rest of the way." And he looked at me, and tears were coming down, and he said, "Would you?" And I said, "Yes."

And so I became the driver. And so we're making our way from 30 miles out of Houston to Fort Monmouth, New Jersey. And we're driving and driving, and he wants to stop at some-place, I think it was Tennessee, at some American Legion or VFW Hall. It was in Tennessee, I know. That was his big thing. He knew people in Knoxville, Tennessee, that were in the VFW Hall or American Legion, I don't know which one. But that was our, that was his interim destination. And I was all signed up for it, because I thought, "Boy, I gotta get this guy with some of his peeps, you know, because he's so --" I don't think I'd ever seen anybody who was such a fragile, emotional, on-the-edge-of-suicide wreck as he was. And I had seen some fragile people who were on the edge by that time, including my mother.

So the goal was to get to Knoxville, Tennessee. And we're driving and driving, and he drifts in, he drifts out, he sleeps, he's sleeping a lot. And we're in the mountains somewhere in Tennessee, and I turn the radio on to keep me, kind of, in the game, because it is snowing, and it's a hard snow, and (a) I had never driven in the mountains before and (2) I had never driven in snow before. And this snow came in at angles, and you couldn't figure out, you know, where the road was. And I thought, "Jesus."

And I turned the radio on, and all of a sudden, I'm listening to the radio, and it's talking about, "Hey, come to the UT Bookstore, get your orange and white jerseys," and so on. And I'm, like, really disoriented now, because I'm thinking, "Woah, is this bouncing off, you know, the clouds or what?" And at some point it finally dawned on me that this wasn't the University of Texas they were talking about, this was the University of Tennessee, which has the same colors as the University of Texas! And so that settled me down a little bit.

Anyway, we made our way into Knoxville. We found the, or I found the, whatever, American Legion or VFW Hall. We went in there, and all he wanted to do was to drink and drink and drink. And so -- that's most of, that's really all I remember of the trip to New Jersey. Because after that, he mostly just slept and slept, and I just drove and drove.

And I found our way to Fort Monmouth, New Jersey. No, he was going to Fort Dix. So I dropped him off at Fort Dix, and then I was gonna try to make my way to Fort Monmouth. And he says, "Obviously, I can't drive. You take my car, just get it back to me in a week or two, but take it, do what you need to do." So I took the car from Fort Dix, New Jersey, to Fort Monmouth, New Jersey, which was this little tiny fort. It was basically a cryptographic school -- it was a cryptographic school and cryptographic repair school. I think David was in the cryptographic repair end of all of this.

But they had a guest house, where people could, visitors could stay, like a little hotel, on the post. It wasn't a hotel, it was like a big cabin or something. But it probably had, like, 15 rooms and then a nice day room. And so I'm staying there, and David and I are meeting up every day to talk, and I was probably there for about a week.

Of course, the second night I was there, there was this woman, young woman, probably 20 years old, and we're sitting in sort of the day room, watching TV, and she's married to one of the soldiers there. And she scoots over, and all of a sudden there's all this sort of petting going on. And it's starting to get out of control. And so she said, "I'll be in my room, I'm in room such-and-such." And I sat there thinking and thinking and thinking, and I thought, "No. No, there's something not right about this. I mean, there's just something not right about it." And so that was the end of that.

Near Death in New York City and New Orleans

During the course of my visit to Fort Monmouth, David got a weekend off, and he wanted to go to New York. So we went to New York. David was gonna show me all around.

So we went to some bar there that he'd been to before, because he'd been up there for awhile, he'd been up there for, I don't know, four or five months. And we get into this bar, and there's some -- I think they were -- well, according to David -- I was never quite sure, I didn't know, I was kind of in an alien culture -- but there was this group of Puerto Rican gang members, according to David. And somehow we got into -- I say "we," me and one of the Puerto Ricans -- got into some kind of little tiff, I'm not even sure what happened, but I knew I was pissed off. So the little gangbanger said, "All right, we're taking this outside." And I said, "Fine!" He said, "I'll see you in the back alley!" And I said, "I'll be there."

And I would! I was heading that way. But David yanks me up by, you know, the arm and says, "He's not alone. I've been watching -- he's got five, six other guys with him. You go out there, you're gonna get gutted." And I said, "I'm going!" I said, "I'm not gonna put up with this shit." He said, "You don't realize where you are, and you don't realize who you're dealing with. You've got to think about this." And so I'm heading out the door, and he yanks me back, and he says, "I'm not gonna let you go out there." And I said, "Okay."

So I didn't go out in the back alley, I didn't get gutted, and I give David Hefner credit with having the more solid vision of what was going on, because to me, it was just another somebody getting up in my face, flunking the attitude test. So that was New York.

Then we go back to Fort Monmouth, and of course, little hottie tottie, she was gone by then. And so I said, "Well, I need to get on the road." (Laughter) And quite frankly, I do not remember how I made my way from New Jersey to Louisiana. I don't think I was hitchhiking. I had gone back and given that guy his car back at Fort Dix. But then I had to go from Fort Dix, New Jersey, to Louisiana, and I think it was by bus. I think the bus ticket was less than, or somewhere around, to get to Houston, was like $20 or $28, something like that. And I had barely that amount of money, or whatever it was. I had very little money with me.

So I get to New Orleans, and I'm in New Orleans. It was the first time as a young adult, 17, that I had been to New Orleans. And I was down in the Quarter and then went wandering around, because in the French Quarter, everything was so expensive. I started walking down some of these side streets, and all of a sudden things were getting cheaper and cheaper and cheaper.

And I walk into this bar, and I look around, and there's like -- it looks okay, there's some, you know -- it's not a big bar, it's probably, the whole bar was probably about twice the size of our bedroom. But there was nothing but girls in there! And I thought they were probably just prostitutes, you know. But the drinks were cheap, and they would serve me, and so I ordered a drink. And I'm sitting at the bar, and this really, really hot chick comes up and sits next to me, and says, "You think I'm gonna ask you to buy me a drink, don't you?" And I said, "I don't know what you're gonna do." And she said, "I want to buy you the next drink."

And she starts flirting with me, like, crazy flirting. And I'm thinking, "Hmmm. New Orleans is turning out pretty good so far!" And so we're there, drinking and flirting, and all of a sudden, this other woman walks up, who looked like your stereotypical kind of dyke lesbian, and she gets up in my face. And she's like, "What in the hell are you doing?" And I said, "I'm having a drink with this woman." Or whatever I said. And she pulls this knife out, with a blade that's about seven or eight inches long, and she grabs me by the shoulder, and she puts the knife up to my throat. And she says, "That's my woman. You're not getting out of here alive."

And I thought, "Huh. I wonder what I've just walked into." And I said, "Woah. What are you talking about?" And it became clear to me at that point that this was a gay bar, a lesbian bar, and the woman/girl who was flirting with me got all crazy weird, like, "Please don't kill him! Please don't kill him!" And I'm thinking, "I think this may be my last day on earth." And so she takes the knife and she pulls it back a little bit, because she's gonna stab me with it, and when she tries to stab me with it, I grab her arm, I toss her on the floor, I get the knife out of her hand, and I run like hell out of that bar! And that was how I almost got my throat slit in New Orleans.

A Teacher, Two #2 Pencils, and College

This is a strange story in a certain sort of way, because, you know, there are things in people's lives that are pivotal points. They don't even necessarily recognize them at the time. But there are things that alter the course of one's history. And what I'm about to talk about now is one of those things.

I was in my first semester of my senior year in high school -- in a high school I didn't want to be in, that I had tried to get out of. But I had an English class, and I really, really liked this teacher. She was extraordinarily good and engaging, and she even got somebody like me involved in what was going on. So I actually was trying -- I mean, not trying hard. I was drawn to, because I was interested -- it was, like, one of the few interesting classes that I had in school.

And at one point during that first semester of my senior year, it was a Friday afternoon. And, you know, that was the last class of the day. And everybody starts walking out, and she calls me by name and says, "Can you hang back a minute?" And I said, "Yeah." I wasn't even up from my desk yet, I was just putting my stuff together. And everybody's gone. She walks over and she puts two sharpened number two pencils on my desk. And she said, "Do you know what these are for?" I said, "Well, I mean, I don't usually use pencils." She said, "Nope. There is an SAT test tomorrow, on Saturday." And she told me where it was. And she said, "I paid for you to take this test, and you will take this test, and this is all you need is your two number two pencils."

And I have to be really honest, my high school grades were terrible, because I skipped so much school and didn't pay much attention to anything, and I was off and wandering around, and all that kind of stuff. But she said, "You have to promise me you'll go. I paid the money. And you don't owe me for it. Go and take the test."

So the next day, on Saturday, I went and took the SAT. And when the results came back, the test scores were, you know, however their calculus is, these test scores were very, very high. Could have gotten me into almost any place I wanted to ever go. And I thought, "That wasn't such a tough test!"

And I think one of the reasons why she had done this was, she had access to my records, and I had taken the PSAT in, like, my sophomore year, that had me in, like, whatever, the one percentile or whatever. So I took it, and it was on the basis -- it was not on the basis of my -- it was notwithstanding my grade point average in high school that got me into college. It was my SAT scores. And but for that, I'm not sure I ever would have even bothered to go to college. Because I really wasn't even thinking in those terms before.

And so I started college, and that first semester of college -- before I got sick and got dragged into the Army -- that first semester of college was probably my favorite semester of college, because all of a sudden I realized I was where I belonged. And I dug into it, made the Dean's List, and had a really high, you know, G.P.A., and then of course I got sick and got dragged into the Army.

But once I got out of the Army -- and while I was in the Army, of course, I was taking classes at various posts and places, they were all being amalgamated at the University of the State of New York in Albany. But I came back from Vietnam and started in at the University of Houston again, because that's where I was having to take care of family business and everything. And somewhere in that semester when I first came back, all of a sudden she appeared before me in, like, the Student Union. And I only vaguely recognized her, and even to this day I don't remember her name. But she sat down, we started talking.

Oh, and I forgot to say that in my second semester of high school -- I mean, my last semester of high school -- she had gotten fired because of me. I wanted to do this report on -- we had to pick a book and do some report on it -- and I picked Voltaire's *Candide*, but juxtaposed with a recent, really, really, raunchy book that had come out called *Candy*. But it was really a parody -- *Candide* was a parody, and this was a parody of *Candide*. And I wanted to juxtapose that and talk about it. And I did. And I got like an A+ for it. But somebody complained to somebody in the school, and she was actually fired for allowing me to use this pornographic, what they considered pornographic, book, *Candy*, in high school. Some parent or somebody complained, or something, so she got fired.

So anyway, I ran into her in college, when I came back from Vietnam. And she was working on her doctorate in psychology. And that was all fine and dandy. Of course, I was married, I had at least one kid at the time, Sam. But she started getting all flirty, and really just, really, really pressing hard for us to get together. And it was confusing to me. I was tempted, but I had to -- I had this family. And I said, "I can't do it." So that was sort of the end of that.

But, but for her, I never would have gotten into college, I never would have graduated from college, I never would have gone to law school, I never would have been where I am right now.

Red Adair and The Houston Chronicle

I graduated from high school in 1967, Waltrip High School -- same high school that I got an award in for five consecutive days of attendance in the same week in my entire high school career there. So when I graduated from high school, I figured out -- oh, and I had been accepted into the University of Houston and was gonna start my college career. But I needed to work because, not only did I have to support myself, I had to support my mother and my two younger sisters, Candy and Susan. Because, of course, my father had moved on.

So I needed a job. And I had applied to -- and here's how idiotic I was. I was driving down Southwest Freeway in Houston and saw a bunch of oil company things that were there. And I just stopped in (laughter) and walked in. And one was, I don't know, I want to say, like, Tesoro Energy, but I'm not sure that was actually -- it was one of the oil companies. And they treated me -- I mean, I was a high school kid, right? And I basically walked in and said, "I'd like a job." And they said, "What can you do for us?" And I said, "I don't know, I don't know anything about you." And that interview didn't go very well (laughter) because I just saw them on the freeway and I stopped in.

And I'm driving away from there, and I see this other place, and it was Red Adair's company. And I had actually heard of Red Adair before. Red Adair was this nationally, internationally-known oil well firefighter, because oil wells blow up and you have to call somebody, and Red Adair was, like, the premier thing. And I thought, "Huh, I can do this. I don't know what it is, but I can do it."

And I stopped in there. Pulled into the parking lot, went up to Red Adair's suite in whatever this office building was. And the receptionist was so nice, and she said, "May I help you?" And I said, "Yes, I'd like to see Red Adair." And she said, "Well, do you have an appointment?" And I said, "No." And she said, "Well, what is the nature of your call?" And I said, "Well, I'd like to talk to him about going to work for him." And I was, like, 18 at the time, I guess. And she said, "Well, okay, can you have a seat over there?"

And I took a seat. It was a huge, you know, waiting room, and I took a seat in one of the seats. And she called -- apparently called into the office of Red Adair, and then she said, "Well, Mr. Adair has a few minutes, he's willing to talk to you." And I said, "Great." I mean, to me, it wasn't like, "Oh, I snuck in

here." I thought, you know, of course he'd be willing to talk to
me! (Laughter)

So I get in there, and Red Adair had this enormous reputation in the oil well firefighting business. And I walked in and
it was this huge office, probably the office was, like, at least,
at least 900 square feet. I mean it was probably like the size of
half of our house that we live in right now. And it was all done
in red. There was red everything, you know, red leather chairs
and couches and so on. And Red Adair was sitting there, and
he said, "Come on in."

And he stands up, we shake hands. Red Adair was actually
probably about five inches shorter than I was. And I thought,
"Woah." I was expecting, you know, somebody tall. And as it
turns out, as a side note, there was a movie made of Red Adair
later, who was about five foot two, and the actor who played
him in the movie was John Wayne, who was about, I don't
know, six foot two or three, right? Because they weren't gonna
have some little guy playing the real guy, right?

So we started talking, and you know, we were talking about
this and that, and Red Adair was just so, so interested and genuine in listening to everything I said. And he said, "What experience do you have in firefighting?" (Laughter) And I said,
"Well, about the only experience I have in fire fighting is, accidentally, I was involved in helping to fight a couple of little
brush fires, one in Houston, one somewhere else." And he said,
"Well, that's kind of interesting."

And we talked, and he said, "Well, you know, what's your,
do you have any professional fire fighting background?" And I
said, "Well, no, not really, but I think I can do anything." And
he says, "I like that attitude!" And he said, "But here's the deal."
He said, and we talked, we probably talked for 30, 35, maybe
40 minutes, I don't know, it was a long meeting. And at the end
of the meeting, he said, "Look. I like you. But I can't hire anybody to work as a firefighter for me unless they've had at least

five years of firefighting experience -- either in, with a fire department, or with the military, or whatever." And he said, "But I will tell you this. If you go get that firefighting experience, I will hire you." And I said, "Oh." And I was, kind of, a little deflated, you know. And I said, "Okay. Well, I thank you so much for, you know, at least hearing me out." And he said, "It's been my pleasure."

And I was about to leave, and he said, "Wait a minute." He said, "You know, I've got a couple of racing boats. I keep them out at Clear Lake. I've got a boathouse, and the boathouse has a little apartment in it. And you know, do you know how to drive a boat?" And I said, "Well, I've driven a little, you know, motorboat before." And he said, "Well, if you want it, I will give you a job. And the job is that you will take my motorboats out and run them every day or two, and you can live in the apartment that's there. And it's good pay. And so if you want the job, let me know." And I said, "Well, okay, Mr. Adair. I've got one other job application that I'm waiting to hear from, it's at the Houston Chronicle." And I said, "If I don't take that, I'm certainly gonna take this, because," I said, "kind of my interest is in journalism, but you know, this would be great for me while I'm in college." And he said, "If you want it, you've got it."

And interestingly, that *very same day*, I got word from the Houston Chronicle that they wanted to hire me as an "editorial assistant" -- which was, in fact, kind of a glorified copy boy thing. But that was where my heart was, so I reluctantly turned down Red Adair's very generous offer to take the Houston Chronicle job. And I went to work for the Houston Chronicle and started out as, yes, a copy boy. And a copy boy at the Houston Chronicle was someone who worked in the City Room, and all the editors and writers would holler out, "Copy!" And you'd have to go grab their copy and send it down a pneumatic tube to the printing place.

But as time went by, in taking that job, I was kind of ooching along, and they promoted me to the next phase, which was going down to the Stock Exchange in Houston everyday, and getting all the Stock Exchange calculations and numbers, and bringing that back, and writing something up about that. And then, it kind of expanded, to where, okay, I was going to be retrieving obituaries from the morgue. And all newspapers have a system, and a place, for famous people in town, where they've already done up some of the copy for a potential obituary. And none of this was online at the time, all of this was just by hand and typed up somewhere. And I was sort of writing some of the obituaries. And then I started getting some reporting gigs. So my copy boy position finally morphed into an editorial assistant position, though never a reporter position, even though I was doing some of that.

And quite frankly, the -- while I always regretted not taking the Red Adair position, because it would have been so cool -- I could have had girlfriends out there at the boathouse and everything else, and riding boats, and taking them -- that appealed to me. But from the standpoint of what really I was interested in, the Chronicle wound up, working at the Houston Chronicle wound up being something that allowed me, once I was drafted and dragged into the Army, to parlay all of that into a position as a combat journalist in the Army, which actually wound up being my salvation in a way, from being sent to Vietnam as a "machine gunner." But even to this day, I always kind of wonder, what would have happened had I gone that other direction?

Chapter 3

The Army, Stateside: Ages 19-20

College, Illness, the Draft, and Enlisting

Because of my high school senior teacher sending me off and paying for me to take the SAT, and the results of that being the thing that got me into the University of Houston -- the first semester I was there, it was glorious in a certain sort of way, because I had hated high school. And all of a sudden, this was a place of learning. And I remember walking around the University of Houston library, which had every great thinker ever known to man up until that time, busts of them all around the library, at the top, outside. And I went in, and it was like, "Okay, this is where I was supposed to have been a long time ago. I should have been here before."

And so I started my classes, and I don't remember all the classes I took that first semester. One of them, one of the more interesting ones, was Asian Philosophies, except they called it Oriental Philosophies at that time. And I was exposed to Taoism, Buddhism, you know, a number of really ancient oriental philosophies, which really kind of resonated with me.

140

And I wound up finishing up the semester -- pouring my heart into it, you know? I wasn't living in the boathouse of Red Adair, but I was still working part-time, or, significant time -- between part-time and full-time -- at the Houston Chronicle. And I was just in a good place. Everything at that moment was in a good place. My mother was off in a mental hospital in Austin, my sisters were kind of under the care of my father and his new wife, and so I had a little respite. And I made some hay out of it. I wound up with some, you know, I mean, the usual stuff -- making the Dean's List, and really good grades, and everything like that. And I thought, "Life is gonna be good from now on out."

And the Christmas holidays came around, and over the Christmas holidays, towards the end of the Christmas holidays, probably about, you know, between Christmas and New Year's, I came down with what was ultimately diagnosed as Mononucleosis and Scarletina -- which is sort of like Scarlet Fever -- arising out of the mono. And I was bed-ridden for about four weeks. And by the time I was not bed-ridden but trying to come back, it was five or six weeks into the new semester. And I thought, "There's no way I can catch up with this semester. I need to drop those classes and I'll jump back in in the summertime." So I dropped the classes that I had for the second semester.

And within two weeks, I got a letter from Lyndon Baines Johnson. I usually describe it as a letter from Lyndon saying, "Sorry, Ben, we're scraping the bottom of the barrel, but we're losing the war, and we're dragging you in." And there I was, I had my draft notice. And I talked to David Hefner, who was already in the Army, and he said, "Don't let them draft you. You've still got time to enlist, and if you enlist, you can sign up for a school, a particular school." And he said, "My school, that I'm in right now, is intelligence and cryptography." And I thought, "That's interesting." Because I'd been up and seen him at Fort Monmouth, and I thought, "If I wind up there, that's pretty cool." So that's what I did. I went ahead and enlisted and chose a school.

The night before I left for the Army, my mother was back in town from hospitalization, and I had decided I was gonna take my two sisters and my mother out to dinner and a movie. Because they were absolute wrecks. And so I tried to find, think of something that would be good for, you know, girls and women. I took them to dinner and that went okay, although they were all still antsy. Then I took them to the movies. And the movie was *Gone with the Wind*. And it did not go well. (Laughter) I had no idea what *Gone with the Wind* was about, I thought it was just about strong women or something. And of course, they were in tears, so they were just, like, horrible wrecks. And I wouldn't let them -- I mean, nobody could take me -- but I wouldn't let them come with me to the induction center in Houston the next day. But that was my parting shot, leaving them in a state of, you know, complete depression and high anxiety.

So, came time to be dropped off at the Federal Building in downtown Houston. My father wasn't available, of course, and nobody was available, but Rick Martinelli -- sort of one of my surrogate parents along the way, who had worked for my father forever as a pharmacist, and he and I were really, really close -- he took me, he drove me to the Federal Building to drop me off. And it was almost a weepy experience, but not quite. But it was touching. He was so scared, because he knew where I was headed.

So, I went into the Federal Building, and we spent, like, eight or nine hours going through this and going through that, or just sitting, or doing nothing, or whatever, and going through this thing or that thing. And finally, after -- I think it was the end of the day -- buses showed up. And they took us to different places, but the bus I was on took us to the airport, and we were flown to El Paso. And there probably weren't -- because there were lots of basic training places. Most people went to Fort Polk in Louisiana. But somehow, I wound up on the Fort Bliss side.

And we got out there, and I think it was in late May, so it was May, June, July, and part of August, that I was in El Paso. And that was a summer in the desert in El Paso, and the temperatures ranged from about 120 to 140 degrees a day.

Basic Training Begins

So I arrived at Fort Bliss, Texas, in 1968, the beginning of summer. It was either May, June, and July, or June, July, and August. I think it was May, June, and July. And I got there, and -- I would say that, to short-circuit a whole lot, if anybody really wants to have a good flavor of what basic training is like, they should just watch the movie *Platoon* or *Full Metal Jacket*. But I'll tell you a couple of little snippets of stuff that happened in my basic training.

One was pretty funny. Actually, the first night I got there, we were assigned to our barracks. We hadn't been processed through yet, we hadn't gotten through all the shots, issuance of uniforms or anything. But I was assigned to fire guard duty during the night. And you have to remember, we were in Fort Bliss -- this was in the middle of a desert. And all of our barracks were concrete. And all of the beds were -- about the only thing that could ever fucking burn would, you know, be something like bedsheets. (Laughter) But still, I was assigned to fire guard duty, and my job was to carry this bucket of sand through about four or five different barracks, walking through the barracks at night. My shift was at, like, 3:00 in the morning, or something like that, three to five, or something like that. And I'm walking through barracks, and actually, it wasn't the worst thing in the world, because at night, in the desert, it cools down a little bit. But I was thinking, "This is pretty funny. This is what I thought the Army would be. Just stupid little stuff like this."

So at one point, in one of the barracks, there was all this squeak, squeak, squeak stuff going on. And I'm thinking, "What in the heck is all that?" And I go over and look, and here are these two guys going at it like crazy in their bunk. And I thought, "Well, nobody gave me any orders on what to do about this. I mean, what do I do? It's not a fire. But I've got a bucket of sand. Should I throw sand at them? Why am I the morals police here? Nope, I'm the fire guard." So I just let it slide. So that was the first night in basic training.

And the second day, they start processing us through. There was a ton of stuff that happened over the next two or three days before we actually started training stuff. But, you know, one, we had to take all these aptitude tests. And fill out tons of weird paperwork, and you know, next of kin, and all that kind of stuff. But it also came time for haircuts. And so, you know, everybody's lined up, like, I don't know, 140, 150 people lined up, and they're going in, you know, two or three or four at a time, to the barbers. And I get in there, and I've got hair down to, like, about my shoulders. And the barber -- and they're all male barbers -- and they throw the little thing over you and then he said to me, "How would you like it?" And I said, "I don't know, maybe trim it up just a little bit in the back." And he said, "Got it." Then the next thing I know, it's buzz, buzz, and within about three or four minutes, I was bald. (Laughter) And, you know, all my hair's down on the floor. And I thought, "Okay, I get it. Ha, ha, ha. This is their little joke they love to play. They probably say this every time somebody comes and sits down in that chair."

So that was the first day, and then they issued us uniforms. Of course, we'd already been assigned to one of the barracks. And I could see immediately that, in the barracks, people were already jockeying for their little pecking order. And it was really, from an anthropological standpoint, kind of interesting to watch, how people start trying to organize, strangers try to start organizing.

There was a group of about four or five who were setting themselves up to be the alphas, and I thought, "This is kind of interesting." And I'm watching them, I'm paying attention to them, and they're a bunch of dopes. They're assholes. And I'm thinking, "Okay, I know who I've got to look out for now." And there will be a reason to have to confront what I call the Asshole Group later. But they were posturing and huffing and puffing, and the drill sergeants made them the, you know, trainee sergeants and corporals and stuff. They were gonna be in charge of us when the drill sergeant was not there. The drill sergeants had their own little room at the end of the barracks.

So that was actually my first day in the Army, nothing spectacular. Well, first night and day. Nothing spectacular, except that it was like, "Hmm, yeah, you're definitely, you're not in Kansas anymore." But I spent my time sizing everybody up. And there was this one kid, Allen Crane, and he was this tall, shy, mentally kind of slow kid, and I focused on him immediately. Because I knew that -- because I knew how bullies operated. I knew that he was gonna wind up being easy pickings for anybody that wanted to pick on him. So I didn't say anything to him, I didn't talk to him, I didn't meet him, I didn't say "Hello," I didn't do anything. I just decided, "I'm gonna keep my eye on this kid."

Oh, and then, we had also gone through and gotten our series of shots. And they used these guns. Some of them were needles, some of them were guns that injected you with six or eight or five or ten, I don't know how many different things. But you'd walk by and -- what they tell you is, "Do not flinch, because it'll tear your arm, half your arm off." And it was true,

I mean, if you did. And some guys passed out, some guys flinched and had all this flesh torn off of them.

I went through -- and I hated shots, by the way. But by the time I got to the Army, I'd had so many shots that I was pretty much inured to them. But as a child, a young child, I was -- I would get hysterical at the idea of getting shots. And I think it's because my parents put me through some kind of allergy testing when I was about three or four years old, and it was over a series of weeks and weeks and weeks, and I had to go back every week, and it would be hundreds of shots, or little pin pricks, but they seemed like shots to me.

But at any rate, we did all of that, and I'll skip just a little bit ahead, because within about a week or so, after we started being made into real soldiers and warriors and killers, I all of a sudden was running this really high fever and was delirious. And they had to haul me to the dispensary. And their diagnosis at that time was, "You need to call -- who is your next of kin?" And I mumbled whatever, my father or my mother, whoever it was. And they said, "Well, you need to call your family and tell them that they need to get here by tomorrow or the next day, because you have spinal meningitis, and you're not gonna make it through the end of the week." And I thought, "Well, this is a great start!" (Laughter)

And so it turns out -- I did not notify anybody, because I didn't really want anybody, you know? I did have this vague, delirious thought that maybe I would call one of my former girlfriends and have her come and watch me die or something, because I thought that was romantic. But I didn't call anybody. And within two or three days, I was fine. It turned out that I had had a severe reaction to the flu vaccine that they had given me in the shot process. Which is one of the reasons why I have never, ever, ever taken another flu shot, from that time until now. But, yeah, that was the first time the Army told me I was gonna be dead. (Laughter) It wouldn't be the last time.

20-Mile Forced Hike in the Desert

So we're in the Army. We're in the desert -- El Paso and New Mexico. We're going on a 20-mile forced march. And it's a whole battalion -- it's, like, four companies. And I had already been warned about, from David Hefner and others, "Don't ever volunteer for anything in the Army. It will always go bad to volunteer."

But they were -- I'm assessing the whole situation. And there were hundreds of people -- I mean, a battalion-sized group is large. And we had been learning, you know, we had been marching, and doing close-ordered drills and everything for, you know, a few weeks. And then we were gonna go on this 20-mile forced march through the deserts of El Paso and New Mexico -- White Sands, New Mexico.

So somebody said, "We're looking for volunteers. Who wants to be flank guards?" And I said -- I raised my hand. Because what I knew was that I didn't want to be in the middle, in the clump, of all these hundreds of people marching. And the temperature was between 135 and 140 degrees. Because there was no shade. It's in the sun, that's what it is, in the desert, during the day time.

So my job as flank guard was to be off, you know, 50 or 100 yards away from the main group. And there were a number of flank guards. I don't know how many, but I wasn't the only one. There were many. A number. Ten, I think. And all I had to do was to kind of be on the lookout for enemies. And so what I figured out I could do was to kind of scoot along a little bit, for 20 or 30 yards, and then I could kind of sit and rest a minute. This was separate and on my own. And I always looked for "on my own."

But during the course of this 20-mile forced march, more than half the battalion fell out with heat stroke, and some serious. A couple died. One or two died. And they were hauling people back in ambulances and stuff. But because I had this -- wasn't caught in the middle of all this -- not just the heat of the day, but the heat of the bodies -- I was able to make it kind of a -- as I look back on it now, it wasn't then, but I look at it now as, like, a walk in the park compared to what the main group of everybody had to do. So there was one or two more deaths there, and many cases of heat exhaustion and heat stroke.

Oh, and one of the things that helped me, oddly, was my growing up in Gonzales and going out and trying to become -- basically learn the way of the Apache Indian, which meant learning how to go longer without water and still be able to salivate. So I had found a couple little stones, and I would suck on those stones, and so I was able to conserve my water. And I only had -- well, actually, on that particular march, we had two canteens of water. Usually it's one canteen, but this was a big thing. And by the time we finally finished this 20-mile forced march, there were only about 50 or 60 people who straggled in that hadn't had to be hauled back for one thing or another. And I still had half a canteen of water when everybody else had long since been out of water.

Grenade in the Bunker

They were training us to kill. From the very first day we ever went into the Army, before we ever held an M-14 rifle, which is what we trained on for awhile, or M-16, which we trained on later -- but every bit of the training, in any context, was training to kill and to dehumanize the enemy we were supposed to kill. And of course I had many internal reactions to that. On one hand, I bought into *nothing* of the brainwashing because I could see it so clearly. We would spend hours running every morning at 5:00, singing all these ditties -- "I want to be an airborne ranger, I want to live a life of danger, I want to go to Viet-

nam, I want to kill a Viet Cong. Kill! Kill! Kill! Kill!" Kill was all
day, everyday, in basic training. And it really didn't, didn't really enrage me. It was just, like, I saw the fucking joke. And I'm
thinking, "God, this is just insane."

So that was sort of the entirety of the undercurrent of basic
training. But of course all the other training was -- everything
from machine guns and crawling through machine gun fire
and throwing grenades and how to bayonet people -- oh, straw
dummies. I once wrote a short story called *Straw Dummies*.
And it was kind of about basic training. And it was kind of
about these straw dummies that we would spend hours stabbing with, approaching and stabbing with bayonets. And of
course we had all this hand-to-hand combat training. And all
the usual stuff.

But one thing that kind of sticks out was the day that we
were having grenade throwing. And this was in the desert. Of
course, everything at Fort Bliss, Texas, is in the desert. I mean,
the running's in the desert. The training's in the desert. I mean,
everything's in the desert.

But they had these bunkers built -- huge thick concrete, or
cinderblock and concrete, or whatever kind of bunkers. And
there were a whole bunch of bunkers. And we'd be out there
with a drill sergeant in each bunker with whoever was going to
learn how to throw the grenades. And it was basically how to,
you know, pull the pin, when to release it, when to throw it,
and how to throw it. And this was no more challenging to me
than just, like, throwing a baseball or a football or something
like that.

But each bunker -- they didn't do it all simultaneously.
They did one at a time. And we got to my bunker, I threw
my grenade, and it goes out to where it's supposed to go into
the sand and it blows up. And then the next guy in the next
bunker, who happened to be Allen Crane, throws his grenade.
And it goes into -- oh, the bunkers were open at the top. It falls

into my bunker, right in front of me. And somebody -- the drill sergeant in the other bunker is yelling, "Oh fuck!" And my drill sergeant, that was standing in front of me, saw this grenade and he kicked it over into a sump that went all the way around the bunker, that was about six or seven inches deep. And had he not kicked that grenade into the sump, when it exploded -- and by the way, I was deaf for about three days after that explosion -- but had he not done that, I and my drill sergeant would have been blown to smithereens.

And that was poor Allen Crane who had done that, who was the biggest -- every unit has sad sacks. And Allen Crane was the saddest of all sad sacks. I don't think you could come up with a sadder sad sack than Allen Crane. He did not belong there. He should never have been allowed in the Army. He should have been treated like the fragile, gentle, scared, mentally slow person he was. But no, this was war, they were running everybody through there.

And at one point, one of the bullies -- after that episode -- one of the bully dudes that was trying to harass poor Allen Crane came up to me and said, "He almost killed you. What do you want to do about that?" And I said, "I don't want to do anything about it, he didn't kill me." And he said, "No. We've got shit planned for him. We want you in." And that's the beginning of the next story.

Bullies Attack Allen Crane

Well, Allen Crane was so sweet and so timid and so -- I don't know what. He just invited abuse because he was so timid. And people took advantage of that. And yes, he screwed up. I mean, yes, he almost killed me. But -- and I was encouraged by this certain little group that was sort of in quasi-official -- had been given temporary ranks of, like, sergeants, but they weren't really sergeants -- they were just recruits that were given the

rank to, kind of, maintain peace in the barracks. And they --
I was getting all these, you know, "He almost killed you. We
gotta do something about him." And I said, "No, we don't need
to do anything about him. I don't need to do anything about
him." They said, "Well, he's screwing up everybody and we're
all getting in trouble because of his mess ups."

So one night, in the barracks, Allen Crane -- and I kept an
eye on him. He was, like, the next bunk over from me. And I
saw him heading to the latrine in the middle of the night. And
he gets to the latrine, and all of a sudden I'm watching all these
four or five people, that were trying to clean up the screwups
in the outfit, follow him to the latrine. And I head out to the
latrine.

I walk in, and they are beating the holy shit out of Allen
Crane. And so I lay into all of them. And I'm just going like
a ball of fire. And I'm thinking, "I'm probably -- poor Allen
Crane and me are both probably dead." And then at that point,
Casey and two or three others, that were of like mind to me,
come weighing in there. And we just start kicking ass and taking names. And it is not pretty. I mean, people went to the hospital. But none of us. And neither did Allen Crane.

And it was after that that I was called into the Commanding
Officer's office a few days later -- after all the reports and stuff
had been done, about the melee -- where he wanted me to go
to Officer Candidate School.

Hand-to-Hand Combat with a Bully

After the latrine incident -- and I don't know if we're talking
two days after that or a week after that -- but we were having
hand-to-hand combat training. And the Army's serious about
hand-to-hand combat training. And when you're out there actually practicing it with people, you're really applying it to people.

So during that training, one of these people -- the biggest giant of the people who had tried to beat up or kill Allen Crane -- picked him out as a partner. And he beat him half to death.

And I walked up, and I said, "Back off of him. You're mine. We're gonna go at it." And of course, you know, the advantage that I've always had in life is that I am -- against, you know, big guys -- is that I'm small, but I am extraordinarily well-trained, mean, and better, when I have to be. So I picked him out. And he got injured pretty badly in the fight, and was hauled off to the hospital.

And after that -- after that -- nobody in that entire basic training unit ever, *ever* messed with Allen Crane again, and *never* tried to mess with me again.

Recruit Killed by Machine Gun Fire

Well, this is going to be a short story, because I don't like to re-tell it. I don't even like to think about it or revisit it. But one of the big training courses we went through was crawling under concertina wire with machine gun fire -- live machine gun fire -- going over us. And it was a pretty hairy kind of situation. You didn't know if some round was gonna hit you, or whatever. But the whole idea was that we had about three, three-and-a-half feet of space underneath the concertina wire. And we had to be working our way on our backs underneath all of that as live machine gun fire was firing over us. We were on our backs -- you could push with your feet and dig with your elbows.

But at one point, all of a sudden this kid, who was two or three people behind me, freaks out, stands up, and is just cut in half by machine-gun fire. And the upshot to all of that, after it was all said and done -- you know, the processing part of all that was, we were all gathered together later on, a day or two later, after the investigations, and the processing was, directed to us was, "Let this be a lesson to you. Don't fucking stand up.

Don't disobey an order. Don't ever disobey an order." And that was the lesson.

AWOL from Basic Training

So I had relatives that I had never met before, but they got in contact. They lived in El Paso. The Plumleys. Leo and Imogene Plumley, I think. And their son was in the basic training cycle right before mine. And somehow or another, somebody in the family who knew them got in touch with them -- I don't know who it was -- but they made contact and came out to see me on a Sunday. On certain Sundays, you could have visitors come and spend thirty minutes. So they came to visit me, and they talked to me, and they were the sweetest people in the whole world. I don't think I had ever met people as sweet as they were. Or maybe it was just in my circumstance, that, you know, anybody less than a monster seemed sweet. I don't know.

But they were very nice, and they said, during the course of that talk, "You know, we're going to be out of town next weekend. And if you'd like -- and here's the address and everything -- if you can get away" -- like anybody can get away in basic training, because it really doesn't happen -- "but if you can get away, we'll leave the key under the front doormat, and the refrigerator will be stocked with food and soft drinks and beer, and the TV -- you can watch something."

So I had this friend, a soldier in my unit, we actually both came from Houston. We traveled to Fort Bliss together. He was an interesting character. He was a pilot already, and he was, like, 18 or 19 years old. But he started flying when he was, like, 10, 11, 12, something. Anyway, he had thousands of hours of commercial flight hours. He made his living as a pilot. And all he wanted to do was to fly, fly, fly. And of course, we weren't flying -- he wasn't flying -- during basic training. And all he wanted to do was become a pilot in the Army, either fixed-wing or helicopters, it didn't matter to him. And he was a shoo-in, with that kind of resume.

So at any rate, I told him about this offer, for the weekend. And he said, "God! If we slip out of here, and if we can make it, if we can get to the airfield -- the civilian airfield -- I can get a plane, and we can fly all around and look at El Paso and the desert and everything else." And I said, "Sign me up!"

So we went AWOL on a -- I think it was either a Saturday or a Sunday, I don't remember which one. And we go flying for about two hours. And we're flying everywhere. And then he dips into Mexico, just to show he can do it, and then dips back. All that kind of stuff.

And so we get over to the Plumleys' house finally, and it's true -- the key's under the mat, the refrigerator's full, it's got Cokes and soft drinks and beer. The TV is there. And we spend -- so we were traveling and flying for two to three hours, and then we spend another two or three or four hours at that place. And it was glorious. It was almost like not being in the Army momentarily.

And we made it back. We didn't get busted or anything like that. We had skated somehow. And that's because Sundays were really -- nobody was paying a lot of attention to anything, we figured that out.

But that's not quite the end of the story. I never had contact with the Plumleys again after that. I went off to Vietnam. Their son went off to Vietnam. He died, got killed in action, the first year I was in Vietnam, in 1969. And I got one letter from them, and it was heartbreaking. I don't even remember what it was, except that, "Our boy is gone." And it just broke my heart.

But that was the end of all of that, until later, a few years later, when I got back from Vietnam and had been back for a little while, around 1974. When I got hired to work on *Green Eyes*, the movie project, I had to go out to California. I had no money, I had nothing, couldn't afford to fly. So I decided to drive. And I had to go through El Paso on my way to California. And I thought, "I don't know how to face these people." I had never figured out how to face these people that had lost their only son in Vietnam, and I survived. I carried quite a bit of survival guilt along with me for many years. But I thought, "No, this just isn't fair. I need to thank them." I never had a chance to thank them. I mean, we left a little note.

So we met up, and we're talking, in El Paso, in their little house -- same one I was in that they so kindly afforded me the opportunity for a little break that Sunday afternoon. And they were talking about their son. And I said, "I am so sorry."

And they said, "Well, the strangest thing about the whole thing was, that his dog" -- and the dog was still there, and he wouldn't leave my side. They said, "It's funny that the dog is so taken with you. He had that dog for years and years, he grew up with that dog." The dog was very old. And they said, "The night -- we didn't know he died. But the night he died, the dog started howling and crying and whining and scratching, and scratching at the door, and just going batshit crazy. He was unconsolable, and we didn't know what to do."

And the next day or two, they got word that their son had been killed in action on that very day that the dog went crazy. And it was one of the most eerie stories I had ever heard. But it all seemed so very right and normal. And that was the second time and the last time I ever saw the Plumleys.

Advanced Infantry Training at Fort Dix

So I originally had a school picked out that I was gonna go to, which had to do with intelligence and cryptography. But they convinced me that I needed to go to Officer Candidate School, and after 12 weeks in Officer Candidate School, I would be able to transfer into any arena of the Army that I wanted to. That was pretty powerful stuff, and I said, "Sign me up!"

I finished up basic training. And when I finished up basic training, they put me on a commercial flight to New Jersey, because -- only one or two of us were going to New Jersey. That was where Advanced Infantry Training was. Because this was going to be Infantry Officer Candidate School, because they said that was the "only one open at the time." They had Infantry, they had Artillery, they had all these Officer Candidate Schools. But they said that was the only one open. That should have been kind of a fair warning because I found out later, the average lifespan of a second lieutenant platoon leader in combat was about seven seconds. (Laughter) So they had a real need for more second lieutenants. Of course, the average lifespan for anybody in combat was between six and ten seconds. So what's the difference, right?

But I had spent months in the sun. There was no such thing as sunscreen, there was no such thing as anything for sunburn. My nose, my lips, my ears were all solid, black scabs. And they put me on this commercial airline flight to New Jersey. And whoever was sitting next to me changed their seat. And the flight attendants -- stewardesses in those days -- were keeping their distance from me. And it dawned on me, "They think I've got, like, leprosy or something." It was that bad. And it looked that bad.

So anyway, make that flight. And somehow or another, I don't remember how, I got bussed to Fort Dix, New Jersey, for Advanced Infantry Training. And the first couple of days we were there, you know, it was the same drill. It seemed like Basic Training II. It was, you know, everybody making formations at 5:00, 5:30 in the morning. And then, during these formations, they would start assigning all these duties to everybody for the day.

And it dawned on me -- and I'd already made contact with a couple of people, I don't remember who they were -- but it dawned on me that, "Hey, if I sneak off to the latrine during this formation, while they're assigning all these crap duties" -- K.P., kitchen police, and all this stuff -- "then I'll just hide in there for fifteen minutes and they'll be done." Because when they assign what they've got to assign, everybody else gets to go off and just spend the day, if they didn't get called out, right?

So I head to the latrine. And I wasn't the only one -- there were about four or five of us. And I didn't even know them, but they all had the same idea. So we're in the latrine, we're kind of hiding back in the latrine, and in comes this, you know, sergeant, and busts us. And says, "Okay, you're going there, and you're going there." And he pointed at me and said, "You report out there, you're going to truck driving school." And I thought, "Okay." It sounded horrible to me, but it wasn't as bad as what the others had been assigned to.

So I go out and there's a group of us that are trucked out to the woods. Fort Dix is huge, it was a great, grand forest out there. It was thousands and thousands of acres. And we get out to this place where we're gonna have truck driving school, and they're going to teach us how to drive Deusenhalfs. These are the big Army trucks, like two-and-a-half ton trucks. They're big, and you haul troops and stuff in them.

And we get out there, and the guy in charge is a Spec Four, which is like a corporal or something like that. And he's the one that's gonna be our trainer and instructor. And he gives us the lowdown of what it's going to be like. He says, "Here's the deal. The pogey trucks will be out here for breakfast and lunch." These were, like, food trucks! Not Army food trucks! He had some deal with somebody that was bringing, like, actual, little food trucks out there! And he said, "Is there anybody here that's not good with the smell of weed?" And we could tell this old hippie was -- this was not going to be your usual Army stuff.

But anyway, we learned to drive these trucks and we get licensed to drive these trucks. I think that school was, like, two weeks long. But meanwhile, we're doing all this other stuff, going through advanced infantry training. The school was, like, a half a day, and then a half a day of shooting, fighting, and so on.

Well, as it turns out, part of the advanced infantry school was this big, huge war game, with, I'm going to call them, blue armies and red armies. I think that's what they were. Blue or white. I don't know. Anyway, two different armies. And each army has -- and everybody's using weapons, but not lethal weapons. They're shooting, like, blanks and markers and stuff. If anybody gets hit, then they're dead. They can get dead or captured or whatever. But, because I was licensed as a truck driver -- and there were only about seven or eight of us -- we were gonna be in charge of hauling people back and forth, like out to where they were going, and if they get killed, we would haul them all back.

And so we're in the middle of all these war games. And my color -- the team I was on -- we were supposed to be neutral, but the team I was supposed to be on -- let's say it was the red team -- there was the other team that had all of these red team people in a prisoner-of-war camp. And I went over there, I'm driving over there because nobody can shoot at us, because we're supposed to be neutral, right? So I'm checking out this prisoner-of-war camp. And the Army liked to do things really realistic. And they had all this torture going on. They had this concertina wire all the way around the prison camps. They were torturing these people. And I thought, "Wait a minute. Those are my people."

So I had this bright idea. And all the people they were torturing were down in holes. You know, they had them, like, in tiger pits, or something. So I went over and hooked up to the concertina wire that ran around this whole thing. And it was probably about a hundred acres, 50 acres. I hooked up to the concertina wire, and I just started dragging the prisoner-of-war camp out. And everybody, all the people on the other team -- my people are all down in holes -- but they're all being forced to run, because I'm pulling them all away, right? And then, I get them all pulled away, and I get all my guys out, and I haul them back. And so they're all safe. And I'm getting into the war now!

And so, then I had this bright idea -- I'm driving back out to pick up whoever the stragglers were, and here's a whole bunch of people from the other team that are marching down, going after, you know, my team, somewhere. So I stop, and I say, "Hey! They said it's over! Hop on in!" So I get everybody in the truck, in that whole platoon or whatever it was, and I take them and dump them off at one of our prisoner-of-war camps! And I got in some trouble for that. (Laughter)

But -- I thought I was in more trouble than I really turned out to be, because the officers that were, like, you know, originally yelling at me, said, "Yeah, but you know, we really appreciate your initiative. It's no wonder they're sending you to OCS." So I skated that.

And during the time I was there at Fort Dix, we got actually a little weekend pass one day. And there's this kid from Asbury Park, New Jersey, and he said, "Let me show you -- I'm going to take you to get the best submarine sandwich you've ever had in your life." So we went for a weekend to Asbury Park. And it was true. I wish I could remember the name of the place. I will never forget that was absolutely the best submarine sandwich I ever had in my life, even including Thundercloud Subs. It doesn't even, it can't even hold a candle. It was just beyond great.

But while we were there, we went to this little club. And it wasn't the Stone Pony. But it was another little club. And we're

watching this little band play in there, and they're just raising beautiful hell and putting a block under it. And after that
was all over, I was saying to the guy that took me there, I said,
"These guys, they were pretty good. They might make it someday." I said, "Who was that?" He said, "Well, I don't know who
all they all are, but that guy's Bruce Springsteen." So that was
my first encounter with Bruce Springsteen. And that would
have been in 1968.

So anyway, I survived Advanced Infantry Training. And the
next phase after that was Officer Candidate School.

Infantry Officer Candidate School Begins

So I was inveigled to go to Officer Candidate School because
I had the promise of being able to spend half of OCS in infantry and then be able to automatically transfer to another
branch of the Army, which would not have been infantry. But
Infantry Officer Candidate School was the only one open -- at
least, they said.

So I get to Fort Benning, Georgia, for Infantry Officer Candidate School, and actually, it was kind of interesting, because it
was a little higher level of people. Most everybody in OCS had
undergraduate degrees. So it was a good mix of people. I didn't
have an undergraduate degree at the time -- I only had one semester of college at the time, because I'd gotten yanked out,
right? But I started meeting some people that were pretty easy
to bond with.

OCS was tough. Hard. Intense. Hours and hours and hours a
day in either physical training, combat training, weapons training, ordinance training, defusing-bomb training, studying the
Uniform Code of Military Justice -- which I found fascinating.
I had the entire -- on all of our desks in our little -- we had
rooms, two to a room. And we each had a bunk, we each had
a desk, and lamp, and everything. And every desk had the en-

tire Uniform Code of Military Justice on it. And I spent a lot of time reading it.

And my roommate was a guy named Al Divicek. And there were a number of people that I actually became pretty close with. Of course, it was a lot longer -- 24 weeks, right?

So I'm trudging through Fort Benning, and it's grueling. It's tough. I mean, it's not completely unmanageable. But there were a couple of things that pop up that are probably worth mentioning.

One was the day in February of 1969 where we were all trucked or marched out to the Chattahoochee River. It was like 13 or 14 degrees outside. And we got there, and the exercise was this: Strip naked, jump into the Chattahoochee River, and you can't come out until you, either individually or group-wise, have created five field-expedient flotation devices, out of whatever you can find in the river. And in we went.

And eventually, out we came. And we were all suffering from hypothermia. But when we came out of the river, we were made to stand at attention naked, in this whole line, and I will promise you that, if anybody was looking below the belly button, they would never have known that we were males. Everything had receded in self-defense up into the body somewhere. And it wasn't that it was so humiliating, because they humiliated you daily in the Army. You got used to being tested on humiliation. But half of the entire unit came down with pneumonia. And the Tac officers -- they were the drill instructors at the officer level -- the ones in charge of that debacle had to face some disciplinary action.

And all during that period of time, by the way, my studies and formulations of my opinions on the war were getting more and more solidified. I was reading everything I could get my hands on. I was reading every history. I read Frances Fitzgerald's *Fire in the Lake*, which was a remarkable book -- I think probably still an absolutely remarkable book to see what led up to the Vietnam War.

And it was also at Fort Benning where one of our hand-to-hand combat instructors was an aikido blackbelt. And he singled me out at some point, and we became buddies. And he said, "It seems like you've known this forever. How can I help you develop what you've got?" So there was that relationship, which was good.

And there were all sorts of other relationships that happened. One of the guys there -- and all these guys had gone to all these Ivy League colleges and everything -- and one of the guys was a guy named Dolph, who was a fencer in college, a collegiate award-winning fencer, and he was a hoot. And all these guys were really arrogant -- you know, I mean, they were all most proud of themselves. So it was sort of an elite group.

Oh, and one more thing -- when we were going through training in APC's -- armored personnel carriers. And they were going through the river. And one of the APC's -- not mine -- it flipped over in the river, upside down. And we all got out of our own APC's, trying to get these people out. But nobody made it out alive of that APC. They all drowned. And the lesson from all that, according to our Tac officers, was "APC's are dangerous vehicles. They're not perfect. Expect this to happen from time to time."

Erdle, Goat Hill, and Playboy Bunnies

When I was in Infantry Officer Candidate School, the first 12 weeks, I was just balls to the wall, doing everything. And when I found out that I would not be transferring after that to the OCS of my choice, like they told me I could do during basic training -- that was sort of a line of demarcation in my mind. It was at that point where I knew that that was, like, the 27th time, or the 50th, that the Army had fucked me. And I sort of started checking out. I mean, I was still in the program, I was doing what I needed to do, but it was like, "No, I'm not invested in this anymore. They screwed me."

So in about the 15th, 16th week, I was talking to a couple of my buddies -- Dolph and Divicek. And there were a couple of other people. I gathered this little group of -- you know, not anarchists, but they were anti-war. And I found this place in Columbus, Georgia -- it was this little hill, and it was called Goat Hill. And there was a place for rent up there, a house, which was maybe $150 a month or something like that. And I gathered all these guys together, we all pitched in, and we rented it. Or, I rented it.

Of course, technically, we were not allowed off Fort Benning the whole time we were there. But I had been appointed, or anointed, or something, to head up the committee that was gonna find dates for all of the officer candidates for the Senior Ball, which was the big end of school ball. As you can imagine, there's a lot of guys that couldn't find a date on their own (laughter) if they fell out of the sky. But I thought, "Okay, this is my new headquarters, on Goat Hill."

And people started coming and going from Goat Hill. I mean, they couldn't believe we had snuck off out of Fort Benning and had this place out there. But that was my headquarters. And apparently, none of the officers in charge or anything -- I mean, it's not that they -- it's like they were looking the other way, I think. Okay?

So this became sort of ground zero for anti-war protestors. And women. And those who just hated the military. And during that period of time -- and I stuck in, until the whole 24, 25 weeks of OCS, before I refused my commission. I was bound and determined not to be a drop-out. For some reason, at that point, when I saw people dropping out of OCS -- and there were a lot of them who did because they just couldn't cut it -- I didn't want to be in that "couldn't cut it" group. I wanted to be

-- I had a higher moral ground purpose for hanging in there, in my own mind. For whatever that's worth.

But one of the people who showed up there was some local girl, woman, young woman, named Erdle. Erdle was -- from her very name, I think you can almost imagine her. She was one of the most physically unattractive women you would ever see. But she was sensitive. And she had had a hard life. And we adopted her into our little group. And she and I were buds. And she was big. I mean, she was probably six feet tall, and not fat, but very, very stocky.

But there were so many guys coming through our Goat Hill compound (laughter) that she was at some risk. So I became her protector. Because she said she wasn't there for all of that, and I said, "I understand." And I said, "Anytime you've got any kind of thing going on that you need help with in that respect, let me know." So I became Erdle's protector. And I actually became close to Erdle, because she was just so -- she was the kind of person that the world was not going to like. But there was just so much to like about her, once you knew who she really was. So I was very protective of her.

And actually so protective that -- well, let me put it this way -- the guys at Goat Hill -- I mean, there were probably 10 of us living there at that time. And somebody came up with this deal, behind my back, where they were gonna raffle off Erdle for sex to whichever officer candidate threw their names in the hat. And I didn't know about that until the very end -- or, close to the very end.

But during that period of time at Goat Hill, I was sneaking off -- I was just living off campus, which was verboten. But we were having a ball. We were living the high life. And my job was to go find dates for those that didn't have dates. So I was taking trips to Auburn University, talking to sororities there, pitching this thing, you know -- "these are all soldiers, officer candidates, that are going to be going off to Vietnam, proba-

bly gonna die, can you come and dance with them at the ball,"
right?

And then I had this bright idea of going to Atlanta -- I went
to the Playboy Club in Atlanta. And I met a couple of the Playboy Bunnies and, you know, explained to them what was going
on. And they just took this on as a project! They -- between
Auburn and the Playboy Club -- especially the Playboy Club in
Atlanta -- they gathered together so many hot women (laughter) for these guys! (Laughter)

And the weird thing was, I wasn't even planning on going
-- and I did not -- to the Senior Ball. Because I knew by that
time I was checked out, right? But I was doing my job, doing my
duty. But as it came closer, and as the night of the Senior Ball
happened, I wasn't at the Senior Ball -- but all of a sudden, 20
or 30 people came cruising into Goat Hill because one of the
things that I didn't know, other than this lottery that they had
put out for free sex, was they also had -- and this just broke my
heart -- but they had a voting thing on who was the worst pig
of women at the Senior Ball. And Erdle was selected for that.
So the night they all came out to have serious series sex with
the pig, Erdle, I snatched her up, I took her off. They were all
left to their own devices.

And I've always wondered after that whatever happened to
her. I've tried to Google the name a couple of times but I've
never found anything that made sense. But essentially, yeah,
she dodged that bullet when I dragged her out of there.

The Playboy Bunnies, on the other hand -- they didn't all
show up at Goat Hill, but they all showed up for the Senior Ball,
I understand. And that was, like, one of the biggest hits of all
of the OCS cycles that had ever happened. So I had, you know,
some cache (laughter) for setting that up.

But for me, Goat Hill was a respite and a place where I went
to think and read and write and be away from the Army. And

also ponder my future in the Army, which I did very, very seriously.

Dahlonega and the Okefenokee

There were periods of my time in the military -- especially during Officer Candidate School, which was, like, I don't know, 24 or 25 weeks long -- where everything blurred. I was, like, just -- sometimes just marking time, and sometimes just going through the motions. And just, wherever they sent me, whatever they did, I just did it, because I wasn't invested anymore.

But there were a couple of things that did have me invested, and believe me, it wasn't the "dismantling land mines" section, and it wasn't certain other sections. But during the course of that time in Officer Candidate School, they sent us for a week or so to Dahlonega, North Georgia, which was the Ranger Training School, and also to the Okefenokee Swamp for swamp training.

And later, after that, of course, after I was out of Officer Candidate School, I went down to the Panama Canal Zone after that, which was still kind of a blur. Because I had checked out, to some level. I mean, I wasn't checking out of the training -- I just checked out of -- we got on a plane, and they sent us somewhere, and we did whatever we were supposed to do, and that's what I did.

And the Okefenokee Swamp was basically just marching through the swamps. Given a knife and three days, no guns, but we had to survive on our own, separately, for three days and make our way from Point A to Point Be in three days and not die. That was basically the drill.

And we had to learn to eat, you know, everything, worms, insects, fruits and berries that didn't kill us. And trudging through the swamps with the alligators and the snakes and all of that stuff. And the truth of the matter is, as I'm talking about it now, it's just a vague memory. And I guess maybe it's a vague memory because by the time I got to Vietnam, I was tramping through the swamps and rice paddies and jungles of Vietnam, so all of that stuff seemed like child's play. But somehow I survived it. I think most people survived it.

I survived the Okefenokee Swamp. I survived Dahlonega, North Georgia -- except that Ranger Training had all this rappelling down mountain sides which really scared the holy hell out of me, because I have a thing about heights. But I somehow managed to bull through all of that and suck it up and do it. The Okefenokee Swamp is more memorable because we were eating crickets and worms and snagging fish with our knives, all that kind of stuff. It wasn't even so much that I survived it -- I just endured it.

There was also a time when I had to jump out of an airplane. I've only parachuted out of an airplane one time in my life. And it wasn't as scary as the swamps or the mountains, but it was, as somebody said to me in the Army, "Why would anybody jump out of a perfectly good airplane?" (Laughter) And I've always remembered that, and I thought, "Yeah! What kind of insanity is it that comes across people that they would jump out of a perfectly good airplane?!" But of course, you know, that was all part of the training.

Refusing my Commission

So there was only one more week of OCS after the Senior Ball. And I had already decided what I was gonna do. I wasn't the only one. For various reasons, there were -- as I recall, there were about five. Three of them -- I remember clearly two or three others. One was Joseph Dubray, who had once been a Lutheran minister before he was pulled into the Army. The other was a guy named Lawrence Dolph. He was a fencing champion in college, Princeton or Rutgers or something. But most of them were based on conscientious objector status.

Before I was making my determination about everything, I had considered conscientious objector status. And I had written my Uncle Benny, the Methodist preacher, and told him that I was planning on resigning from OCS and was contemplating conscientious objector status. He wrote a letter to John Tower, the Senator from Texas -- who was a huge hawk and kind of still in the McCarthy arena -- and reported me. And Tower set in motion an investigation that would actually take place after I left OCS. But my Uncle had sent me a letter copying me on the letter he had sent to John Tower accusing me of being a Communist and Communist sympathizer.

So anyway, I gave notice that I was refusing to accept my commission. And this was in the last week of OCS. And I had gotten through fine. And because there, like, were five different people, the news was starting to get out, and the Army was really concerned at that point, about -- "Oh my God, five potential officers refusing their commission based on their opposition to the war in Vietnam?" They were really scared of all the controversy. They were gonna bend over backwards to not let that happen.

So everybody had to appear before a panel. As I recall, it was a panel of -- let's see, a full bird Colonel was at the center of the panel, then you had two Majors, then you had two Captains, and then you had two Lieutenants. And this was all individually. So I had my day in the sunshine, and I'm sitting at a table by myself. And they're at this, like, a Supreme Court bench or something.

And they're going on and on, the junior officers. The Lieutenants and the Captains are all, in various ways, being very hostile, and they're peppering me with all these questions. "Let us ask you this. If your mother and sister were being raped by somebody, would you refuse to kill them?!" And I said, "Well, probably not. But you misunderstand what I'm saying. What I'm saying is, I'm not applying for conscientious objector status. I know I'm capable of killing somebody. That's not the point. My point is that I have studied this war, and the history of this country, and the history of the wars leading up to this war. And I will tell you, I think that this is a wrong and immoral war. And I am not going to put myself in the position of ordering 19- and 20-year-olds" -- of course, I was only 19 or 20 -- "but I'm not going to put myself in the position of ordering 19- and 20-year-olds to do something in this war that I know is wrong because I believe the war is wrong." Essentially that was the argument.

And boy, the junior officers, you know -- "Well, you're just a coward! You're afraid! You know within a week, we're going to be sending you to Vietnam as soon as this is over, and you're going to be sent over there as a machine gunner! You're not going to get out of this war!"

I said, "Wait a minute. You don't understand. I can only control what I can control. And what you do to me, I can't control. I'll have to live with it or die with it. Doesn't matter to me. But I have to do what I think is the appropriate thing to do right now."

And one of the officers, Lieutenants up there, was a graduate of the University of Houston. And his spiel was, "You dropped out of school after one semester! You're a loser! You had an opportunity here, and you blew it! You were a loser then, you're a loser now, and you will be a loser for the rest of your life!" It was that kind of thing. "Unless you accept this commission!" You know, and so on.

And all of this was going on, it was getting pretty hot, and pretty heated. There was more to it, but you get the general flavor. The Colonel had never opened his mouth. But as this Lieutenant and one of the Captains were just yelling and screaming and throwing insults and invectives, the Colonel said, "Stop.

Stop, everybody." And he looked at me, and he said, "Candidate Cunningham, I've listened very carefully to everything you've said. Quite frankly, it makes a lot of sense, from your perspective. I don't agree with everything you've said, but I respect it. This tribunal accepts your refusal of your commission."

And one of the other officers tried to pipe up and say something, and the Colonel said, "I thought I said silence on this podium." And shut it down. And that was my refusal of my commission.

They sent me to a holding company where I was supposed to stay for a week or two before they shipped me to Vietnam.

The 13th Public Information Detachment

So I refused my commission and resigned from OCS in the 24th week. A number of people thought I was absolutely insane for doing that, but they didn't understand where I was coming from.

So I was put into a holding company. That's where you go when you're between assignments, basically. And, of course, the promise that had been made to me by this panel that I had to appear before was that I would be there for a week or two and then be reassigned to Vietnam as a machine gunner. And that was all, to me, like, "Why even bother to tell me?" Because, you know, I'm in the system, I have no control over the system. Just, you know, whatever will be, will be.

So I'm there, and during the first week -- there was nothing to this holding company. I had nothing to do, I had no details, I had nothing. You're just waiting for your next orders. And I thought, "This is a nice little break and vacation." So I started wandering around Fort Benning. And I come across this little bitty building that says "13th Public Information Detachment." And I'm wondering what it is.

I walked in and started talking to this guy, and his name was Ron Johnson. I don't know whatever finally happened to him. But he was a -- it turns out this little outfit was a little journalism outfit. And I started talking to people there. And I was kind of interested. And they said, "Have you ever had any journalism experience?" And I said, "Yeah, as a matter of fact, I worked for the Houston Chronicle before I was dragged kicking and screaming into the Army."

They introduced me to the Commanding Officer of the outfit, who was this Major. And he said, "Why are you trying to get on with us?" And I said, "Well, I'm not necessarily trying to get on with you. I'm waiting to be shipped to Vietnam." And he said, "Well, how'd that happen? Because I see from your file here that you were in OCS, and I see that you finished OCS, and that you sailed through OCS. But other than that, I don't know why you're here." And I said, "Because I refused my commission." He said, "Oh. Why?" And I said, "Short version is, I'm opposed to the war. No sir, I'm not a conscientious objector. But I am not going to lead people my age and younger and order them to do things that I don't believe in." He said, "Okay."

So another week went by, and I heard nothing. I thought that was just a little sidebar kind of deal. And the next thing I know is that the Commander of the outfit -- and it was a very small detachment, it was less than 20 people. And I was ordered to his office. And he said, "We're offering you a job. We wouldn't be offering this job if there hadn't been a recommendation from someone upstream." But he didn't say who. But to this day, I think it was the Colonel that was in charge of that tribunal.

And so I started working as a journalist for the 13th Public Information Detachment. The 13th Public Information Detachment was established during the Domincan Republic conflict back in the 1960's, I think. And its whole purpose was that we were on call 24 hours a day, 365 days a year, to respond to any kind of military situation that happened in the southern hemisphere. And nothing had ever happened in the southern hemisphere since the first time the 13th Public Information Detachment had been established.

So we had to find other things to do. So one of the other things we did -- the main thing that we did -- was to write articles -- and we had photographers also -- so we would do stories for the Army *Stars and Stripes*, which was the Army-wide news organization, and the Fort Benning *Bayonet*. (Laughter) Oh, what a surprise that name was! Because everything in the Army is bayonets, when you get right down to it. (Laughter)

So I started writing articles, and I'd done a number of articles that were very, very well received. I did one article on parachute packing. And as part of that article, I had to jump out of an airplane with a parachute that had been packed by the parachute packing units, that I didn't even know existed! I mean, I never knew, or wondered, where parachutes -- you know, how the parachutes came to be. But I had had some previous experience, in the military, of jumping out of an airplane once or twice. I had to have some credibility with these parachute packers. And I was hoping that whoever had packed my parachute had not fucked up really badly. And he hadn't.

So anyway, I wrote this long, long article on parachute packing. And that led to somebody coming to me who was a sergeant in some other unit who was about to get out of the Army. And he was in the public information realm. And he explained to me that he was about to get out of the Army and he had been engaged already by *National Geographic* to go to the Amazon to do the photography for this whole project in the Amazon. And I had also done an article on him and on that. And he came to me and said, "*National Geographic* wants you to come also. They want me to be the photographer, they want you to be the writer." And I said, "Well, I'm sort of indisposed at the moment. (Laughter) I don't know what's gonna happen. I mean, you're getting out of the Army. I'm not out of the Army yet." And he said, "Yeah, well, if something changes, let me know." So that Amazon trip was something that I missed.

And then also, as part of all of that and my writing for *Stars and Stripes* and the Fort Benning *Bayonet*, when -- there was a small ship, I forget what it was now. The North Koreans had stopped some American ship, a small gun boat, I think. And it was threatening to be a huge flashpoint for a new war with North Korea. And I was no fan of Richard Nixon, who was President at that time. But he made a decision that I approved of. And I wrote an editorial about it. And in the editorial -- in my mind, I was approving of Nixon -- but I had put in the editorial all the reasons why I detested Nixon.

So that editorial got published. Next thing I know, I've got Army C.I.D. coming to me and putting me in custody and going through my locker, because I had written this editorial that was, in somebody's mind, not friendly to the President of the United States. And in my locker, they found a hunting knife. It was actually an Army knife that belonged to me. So they were threatening to court-martial me, as they put it, "not for writing the editorial, but for the weapons we found in your possession that could be a threat to the President of the United States."

So at that point, somebody suggested that they do an Article something or another, which was -- there were variations in degrees of the crime. And the basic one was an Article 15, which was like a Class C misdemeanor. The other was an Article something, and another -- and they were going to charge me with this highest charge, Article. Of course, what they didn't realize was, I had spent, you know, 24 weeks in OCS, with the entire Uniform Code of Military Justice, and I had studied it. So I said, "Eh, okay, well, I demand a general court martial."

And that threw everything into a fucking loop, for everybody. Because a general court martial is a big deal. That's like, you know -- it's the highest level. But as an accused, you have the right to demand it. So they went through this exercise, and they said, "Okay, okay, okay," and they kept bringing it down, one Article at a time, back to an Article 15, which was the lowest. And I said, "Nope. Nope."

So they wound up dropping all of those charges. (Laughter) Because they had nothing. They had absolutely nothing. And I got my knife back!

Oh, and during all this time, I was also making runs to get the *Great Speckled Bird*, which was an underground newspaper out of Atlanta, Georgia. I was making runs, and contributing to it, and bringing it back to Fort Benning and putting out massive issues of it in different places. This was totally against the law. And that's what they were really after me for on the "Nixon editorial." They were trying to get me for what they couldn't prove otherwise.

Yeah, so, anyway, I was in that unit -- the 13th Public Information Detachment -- for about four or five months. But I thought, at the time, "I have dodged the war! I am now assigned to the southern hemisphere. And this is all working out."

That did not come to be.

Arrested in Dothan, Alabama

So while I was in the 13th Public Information Detachment, we were just on our own. Everybody knew the drill. We lived where we lived, we did what we wanted to do, nobody cared.

So weekends, I would generally take off -- sometimes long weekends, because nobody cared. So one of my buddies in the unit, a black guy, we got kind of buddy-buddy and close together. And we decided we wanted to go down to Panama City Beach, Florida. And I had been telling him that I had been down there before, relatively recently, a few weeks before that, and there was an old, very small amusement park. And one of the things they had was a roller coaster, and they built these mountain things that the roller coaster went through, out of cement and everything. But it was abandoned. The whole place had gone out of business.

And I'd been down there before and we camped out -- I mean, me with others -- we camped out in the place where the roller coasters were, because it was like caves. And we'd just get up on a little ledge in there, and camp out, and it was great. And Panama City Beach was beautiful. Absolute perfectly white, fine sand, and the waters were crystal clear, you could see all the way to the bottom, you could see fish swimming. Panama City was beautiful.

So I'm telling him all about this and I said, "Let's go down there this weekend." And he said, "Great! Okay!" Of course, we didn't have any transportation, so we were gonna hitchhike down there. And we had to go through Georgia, Alabama, and then into Florida. So we're hitchhiking, we get out of Georgia, we get into Alabama. And then we get to Dothan, Alabama, and somebody drops us off at about the city limits of Dothan, Alabama.

So we're standing there, and got our thumbs out, and all of a sudden this city police officer pulls up, bumps his siren, and we stop. He gets out, he waddles up to us -- it was just as stereotypical Southern fat waddling cop as you could have ever imagined. And he walks up to us, and he looks at me, and he says, "What are you boys doing?" And I said, "Well, we're heading to Florida." "Whereabouts?" "Panama City." He said, "That's a nice place. Well, how're you getting there?" And I said, "Well, we're hitchhiking." He said, "That's what I was afraid of."

He said, "So here's the deal. I'm gonna have to arrest both of you boys." And I said, "What for?" And he said, "Well, I'm gonna arrest him for being a nigger hitchhiking. And I'm gonna arrest you for hitchhiking with a nigger. What do you think about that?" And I said, "Well, I don't think much about that." He said, "Well, it doesn't matter. Get in the car."

So he cuffs us, he puts us in the car. We go to the police station. There's only four or five city police in all of Dothan, Alabama. And we get there, and the police chief is there. And this was a big bust for them. The police chief is, like, puffing up and saying, "What are you *really* doing going through our town? Is this some kind of agitation? Some kind of protest thing?"

And I said, "Well, Chief, don't I get a phone call?" And he said, "Well, what do you mean?" And I said, "I mean, Constitutionally, don't I get a telephone call?" And he said, "Well, yeah, you're entitled to a telephone call."

So he gives me the telephone -- we're sitting in his office, at his desk. We hadn't been put in a cell yet. Hadn't been processed or fingerprinted, anything like that. It's just about as loosey goosey as you could ever imagine. So I called my Commanding Officer. And my Commanding Officer was not only a Captain in the Army, but he was also a Major in the Columbus, Georgia, Police Department reserves. And I got hold of him, and I explained to him what happened, and he listened to me for about 30 seconds and said, "I think I've got it, put the Chief on the phone."

And I hand the phone to the chief, and all of a sudden I'm listening to this one-sided conversation (laughter) and the chief was saying, "Oh! Yes, sir! Oh! Army! Oh! Yes, sir! Yes, sir! I understand! Yes, sir! Hang on just a second!" And then to his staff, "Get those boys a Coca Cola! And don't put them in a cell, just leave them sitting right there on the bench."

And he gets back on the phone, "Yes, sir, yes, sir, I told them. Oh! Okay, hang on!" And then, to the arresting officer, he said, "Woah, woah, woah! Tell these boys that you're sorry, that you made a mistake in arresting them." And the police officer that arrested us -- I mean, he was upset -- and he said, through gritted teeth, "I'm sorry I arrested you." And then the chief gets back on the phone with our Commanding Officer, and he says, "Yes, sir. Okay. Yes, sir. Oh! You're coming here? Oh, you're coming here! Oh! Okay! A couple hours? Yes, sir. Okay! No sir, we're not putting them in a cell. No sir, we're gonna treat them right, we know they're soldiers."

So that was it. A couple hours later our Commanding Officer got there, gathered us up, took us back to Fort Benning, Georgia. And he held forth all the way back on how careful we needed to be hitchhiking through the South. Not just white or black, but just in general. He said, "This is *not* a place you want to get in trouble." So that was my only arrest ever, and it was in Dothan, Alabama.

The Panama Canal and Alaska

Well, I will give a general story of this, because this was part of a classified operation that was a precursor to me going to Vietnam. This was after OCS. I was technically working with the 13th Public Information Detachment. But I had been put in that detachment for God only knows what reasons. I think it had to do with, after I left OCS -- my military occupation specialty had been changed to combat journalist. So I was sent to the Panama Canal Zone theoretically to do a story on the jungle warfare training, which meant that I had to go through the jungle warfare training. And I thought it was all for the reporting, but I think it was part of a bigger plan that I didn't know about then.

Anyway, get down there, and it was pretty miserable. They hauled us out to the jungles. We trained for -- I think it was about a week. And then we were all given only our combat knives and we were dropped off in different places and had to make our way back and survive for a week in the jungles, in the swamps, on our own. It was similar to what happened in the Okefenokee swamp, but it was longer and more intense.

But part of that training -- before we were dropped off -- during that first week, we were out on maneuvers through the jungle, looking for trip wires and booby traps and all these kinds of things. And you know, everybody's got their heads down, looking down at the trail. There was a point person walking point. There's always a point person and a rear guard kind of person. And everybody else is kind of in the middle. And we're walking through these jungles, and the point person is supposed to be trying to find trip wires.

And all of a sudden we hear the point person say, "God dammit!" And then silence. And everybody freezes. We're not sure what to do. And we're calling the guy's name, and he doesn't answer. So a couple of us move up towards him. And we get up to him, and he's dying. There had been -- whatever, I forget the name of the snake, but it was this really super poisonous snake they had down there. And as he was looking down, it was hanging from a tree and bit him in the face. And before we could do much of anything with him, he was dead.

So we had to call for air support and everything. But that was the most dramatic thing that happened during that training. The rest of it was miserable, and everybody thought they were gonna die, because they realized, "Oh, there's really death out here." But everybody else made it back in one piece, separately. So that was the jungle warfare training.

Jungle warfare training didn't surprise me at all, because I had been informed that, no matter what, as punishment for resigning from OCS, I was gonna be sent to Vietnam. So that made sense.

But then, about a month or two later, I was given orders to report for cold weather survival school in Alaska. And I'm a little bit encouraged, because I'm thinking, "Oh, if they're sending me to cold weather survival school, they may not be sending me to Vietnam after all."

So we get to Alaska, and we get to where the cold weather survival camps were, but they were having a heat wave in Alaska. So they had to put us on airplanes and fly us 200 or 300 or 400 miles north of where normal cold weather survival school was.

And that was a trip. I don't even remember much about it, except that it was cold. But it was not as miserable as the jungles. And it wasn't as miserable as the Panama Canal Zone. It wasn't as miserable as Fort Bliss in the desert in the summer. It wasn't as miserable as the Okefenokee Swamp. It wasn't as miserable as the Chattahoochee River in the winter time.

I don't remember too much about it except that seemed kind of like a boondoggle. And the main thing I remember about it is finally getting back to the Anchorage airport, and waiting on the plane that was going to take me back, and the Anchorage airport really impressed me. It had this great, huge fireplace with a fire going, and everybody could sit around it, you could have drinks and talk. But yeah, I came back kind of thinking, "Ha! They've got something else planned for me other than Vietnam!" It was about two weeks after that that I got snatched up while I was home on leave and sent to Vietnam.

Libby Hilliard

Libby Hilliard and I met in high school in the "Home and Family Life" class. I was just needing a credit or two left to graduate from high school or something, and I liked the idea of that class because there were, like, 30 girls and two boys in the class. (Laughter) Go figure. One of the same reasons I took typing class in the ninth grade. So anyway, we were partners in cooking beef stroganoff, or something like that.

And when it came time to graduate from high school, I needed one more credit and I had to take a summer school class. So I took an art class, and I convinced the art teacher that I wanted to draw this tree out on the school grounds somewhere. So our little relationship -- I would go out everyday to paint this tree, and Libby would come and she'd bring a picnic lunch. And we'd sit there and have lunch. So it became a little romance.

When I went into the Army, we began corresponding back and forth. And we had gotten together in Panama City Beach for a weekend.

But then, at some point, I got a two-week or a one-month leave. And the notion was, I was going to go back to Houston and Libby and I were going to get married. Now, you have to remember, Libby's a big woman. She's probably an inch or two taller than I am. And her mother was adamantly opposed to this marriage.

So we were together at my house, where my mother lived at that time, and we're upstairs in one of the rooms that had a balcony that looked over the front yard. And all of a sudden I hear all this disturbance outside -- honking and all this kind of stuff. We go to the window, and Libby's mother is out there, and she's screaming and yelling at the house. And Libby is just so embarrassed she doesn't know what to do. And I said, "Wait a minute, let me hear what she's saying."

And the mother was yelling and screaming -- and I remember, my Aunt Sissy happened to be there that day also. So then my drunken mother and my drunken Aunt Sissy are out in the front yard with a drunken Libby Hilliard's mother. And they're screaming and hollering at each other. And Libby's mother is screaming, "I will never allow this marriage to happen! I am never gonna allow my daughter to marry somebody shorter than she is!" And it was like that, right? (Laughter)

And there were chairs out on the deck. And I said, "Come on, let's watch this." So we're sitting there like it's a movie, and we're just watching these -- and they're all, like, almost at --

they didn't physically ever get at each other -- but they were, like, jumping at each other, and jumping back, and you know, and screaming and yelling, and on and on.

So somehow or another -- I think it was my Aunt Sissy, because she was a bad ass -- got up in Libby's mother's face, and you know, read her the expletive riot act for a good two or three minutes without ever repeating an expletive. And told her that she was gonna kick her ass up and down the street. And Libby's mother got scared and got in her car and drove away, right?

And we were actually planning on planning the wedding. Probably while I was still there. Because I didn't know what my future was in the Army, and Libby really, really wanted to get married. And I'd given her, by that time -- I had come home on leave and gotten her an engagement ring and everything like that. She picked it out. She went to Zale's Jewelers and picked it out. I was like, "Whatever, I don't care." Because I'm still just in sort of a -- I mean, all this stuff is already like a fog to me, right?

So Libby's not going home because she's angry with her mother. So she's gonna stay there that night. She stays there that night at the house. And the next morning there's this big knock on the door. And there's two -- I call them "Men in Black" in my memory. But they were in civilian attire, and they were from the Department of the Army. And they were there to collect me.

The 166th Aviation Detachment

When they got me from my house in Houston, I hadn't even -- I still had, you know, all my stuff, like, back at Fort Benning, Georgia. And they said, "Gather what you can. You need to come with us." And I'm, like, "Am I under arrest?" And they said, "You are to come with us."

So I left. Libby's still at the house where my mother and Aunt Sissy are. I get put in this car and we go to Hobby Airport. They get on a plane with me and we start flying. And we don't go back to Fort Benning, Georgia. And they won't tell me where we're going, they won't tell me anything about what's going on. All they kept saying was, everytime I asked them where we were going, "We can't say."

We landed in Virginia. I was taken off the airplane and there was an Army vehicle waiting there for me. And I got in it with an M.P. And we're driving along. Nobody's telling me anything. And I'm thinking, "What?"

And then we get to Fort Eustis, Virginia. We go in, and I see that we're going into Fort Eustis. And it looks like a typical Army fort. We're driving through the fort, and civilians could come in and out. And I'm thinking, "What is all this?"

And all of a sudden there's this huge compound within the fort that has, like, 14 or 18 feet wire fences around it, with con-certina wire, surrounding this whole compound. And the gates are open and we go through. And I'm thinking, "Oh. I'm in cus-tody. I'm under arrest. This is some kind of prison."

And we get in there, and it was very, very surreal. They drop me off -- and I keep asking, "What's going on? Why am I here? Am I being charged with something?" And there were no an-swers forthcoming to any of that. "Sir, we can't tell you. We are only delivering you."

So I get to this place within this barbed wire deal, and they let me out, and there's an officer there, a Lieutenant Grow. He's -- last I heard, he's still alive, living up in Fort Worth, or some-thing. But at any rate, it was a kind of sequestered airfield for helicopters. It was, like, a helicopter place. But it had all sorts of stuff in it. It was just secret. It had, like, a PX and barber shop and stuff like that. It was like a fort within a fort.

And they handed me over, and this Lieutenant sounded nice. He said, "Welcome." And there was a chief warrant officer there, who welcomed me with a big smile, and said, "Come on in, let's get you settled in." And I said, "What am I doing here?"

And they said, "Oh!" And they showed me these new orders, where I had been transferred to the 166th Aviation Detachment. And I said, "What is this?" And they said, "Well, we can't tell you yet." And so, it turns out that this unit was a special unit that had been -- a secret unit, top secret unit -- that had been created because Richard Nixon -- still in secret, nobody knew -- but he was planning on trying to start the withdrawal of troops from Vietnam. And ostensibly, this unit -- they didn't tell us that at that point, we didn't know. We found that out later. But ostensibly -- we were just told that, "This is a unit that is going to be retrograding and returning fixed and rotary wing aircraft from Vietnam back to the United States."

And I'm thinking, "What am I doing here?" Everybody in the unit -- and Jim Kulczyk was in that unit, okay? But the unit was maybe 15 soldiers and then two officers in charge. And I'm wondering, "What am I doing here?" I didn't get it. But Kulcyk and I met there, and we were bouncing back and forth in terms of "What in the hell is going on?" and stuff. And I was quizzing everybody. "What do you do?" And Jim Kulcyk, for example: "Well, I'm a helicopter crew chief and machine gunner and door gunner." And "What do you do?" "Well, I'm a helicopter mechanic." And "What do you do?" And it's all helicopter, helicopter, helicopter. And I'm thinking, "What am I doing here?"

And I asked Lieutenant Grow. I said, "Why am I in this unit?" And they said, "We can't tell you." And it turns out that the whole unit was -- I didn't know this at the time -- but the whole unit had a dual purpose. One purpose was to do what they said they were gonna do, which was to start dealing with retrograding and shipping back to the states helicopters.

But the other purpose had something to do with me but they didn't know what it was. And that's all they told me.

And they said, "In the meantime, you're slotted into this unit as a journalist." So I thought, at that point, "Oh! Okay. Well, now I'm not with the 13th Public Information Detachment anymore, I'm on some kind of mission to the southern hemisphere! This ought to be cool!"

So we're there for a couple of weeks. And I'm not going through any training. Everybody else is going through all this training, you know, for how to deal with helicopters and cover them with this special new coating, or something, to ship them back to the United States. And I'm thinking, "This is just so bizarre."

And during that period of time, it became clear to me that we weren't going to the southern hemisphere. I mean, they gave us all M-16's, and Vietnam handbooks, and all this kind of stuff. And I thought, "Okay, I think I know where we're going. I don't know why, and I don't know why I'm here."

AWOL on the Fourth of July

So we were supposed to leave, but over the Fourth of July of 1969 -- right before. I thought, "They're shipping me off to Vietnam. This may be the end of the trail." And I decided I was gonna go AWOL. I knew that they were having a big Fourth of July thing at the mall in Washington, D.C. -- the National Folklife Festival. And I had never been to the Smithsonian. And nobody was paying a lot of attention to me. So I thought, "I'm going AWOL." I thought it might be my last few days on earth, my last Fourth of July, my last opportunity to see the Smithsonian. And I wanted to see the National Folklife Festival. And I wasn't sure if I would ever come back.

So I went to the bus station in Newport News. I got on the bus. I had about $12 to my name. Paid for my bus ticket, which was, I don't know, whatever, $3 or whatever.

I got to Washington, D.C., and I had nothing with me except a little journal that I always carried around. I'm wandering around the bus station area, trying to figure out what I'm gonna do next, and I found this fleabag hotel. I went in and asked them how much for the night, and they said $8. This is how bad this hotel was. I said I could afford $3 a day, and they said whatever, okay. So I got this fleabag room up on the fourth or fifth floor for three days. And, oh, god, it was terrible. I mean, there were no bathrooms in the rooms. There was a bathroom down at the end of the hall. And the shower only had cold water.

So I am working with maybe $4 left, and I start exploring around. I didn't know how I would make it three or four days. I go out and I find this little diner. And I'm looking for the cheapest thing on the menu. I was sitting there trying to figure out something on the menu that would leave me with a little tiny bit of money, right? And there was this older guy in his, maybe, 50's -- he looked ancient to me. He was sitting kind of across from me, on the other side of the aisle. He sees me checking my money, and he looks over and says, "May I intrude?"

I thought that was an odd turn of a phrase. I said, "I don't know, what for?" And he said, "I see you're struggling with the menu. You look like a soldier." I wasn't in uniform, but I had a shaved head and everything. I said, "Yeah." He said, "You're headed for the war, aren't you?" I said, "How did you know that?" And he just kind of smiled and came over. He said, "Let this dinner be on me."

We started talking, and he was very obscure. I mean, he didn't say anything about himself. But he started asking me questions. And it was almost like he had read my mind in a certain sort of way. He said, "When are you supposed to leave?" And I said, "In a few days." And he said, "You're struggling with it, aren't you?" And I said, "Yeah." And he said, "It's a hard struggle." And he bought me dinner that night. And that allowed me to, you know, have enough for at least coffee or something in the morning, maybe a meal the next day.

So I get back to my hotel room, and during the night I am awakened by these horrible, horrible yelling, screaming, crashing, thrashing, walls wobbling, people yelling at each other, and then a gunshot, and then more yelling, and something breaking, and all hell breaking loose. And I'm just sitting there in my room, listening to all of this, through the thin walls in the hotel. And then all of a sudden it's quiet. Then within a few minutes I hear police coming through the hotel. And I hear all this stuff going on out in the hallway.

And after about an hour it was all gone. And I'm sitting there holding it in, because I needed to go to the bathroom! And finally, everything quiets down, and I go down to the end of the hall to the only bathroom on the floor, and I get in there, and the toilet cover is broken on the floor, there's blood all over the walls, there's blood all over the hallway. I had heard somebody screaming before I went down there, and I'm thinking, "I don't even know if I'm gonna survive this night!" (Laughter)

So the next morning, I only have about $2 left. I did have a round trip bus ticket -- I was smart enough to buy that. And if I thought that this was going to be a little respite -- to consider "Do I go to Canada or do I go back or whatever" -- no. This was more immediate than that. So I go back to the same little diner, and I was kind of in my mind hoping that that man would be there, but he wasn't. All I could afford was a 50 cent cup of coffee and still have a little money left.

I'm trying to figure out my day. So I thought, okay, well, I'll make my way to the mall. So I did. And it was wonderful. There was everything from gospel music to lumberjacks throwing axes -- I mean, every culture that you can imagine around the United States. And I was looking, watching all of this, and absorbing it, and I was thinking, "I'm leaving a lot behind here, especially if I decide to go to Canada. But one way or the other, I'm leaving, and I don't know which direction I'm going yet."

So by the time I bought something to eat and drink, I was zero broke. And the only place I had to go back to was this flophouse hotel. I went back, and I'm listening to screaming down the hall and people yelling at each other -- no more gunshots, no more blood, that had been cleaned up. Toilet cover was still broken. But I'm sitting in my room thinking, "I have two choices. But maybe I only have one. Maybe my only choice is to get back on the bus to get back to where I'll get paid. And then shipped off." But I didn't want to leave yet, because there was two more days of all this stuff going on.

So I'm sitting in my little room, which was just tiny, and I had hung something up in the closet. And I'm in the closet, and I saw something up on the shelf in the closet. I got something, a stool or something, got up and I found an old book. And I'm thinking, "Well, maybe I could get a couple of bucks for it at a used book store." So I started wandering around the city looking for a used book store, and I found one. I took it in, and the guy I was talking to was studying it and asked where I got it. I said I found it in my hotel room. I was hoping to get, like, $2 or something for it. And he looked at me -- and I could tell he was lowballing me -- and he said, "I could not possibly give you more than $75 for this." And I said, "Can you make it $100?" And he said, "I'll make it $80."

So all of a sudden I had $80. I was rich. I was *rich*. And why the universe let that happen, I don't know. But it enabled me to, kind of, spend the rest of my time -- I saw the rest of the festival, it was absolutely fantastic. And I decided, "You know, everybody that I've met back there at Fort Eustis is gonna get on a plane and go to Vietnam. I don't know what I'm supposed to be doing with them, but I'm not gonna let them down."

So I rode the bus back, got there, and nobody, nobody ever asked where I'd been. It was as if I had never left.

Chapter 4

The Vietnam War: Ages 20-22

The 166th Aviation Detachment

So we were a pretty close unit. Although nobody knew -- even the commanding officer and his second -- nobody knew what my function was. I didn't quite know what my function was until I would go to Saigon, get these orders, bring them back, hand them to them, they would deliver me to some place out in the jungles and drop me off for, you know, two days, four days, six days. I don't think I ever spent seven days straight in the jungles. But I was observing and watching. Or I was dropped off in South Vietnamese military units to advise them on one thing or another. And that's about as far as I can go into all of that, in terms of -- I don't know for a fact that all of that has been declassified.

My official function with the 166th was combat journalist. And actually, "combat journalist" was sort of my M.O.S. everywhere, except for later in MAC-V when I was officially assigned to the Military Assistance Command, my actual job and cover was with the Armed Forces Language School, teaching English to Vietnamese officers. But it was both teaching English and also dealing with transferring command to the Vietnamese. And at that point, in Saigon, my official rank was one rank higher than whatever Vietnamese officer I was teaching.

But that was also where I met two friends. One was Binh, Tao's father. And then Captain Lam. Captain Lam was with the Vietnamese and American intelligence, and that got me pulled into the intelligence realm.

A Rat on My Chest in the Middle of the Night

So this would have been somewhere around September of 1969. We were in Vung Tau, and we had some permanent hootches. And I would repair there when I was in from out in the field. Hootches were these actual wooden buildings that were like little barracks. But it was on the airfield in Vung Tau. And Vung Tau was one of the most beautiful spots in Vietnam. It was kind of like Heaven. It was pretty sane compared to everywhere else, out in the boonies.

So in my hootch, I had a little bitty space, probably about the size of a walk-in closet. It had a bunk and a little table -- that's about it. And, of course, a mosquito net. The mosquito net apparently had kind of a little tear or hole in the top of it, above my bunk.

Well, one night, I'm sound asleep, and all of a sudden I feel something drop onto my chest and stomping, going everywhere on my chest. It's about the size of a cat. And it freaked me out, because I'd been sound asleep. I get up and I'm knocking things around and everything. And it turns out, it was a rat.

And it scratched my chest and maybe bit me. And I thought, "Damn, I'm gonna get rabies." So the next morning I went to the Army dispensary, and I go talk to the doc and I tell him what happened. And I asked if I needed to get a rabies shot. And he said to me, "No, you don't have to worry about rabies. Rats don't carry rabies." And I said, "Oh! Okay."

Well, of course rats can have rabies, they're mammals! Why the doc told me that, I have no idea. I mean, I believed him. And at some other point, I was talking to another doc at some other field hospital, who asked if I'd had any other injuries or wounds. And I said, "Well, I had a rat fall on my chest and scratch the hell out of me a few months ago." And he said, "Oh, okay, and did you get rabies shots?" And I said, "No. Rats can't cause rabies." And he looked at me like I was crazy, and said, "Where did you come up with that?!" And I said, "Well, the doc told me." And the doctor shook his head and said, "Jesus Christ."

So it was just by a bit of luck that I didn't wind up with rabies.

Sea Snakes in the South China Sea

We'd been in Vietnam for three or four months, in Vung Tau. From there, the 166th Aviation would fly me to Saigon, I would get orders, and I would hand these orders over, and these orders were where I was supposed to be delivered to, in different places. It was still all a mystery to me.

But Vung Tau was a really, really good respite spot. As a matter of fact, it was so beautiful there, that it was one of maybe two in-country R&R sites. It was an old French colonial town -- had these great French hotels that were fronting Front Beach, which was on one side of the South China Sea as it came around the peninsula. Vung Tau was on a peninsula. And then there was Back Beach. Back Beach -- the unit -- I don't know who set it up, maybe the first sergeant -- but they thought it would be good if we all had a gathering, and picnic, or, you know, cookout, and beer and swimming on Back Beach in Vung Tau.

So there we were. We're all swimming out in the ocean, everything's good. And all of a sudden, at some point during all of this, I was looking out into the distance, and it looked like the ocean started boiling. I mean, it just looked like it was boiling. And I said to somebody near me, who wasn't even in my unit, "God, it looks like the ocean's boiling." And the guy said, "What?!" And he looked out there, and he said, "Get out of here! Get back to the beach now, now, now!"

And it turns out that there were hundreds of thousands of poisonous sea snakes out in the ocean, coming in towards land. It apparently happened periodically -- I'm not sure what the phase of it all was. And these sea snakes were as lethal as, you know, any other lethal snake on land that you would find -- water moccasins or rattlesnakes. So we're hollering to every-body, "Get back! Get back! Get back!" And we're trying to make it back to the seashore -- and we were probably, at that point, maybe a hundred yards out. And the sea snakes were maybe 300 yards out. But the whole sea is boiling with all of this sea snake stuff.

So we're pulling people in onto the beach, and there were some that were so far out that they got enmeshed in the snakes, and they were killed. I think that was maybe four or five people. But there had been probably a hundred people out there to begin with. And we made it back -- I made it back, Kul-czyk made it back, Huggins made it back, Scotty made it back -- all these people that were in my unit made it back to the shore. Nobody in my unit got killed in that. But it turned out that some did die. And we were lucky enough to survive.

And a couple of the people -- not me -- but a couple of the people that were in my unit said, yeah, the snakes had bounced off of them. None of them ever hit me. Of course, I was swim-ming like a mofo! (Laughter)

Exploring an Old Freighter

In Vung Tau, Back Beach was the more interesting beach. There was this old freighter from some hurricane or typhoon or whatever -- who knows how many years before -- that had been pushed up on shore. It was half on -- three quarters on shore, and a portion of it still sat out in the water. And it was an enormous freighter. And it was just a fixture.

So Jim Kulczyk, Scotty McQueen, David Eastburn, and a couple of other guys, I don't remember who, and myself -- we decided we wanted to climb up onto the freighter and explore the freighter. And it was a long, long climb up. I mean, it was probably three stories high to get to the deck, because it was all out of water, right? And of course the back end was in the water. That would be the bow and the stern. The stern was in the water, the bow was up on land.

So we're exploring this thing, and it's all cool. And we get to the back -- to the stern. And somebody comes up with the grand idea that we ought to jump off -- instead of climbing down, we ought to just jump off into the water and swim back to shore. So Scotty McQueen, I think it was -- he decided to be the first one to jump off. And he jumps off, and it's, like, four stories up from that place. And he hits the water, and he fractures his back. And he's flailing and dying in the water.

My first reaction was to jump in after him, but no, that wouldn't be good. So everybody starts working their way down, off of ropes, down to get off the ship. And we get out there and we haul him back in. And he didn't die. But he did fracture his back.

There's nothing really big and important about that, except that he got to lay up in the hospital for a while. But it taught us sort of a -- well, some of us already knew the lesson. Don't jump! Because the water was only like three feet deep there. And when he hit the water, he went in feet first.

He was in the hospital for a long time, but he healed up and could walk again. But that was -- and we tried. We tried. We tried to talk him out of doing that. But he wanted to show us that he was a bad ass. And I remember specifically -- I don't know if it was me or somebody else -- saying, "You don't know how deep the water is there!" And it turned out it was only about three feet deep there.

A Company-Sized Snafu

I had a lot of discretion in what I wanted to do. I could suggest things and they'd say, "Fine, do that." But every now and again, I would get some order. "Do this." And the order in this case was -- there was an American Ranger unit -- well, I don't remember if it was Rangers or special forces -- but anyway, it was a relatively small American unit, and then a company-sized Vietnamese army operation. And I was supposed to be involved in that operation.

So off they flew me, dropped me in, and we're going along. And I'm looking at -- oh, I think the Vietnamese were also Rangers, special forces. And I'm just stunned. We're going through the jungle. It's a company-sized operation, which is over 150 bodies moving through the jungle. And nobody's paying attention to any kind of protocol. They're smoking, they're joking, they're talking, they're laughing. And I'm like, "This is not a good situation."

But I had no way to get out of the situation. But it was like, "No, no, no, this is not the way it's supposed to be." But anyway, here this grand little troupe goes through the jungle. And I keep talking to the commanding officer, which I think was a first lieutenant or captain in the American unit, and I said, "This is bad. This is bad. Stop everything. Make everybody get quiet. I want to go person to person to person and talk." And he laughed me off. He said, "This is a milk run. We've done this -- we do this all the time."

So here we go, tramping through the jungles. And then, of course, Charlie sees us, hears us, smells us, from a mile away. And Charlie's there. And Charlie ambushes this whole operation. And people are just being mowed down. And it's horrible.

And I'm back there with the RTO -- which is the radio operator -- and the commanding officer and somebody else. And I've got people standing in front of me, and behind me, and on the side of me. The ones in front of me were killed, the ones in back of me were killed, the ones on each side of me were killed. I was left standing. Did not get a scratch.

Out of that 150ish people, there were only eight of us who were not either killed or wounded in that operation. And you can imagine what my report back to the people I was reporting to was, at the military assistance command -- with a special note to -- I think it was Westmoreland at the time. Completely buried, completely ignored. But I thought, "This transfer of operations is not going to be very effective." Which is part of what I was there for, to try to transfer operations to the Vietnamese, and also report on the status of what the American operation forces were doing at the same time.

But there were only eight of us that were not either medevaced or picked up in body bags and flown back after that operation. And since I had quite a bit of control over my own operations, I swore at that time that never again would I go out in any unit that was larger than about six or eight people, and I would have to vet them first to decide if I wanted to go with them.

And it breaks my heart to this day. I wish -- I hated to see that. Because it was -- it still breaks my heart. There was no reason for all that to have to happen. When I was out there by myself, I could find any trip wire, I could smell anything. I mean, I loved it most when I was by myself. That's when I love life the most. Put me together with people I don't know or can't control, and it gets kind of sketchy.

I'll add as a footnote, that I did go out with a South Korean unit one time, that was probably platoon-sized -- probably about 30 or 40 people. This was probably the most vicious and disciplined unit I ever went out with in the whole time I was in Vietnam. They were quiet, they were committed, and they were killers. They showed no mercy to anybody who was the enemy. There were no prisoners, ever.

Sgt. Flint and Kim Hoang

The hootches in Vung Tau were long wooden buildings with sandbags around the sides of them. They had an aisle running down the middle, and on each side, they had these little alcoves, where our bunks were. And there was one little spot where there was a little space for a table, where people could sit and play dominoes or cards or whatever. And they had a door at both ends.

So I had just come back from some four or five day little travails in the jungles, and I was happy to be back in a place that was relatively safe. So me, and Kulczyk, and Scotty McQueen, and Buck the Navajo Indian -- he was the nicest guy in the world unless he got drunk -- but anyway, whoever was there, we were all sitting there at night playing poker.

And in each hootch, there were hootch maids assigned. These were Vietnamese civilian women who were there to basically, you know, wash the bedding, shine the boots, do the laundry, that sort of thing. And Kim Hoang was one of our hootch maids. We had a couple of hootch maids. And everybody called Kim Hoang "Baby San" because she looked like she was 15 years old or something. I didn't know this until later, but she was actually about the same age I was. Maybe a year younger than I was. And she was very shy, but very sweet. She didn't engage much because she didn't know much English at that time. But we all kind of took her under our wing a little bit because she was very sweet.

So one night, the night we were sitting there playing poker, this hootch maid from another hootch comes running in the back door screaming at the top of her lungs and is being chased by Sergeant Flint. And she's screaming, "He rape me! He rape me! He rape me!" And he's flying in, and he hits her at one point, and she flies off to the side.

Jim and I and maybe somebody else stand up. I stop him in his tracks. I said, "What in the hell is going on?!" And he said, "None of your business! She's mine! Get out of my way!" And so on. And I said, "Nope. You ain't touching her." And my little crew kind of gathered around me. And he's glaring at me, and he says, "When I come back, I'm gonna have my weapon." I said, "Give it your best shot."

So he takes off. We had sequestered her. We got her in a safe place. And all of sudden, there's all this hubbub, because, you know, "What's gonna happen? He's coming back!" And so on. I said, "Let him come back."

So he comes flying back in with his M-16 and I knock the shit out of him with a bunk extender. A bunk extender was a metal pole that connected the bunks. They were about 15 or 20 inches long, I don't know. I knocked him out, took his weapon away, called the MP's, had him arrested, and off he got hauled to the stockade.

So the next day, Kim Hoang comes to me, and she says, in her broken English, "He did this with everyone." Because he was the sergeant in charge of hiring all of the indigenous personnel to work as hootch maids. That was his job as a sergeant. And I started questioning her. I couldn't understand everything she was saying, but I could tell it was big. I could tell it was really big.

So the Vietnamese secretary for our unit, the 166th -- her name was Cuc. She spoke very good English. And I explained to her what was going on, and she was horrified. And I said, "I need a translator. I want to take statements." Because all these women were coming forth, you know, one after the other. And I didn't speak Vietnamese well enough. I mean, I knew what was going on, but -- so she became the scribe for all of this. And I built a case. And it was a horrible case. It was terrible. And Kim Hoang had so far evaded him. He hadn't raped her. She said she was afraid he was going to because he kept trying to do stuff.

So I put this whole case together and I presented it to the Inspector General and to the MP's. And Flint was arrested again. And everybody swore that yes, this was the end of his career. This is bad, bad, bad stuff.

And it lingered for -- I don't know, two or three more months. And then I got moved to my real unit, which was the Military Assistance Command, MAC-V, as a military advisor, which is what I really was at the time. And I got moved to Saigon.

When I was leaving Vung Tau, I talked to Kim Hoang and thanked her for everything she had done to help with all of this. And I said, "You know, I'm going to Saigon, my headquarters is gonna be in Saigon. But if you ever need to get in touch with me, if there's ever any more problems with Flint or anybody, let me know, and I'll try to do whatever I can."

And then, after I got to Saigon, and after I checked back in, a few months later, on what was going on -- yes, Flint had been court-martialed. And he'd been demoted one rank. And transferred to another unit way up in the northern part of South Vietnam, where, apparently, he was given the same job. Yeah. Yeah. They busted him down a rank, they took, like, two or three months' pay from him, and sent him off to do the same thing somewhere else.

And a couple months after I had left Vung Tau, Kim Hoang showed up in Saigon.

My 21st Birthday

So I got to Vietnam July 12, 1969. My 21st birthday was October 25, 1969. And the night of my birthday, we were under a -- being bombarded by rocket and mortar fire. And they were targeted well.

So I'm in a bunker. Jim Kulczyk's in a bunker about 40 yards away, I guess. Looking out the front of my bunker, I could see his bunker. And I look out, and when the rockets and stuff go off, and there's all these flares going off and everything, and there's illumination, I can see him standing in the doorway of his bunker, holding something with a candle in it that was lit. And all of a sudden, I see what I think is a smile on his face, and he starts walking across this dead-man zone. Rockets and mortars coming in, right and fucking left. It was a heavy, heavy hit. And I'm sitting there trying to wave him back. I just know I'm going to stand there and watch him die.

And he made his way all the way across, and got to my bunker, and walked in, and handed me a Hostess cupcake with a lit candle on top for my birthday. I told him, "Okay, go back!" (Laughter) And he said, "I ain't going back!" So he stayed there in my bunker. (Laughter) So that was my 21st birthday.

Attending to a Plane Crash

One day, in Vung Tau, Kulczyk and I were out on the tarmac of the airfield. And we're watching this fixed-wing plane coming in. I forget if it was -- I think it was, like, a Mohawk or something. It was kind of a medium-sized airplane that probably could hold 50 or 60 people. Not a jet, but, you know, a prop-driven plane.

And we're watching it kind of coming in, and Jim says, "This approach isn't right." And we're watching it come in, and I said, "Yeah, there's something wobbly about it." He says, "This is gonna go down."

So we watch it and it is heading down, and we're thinking nobody's gonna survive that. We jump in a Jeep and we go to where the plane is gonna crash.

And it crashed in this large rice paddy field just outside the perimeter of the airfield. And we're the first two people there because we were headed there fast. So we're both in the water, heading out to the airplane. And then there's other vehicles and personnel making their way that direction, because we weren't the only ones who saw it. But we're -- the plane is sinking pretty fast, and it's a deeper rice paddy well than people imagine. So Jim and I are just hauling people out right and left. And then other people are hauling them back farther.

We never knew the reason for the malfunction or crash -- it could have been sabotage, it could have just been mechanics, I don't know. But of all the people that were on there, there were only three or four or five people, I don't remember now, who didn't make it out. But everybody else did. And everybody formed a line behind where Jim and I were -- like a conveyer belt -- all the way to the end of the rice paddy -- and it was just shuffling everybody to the next person, all the way down. But the fact that anybody survived surprised everybody by the time it was over.

Catching a Barber Spy

A few days, or a week, something, after my 21st birthday, we're -- and this was while we were at the airfield in Vung Tau. It was for helicopter and small, fixed-wing planes to come in. And our little complex was attached to that, where we had these hootches that we barracksed in.

So one day, Jim and I are out, just, I don't know, just hanging together, doing nothing. And I'm watching this -- oh, and they had civilian Vietnamese workers working in the compound. They called them "indigenous personnel." And there was a barbershop.

And I saw the barber come out of his little shop. These were all, like, little wooden shacky stuff. And I'm watching him, and he'd walk to different buildings, and then he'd walk over to the fence line, the concertina wire fortification. And Jim said, "Well, that's kind of weird." And I said, "Yeah, it is kind of weird."

And I was watching him, and he did that, like, with two or three different, four buildings. And I said, "You know, Jim. I think all this rocket and mortar fire that we've been getting lately is being drawn in by this barber. I think he's counting off steps from all these different locations inside the compound to the fence, and then from the fence they know how far everything has to go inside the fence." And Jim said, "I think you're right."

So we went over and jacked him up. Took him into custody. And sure enough -- we turned him over to some intelligence people there -- and yeah, that was why -- he had been doing that -- he'd been there for, like, two months, as a civilian Vietnamese personnel working there as a barber. And that's exactly what he had been doing.

And once we got rid of him, all of a sudden the rocket attacks and mortar attacks started falling way off base.

Delivering a Baby on an Airplane

So this was in 1969, probably in-country. My missions were given to me as they came along, and were sometimes kind of odd -- not odd, but I just never knew what it was gonna be. And this particular thing was I was gonna be flown out to this area near the Cambodian border, hook up with a couple of CIA people, and we had things we had to figure out.

So one of the CIA agents -- and they were there undercover and had been there for months. And I got there, and the girlfriend of one of the CIA operatives was going into labor. And the chopper that took me out there was gone. But the CIA had its own little airforce in Vietnam, and it was called Air Vietnam. The planes had "Air Vietnam" on the side of them. But they were all CIA planes.

So this guy said, "Okay, we've got to get my girlfriend to a hospital." And I said, "Well, there's a hospital at the airfield in Vung Tau -- a field hospital. And that gets me back close to where I need to be."

So we're flying from the Cambodian border in this little Air Vietnam plane, which had maybe five or six seats inside it. And she goes into heavy labor. And nobody knows what to do. Everybody's going batshit crazy. And she's saying, "This baby's coming! This baby's coming!" Except she's saying it in Vietnamese, and they didn't understand it, but I did. I said, "Tot lam," which is "Very good." (Laughter)

And they're saying, "What's going on?!" And I said, "She's gonna have a baby." "What do we do?!" I said, "Stand back."

I had had some, you know, really basic, basic training in medical stuff in the Army, and one of the things that had been a 20-minute deal somewhere along the way was delivering a baby. So I was trying to recall all of that. And the truth of the matter is -- and we're flying along, and the baby daddy CIA agent is just getting all squenched up -- and I'm more concerned with him than I am with her. She's going through a hard labor, and she's screaming, but that was getting him all upset. "What did you do to her?!" I said, "I haven't done anything to her, just stand back a minute."

And basically, all I really did, was to catch this baby when it popped out. I mean, that was the delivering of the baby. It was not like I was doing the delivery. I just was the catcher's mitt.

But then I had this baby in my hands, and you know, the umbilical cord's still attached. And I am just going frantic in my mind, trying to remember what in that training where they described how you tie off the umbilical cord. I kept thinking, "Is it this way? Is it that way?" And I thought, "Fuck it." I put the baby on her stomach and said, "Hold this baby. We're 20 minutes out."

So we get to the field hospital and everything's fine with the baby, fine with mama. And I'm talking to the doc, and I said, "You know, it's driving me crazy. I was trying to remember how to deal with the umbilical cord." And he said, "Well, it's better that you didn't." He said, "You did exactly the right thing." And he said, "You knew you had to tie it off, but you forgot that it has to be tied in two different places and you cut in between." I kept thinking you tie it, and then you have to cut it above or below. But it didn't make sense to me, so I left it alone. And he said, "You did exactly the right thing. Not only that, but you would have screwed up the belly button, no doubt, if you'd done it. And it worked out fine."

So that was my first, and last, delivery of a baby on an airplane.

Horrific Helicopter Crash

During the course of my two to two-and-a-half years in the military in Vietnam, I was involved in four helicopter crashes and one plane crash. Three of the four helicopter crashes were what I think can be termed "hard landings." Yeah, they did some damage, but nobody was killed or severely injured. I would hurt my back or whatever, but I didn't pay much attention to those.

I was involved in one fixed-wing -- airplane -- crash, but that was relatively -- it turned out okay. We crash landed in a rice paddy, and basically everything was okay unless we got shot or drowned trying to get out of the rice paddy. But nobody died.

The one helicopter crash of the four that was significant was also sad and very tragic. It happened around November of 1969. I don't remember -- I think -- I was catching a helicopter ride from either Tan Son Nhut in Saigon or Bien Hoa airbase. I don't remember which airbase it was; they're both huge.

But we're on this chopper ride, and they were taking me back to the Mekong Delta. And on the chopper was the pilot, the co-pilot, the door gunner, and myself. And I was talking to the pilot before we took off, and he was happy as a clam. He said, "This is my last mission! I go home tomorrow! And this is a milk run!" And it should have been a milk run. A milk run means just a typical, regular old easy peasy deal. And he was gonna drop me off in Vung Tau, and then he was gonna fly back to either Bien Hoa or Tan Son Nhut, wherever it was. And he was going home from the war the next day. And he had told me all about his wife and two kids and all of that.

So we're flying. The flight is good, everything's good. And we get to the Vung Tau airfield, and we're coming down. And we're about 20 feet off the ground, and all of a sudden, everything blows up. What had happened was, Charlie -- the Viet Cong -- had put a hand grenade in the fuel tank, wrapped with black tape. And after a certain period of time, the fuel would disintegrate the black tape and the grenade would explode. And it happened when we were about 20 feet away from landing, coming down. It blew off the tail rotor, which flew into the main rotor, and the main rotor came down and sliced through the cockpit and decapitated the pilot.

I had jumped out of one side of the helicopter. The tail gunner had jumped over the bar where the M-60 machine gun was and had come down. And the co-pilot remained in the helicopter as it hit the ground. And it was a huge crash, a huge fire. We all jumped out. I hurt my back and ankle. The door gunner broke his leg. And when we got down and we kind of came -- got our bearings a little bit -- the co-pilot was fine, and the pilot was sitting there in his pilot seat, with no head. His head had fallen out of his side of the helicopter and was laying on the tarmac. And for some reason that I've never been able to figure out, one of the pilot's boots was off, and just laying on the tarmac separately. I have never figured the boot thing out.

I don't know -- most people have not witnessed close-up and personal decapitations. I've seen many. More than I'd ever want to talk about. And they are so, so discombobulating. Because your first thought is, "This head belongs on the body. How do I put it back on the body?" And that can't be done, of course.

So that was the worst crash that I was ever in. And actually, Kulczyk -- he was not in the helicopter, he was there at Vung Tau, waiting for us to get back. And he came out -- a lot of people came out to try to help. But there was obviously nothing that could be done for that poor pilot. The co-pilot was actually about as unscathed as I was -- a hurt back or ankle. And the door gunner had broken a leg. But we pulled everybody far enough away from the helicopter to where, when the gas tank finally did a second explosion, all of us that were left alive had gotten far enough away from it to survive it.

Refusing an Arm Amputation

I was out for a few weeks in the jungles, working with South Vietnamese Rangers and a couple of other U.S. -- we were all military advisors. And all of this was part and parcel of trying to transition operations over to the Vietnamese. This was barely into 1970, maybe the end of 1969.

I received a very, very tiny, insignificant wound in my shoulder. It was nothing to pay attention to. And I didn't pay any attention to it. But within about a week, it began festering. And within about a week-and-a-half, I had all these red and blue streaks running down my arm, and this thing was just an oozing mess. And I was delirious.

So they medevaced me out to a little field hospital. The field hospital was maybe 1500 square feet. It wasn't tents, it wasn't like a MASH unit or something. It was a pre-fab mobile hospital that -- more like a triage place. Some place where wounded were taken, and then, depending on whether they could be treated there or had to be sent somewhere else -- that was sort of the triage unit.

And I got there, and they gave me the once-over, and the doc came and said to me, "Good news and bad news." And I was feverish, I was half in and out of it. And he said, "The good news is, you get to go home from the war. The bad news is, we are medevacing you out of here tomorrow morning to Yokota, Japan, where they're gonna have to take that arm off. Gangrene and blood poisoning have already set in. You're gonna lose the arm, but it's gonna get you home."

So with that, I'm lying in my little bunk, in the hospital bed, and I'm still in and out of it. Fuzzy, fuzzy, fuzzy. But I decided, "No. No, I'm going back to my unit. I'm not gonna let them chop my arm off. Whatever happens, happens."

So around 5:00ish or so that afternoon, I walk out of the field hospital. And I start walking. And the outfit that I was supposed to be with was probably about 15 or 20 kilometers from there. But I knew where I was going. And I was walking -- and in maybe 3 kilometers, maybe I made it 3 kilometers into this friendly village. Because I could tell I was fading fast, and I knew where this little friendly village was. I got there, and I ran into people that I knew and had established a relationship with. And I basically just collapsed.

And the last thing I remember was them packing this little wound with what, to me, smelled like foul-smelling, nasty seaweed or something. I have no idea what it was. I'm guessing herbs and spices. (Laughter)

But I was out. And I was out for at least a couple of days. I don't know. But I started coming to, and when I came to, the first thing I did was to look at my left arm and see if it was still there. And it was. And then I'm seeing all the red streaks and blue streaks are gone, and the wound is actually starting to heal. It's a little red around it, it's not healed, but it's better, and my arm is still there.

So I was still running a fever and kind of in and out of it. But about two or three days later, I had use of my arm. And I started making my way back to where my assignment was. And when I get there -- it took about another day or two -- when I'm walking into the unit, everybody there -- the South Vietnamese Rangers, the other military advisors -- are looking at me like they've seen a ghost. And I get there, and I tell them what happened. And the ranking commander said, "Your family was already notified that you were missing and presumed killed in action, because the night you walked away from the field hospital, it was hit by rocket and mortar fire, and the entire hospital and everybody in it was obliterated."

Of course, bureaucratically, that took some while to undo. My parents had already been informed that I was probably dead. And I wasn't. And but for -- well, especially, but for the Vietnames villagers, who knew things for thousands of years that modern western medicine doesn't know -- I still have my arm to this day and still use it.

And since then, I always really, really take with a grain of salt what any medical doctor says is the prognosis.

C-4 Explosion and the Beatles

Around December of 1969 or early January of 1970, the 166th Aviation Detachment was transferred from Vung Tau to Tan Son Nhut Airbase in Saigon. And of course, we were leaving behind these people -- all these personnel, including Kim Hoang, who worked for that airbase. It was a sad occasion for some of these people, because I had been somewhat instrumental in getting rid of this monster they had there.

Saigon was a wild and wooly city. At that time, it had a million or two million people in the city. The city was built to hold about 250,000 people, but everybody from the hinterlands were trying to come to Saigon to try to get out of wherever the war -- the worst part of things were. And Saigon was pretty well protected.

Downtown Saigon had kind of a strip of bars and that sort of thing. These were bars, the hookers, you know, "Buy me drink G.I." kind of places. But somehow or another, somebody had said something to us about, "Hey, there's this Filipino band that does brilliant covers of the Beatles." And it was on Tudo Street, or just off, I don't know. But anyway, it was right around there.

So we decided that we're gonna go watch this band one night. And we get in there, and it is a -- it's not a huge place. But it was a long, narrow bar. So we get in there, and Jim wants to get up close. And I said, "I don't want to get up close." So we found a place back towards the -- not in the very back, but a little beyond the middle. So we have our spot, and the band comes on. And it is phenomenal. I mean, they *are* the Beatles. And everybody's just going -- and the place is jammed pack.

And around, I don't know, 8 p.m., or 8:30, or something, we're sitting there, and I don't know what it was. Something was out of whack to me. And I think it had to do with the bandstand, which was elevated up about five feet with just this drapery stuff around it. And I'm sitting there, we're sitting there listening to the band, and something's out of whack, and I'm not quite certain what it was. But I looked at Jim and said, "We need to get out of here." And he was up before I stood up.

And we go out the door, we turn to the left, we've walked down about fifty or sixty feet, and the whole damn place blows out. Charlie had hidden a whole bunch of C-4 underneath the bandstand. And maybe it was the room itself, because it seemed like the room itself was like a canon to me. You know, this is like a perfect canon.

And people, chairs, tables, everything, was blown out -- there were bodies blown all the way across the street into the buildings. And virtually nobody got out of there alive, except two people -- and that was Jim Kulczyk and Ben Cunningham.

And we went back to try to help do what we could, but there was nothing to be done, because -- I don't know how many people -- 200 people, 150 -- I don't know -- they were dead. They were splattered against walls across the way. They were disintegrated inside the place.

But the minute I said, "We need to get out of here," Jim was up, he was ready, we were gone, and we survived it.

A Village Massacre

So this was down in -- I'm not even sure where now. Somewhere between -- between the Mekong Delta and up towards Parrot's Beak, which is where Cambodia kind of comes into Vietnam a little bit.

I was with a small Vietnamese Ranger operation. And there was this friendly village that we were headed to because there were supposed to be Viet Cong heading towards that village. And we got dropped off about -- well, I met up with the Ranger unit about two clicks -- two kilometers -- away from where the village was. And I made my way from the helicopter to where they were.

And we get to this village, and every man, woman, and child had been killed. And they had all of the village leaders -- they had decapitated them and put their heads on sticks, as a warning to all the Vietnamese that were not aligned with the Viet Cong. And that's how the Viet Cong controlled villages.

The village probably didn't have 25 people in it, altogether. And so obviously, we were too late getting there. It's one of those few scenes that stick in my head and I see, every time I think about it.

Training South Vietnames Rangers and Meeting Binh

So part of my mission when I was a military advisor for MAC-V was to advise military officers. My -- I guess you'd have to call it my cover at the time -- was as an English instructor to Vietnamese officers. But this was both a combination of helping them speak better English but also explaining what was happening with the transition of the war. And this was not a dangerous mission at all -- this was kind of fun. Because it was kind of like teaching but kind of like advising at the same time. And I had this rank of one rank higher of whoever I was teaching.

So finally I had the top general in the Vietnamese Army. And it created a little bit of a kerfuffle because I had the next higher rank, and there was nobody higher than the General, besides the President of South Vietnam! So this was a huge conundrum for him. And I told him, "Do not think of me as one rank higher than you or the same rank as you. Think of me as somebody who is really, really committed to giving you all the information I can possibly give you so that, when all of this transitions to you, you will have as much knowledge as I have."

He said, "Yes, sir." And I said, "Don't call me sir. I am taking my rank backwards from you. You are the highest ranking person here."

So we talked, and he said, "If ever you or the people around you need any help, come to me." And I said to him -- and this panned out later on during the evacuation of Vietnam -- I said, "Yes, I understand, but the same holds true for you. If you ever need anything from me, you let me know."

Oh, and by the way, Lieutenant Binh -- Tao's father -- was also part of that pipeline. And that's where I met him. And we glommed onto each other and became really good friends. I wasn't like buddies with the General, but with Binh, and with another Captain in the Vietnamese Army -- Captain Lam. They were probably my two closest people. And Captain Lam was the one who actually got me assigned to that mission, which was a combination of purportedly teaching English to Vietnamese officers, but also the intelligence side of the operation, combined with Army intelligence.

Best Sleep of My Life

After my first year in Vietnam, I got a leave to come home. The first year in Vietnam was the hardest and worst, and I really didn't think I was gonna survive.

So I came home. Of course, my father had already divorced my mother by that time. She had the house that he had bought in this relatively upscale, very upper middle class neighborhood. And that was where Patsy Swayze and her kids lived.

And across the street from us was a kid named Skip. And I had known him while I was in high school, but he was a little older and I think he went to some hoity toity private school. And I liked him at one time. But then one time he just begged to go out with David Hefner and me and one of my other buddies, because he wanted to "get into some shit." Well, we actually fell into some bad stuff that night, but it wasn't enough for us to really respond to. But he grabbed a baseball bat and jumped out of my car and ran back and started beating the hell out of the car behind us. And trying to beat the hell out of whoever was in that car. And we dragged him back. So that was while I was in high school. And I never forgot that. I was leery of him ever after that, and I never had anything to do with him after that.

But when I came home on this leave, he came over and said -- oh, and by the way, his father was a bigwig in one of the oil companies. And he was the honorary consul -- not ambassador -- for Malawi. The nation of Malawi. I don't even know if it's still a nation. But he came over and said, "Hey, welcome home. My dad and I are going down to the coast tomorrow to his boat, and we'd like to take you with us to go deep sea fishing." So I decided to say yes.

And we got in the car and we drove down to wherever the boat was in one of these places down near Galveston in some marina. And they're fiddling around with the boat, getting it all done. And it was a very nice, big boat. It had a bedroom down in the bow of the boat. And while they were, you know, taking care of getting the thing unmoored, and throwing stuff in and everything, I went down and explored the boat, and I found that little place.

I sat down on the bed, and the next thing I know, it's, like, nine hours later and we're coming back into dock. I sat down on the bed, I went to sleep, I was in the deepest, safest sleep I have been in, in maybe my entire life. I was out in the middle of nowhere. I knew nobody could be shooting at me. I knew no bombs could be falling. I knew I didn't have to look for trip-wires. I knew my helicopter wasn't gonna crash. I knew that nobody was gonna be shooting in the middle of the ocean. And I slept like I was in the womb for all of those many hours.

And as much as I didn't like Skip -- because I thought he was some sort of psychopath -- I have never appreciated anything more than that good sleep after an entire year in Vietnam where I probably never got more than two hours' sleep a night for the entire year.

Press Pass at Oakland Army Base

So after my first year in Vietnam, I got this leave to come back home. And then when I came back to go back to Vietnam, I had to go through Oakland Army Base. I got there, and of course I was categorized as an enlisted person. So they put me in a holding company waiting for a flight back to Vietnam. And this holding company was, you know, enlisted men, not officers. And by that time I was a specialist, so I was probably the rank of a low sergeant at the time, but still enlisted. So they were assigning everybody to different duties while they were waiting to get manifested back to Vietnam. And I thought, "This is bullshit."

So I demanded to speak to the commander of Oakland Army Base, and (laughter) got an audience. I handed him my press card and said, "I can't talk about this too much, but I am here basically for the purpose of writing a story about the transition and organization and situation with respect to receiving and sending troops back to Vietnam." I said to -- this was a general, not the highest kind of general, but a general -- I said, "I hear good things about you. And I want to write this story." And he was, like, gobsmacked. He was all over it. He said, "I give you free access to anything and everything and everywhere you want to go."

And (laughter) for that week, I just fucked off. (Laughter) I didn't write a thing. I just went here, went there. Went out to San Francisco, went over to Oakland, went over to Berkeley.

Just kind of exploring the city. But I had gratis free range for everything.

And right before I got sent back, he said, "How's the story going?" And I said, "It's going great! I'll send you something once I get back to Vietnam." And that was the last time I ever had any connection or communication with him. But, boy, did I think having that press pass really paid off!

The Catholic Priest

As anybody who's ever been in any kind of war knows, navigating or traversing even short distances can be a huge and long chore. I had -- and I don't remember where I was coming back from. I think maybe it was from the States after, like, a two-week leave or something like that. And I flew back into Bien Hoa airbase, which was probably about 20 miles out of Saigon. But 20 miles in Vietnam during the middle of a war could be like 200 miles in regular time.

I landed at Bien Hoa and I had no idea how I was gonna get back to Saigon. I exited the gates of Bien Hoa thinking, "Okay, maybe I can shag a ride with some military outfit or something." So I'm standing outside the gates, and I'm kind of, like, just hitchhiking.

And this Jeep stops. And I guess the best way I can put this is -- you remember the psychiatrist in MASH, the TV series? It was a guy like that who stopped to pick me up. Except this was not a Jewish psychiatrist. It turns out this was a Jesuit chaplain. And he picks me up.

And we're making our way to Saigon. And making your way to Saigon over 20 or 30 miles, whatever the distance was, meant not only rough roads, but attacks by the enemy and everything else. And, you know, that wasn't anything we were -- it was just the nature of the way it was going to be. It was going to take a long time. Probably two or three hours to make the 20 miles.

And we would stop, we would hide, we would do this, we would do that, we would get ready to fight. He wouldn't get ready to fight, he was not allowed to fight. But we had started chatting and, you know, getting to know each other, and so on.

And at some point, after about five miles into the trip, he said -- you know, we were talking about just, sort of, life, the universe, and everything, and he was trying to pick my brain on the war. And I was explaining to him that I was opposed to the war. I was morally opposed to the war. I was politically opposed to the war. I was there to do my duty, but I was never going to -- I was going to do my very best to dance around having to kill people. And we were having these great philosophical discussions. He was a Jesuit. He was challenging me on everything, you know? We were going back and forth.

And then he lit up a joint and handed me a joint. (Laughter) And we spent the rest of the trip heading to Saigon smoking and joking and philosophizing. And he made it sound like -- I had the feeling during the whole little trip -- that he was trying to pull me away from where my position was. Because it sounded to me like he was arguing, or insinuating, that no, the war is legal, this and that, and you're here. You need to fight. You need to die if you need to. And so on. This was kind of the arguments going back and forth.

And when we finally got to Saigon, and I showed him where to drop me off, the last thing he said to me was, "You do know, of course, that you're right. It's my job to challenge. But you are absolutely right." And I never ever -- I don't remember his name now, and he would never remember my name now. We were two ships passing in the night. But I will never forget him. And I will never know who he was.

Breaking up with my Fiancee and a Bet with Jim

While I was in Vietnam, my fiancee and I were still engaged. We were writing letters back and forth. But I wasn't sure if we were right for each other. And I was talking to Jim Kulczyk about this. I'd gotten this letter. I don't remember what it was or what it said. But I told Jim, "I can't keep doing this. I feel like I'm leading her on, because I'm not sure I'll make it through the war." And he said, "Well, you're just gonna have to tell her." And I said, "Yeah, but I've got to figure out a way to -- I mean, I don't want to hurt her."

But then I came up with this brilliant idea. It just dawned me that two of my best friends in the world -- my fiancee and David Hefner -- it dawned on me that they both had more in common with each other than either one of them had in common with me. And I knew that David was going back from Okinawa, or wherever he was, back to the States -- he'd been discharged. So I timed it for the discharge.

So I made a bet with Jim. I think it was fifty bucks. I said, "I'm gonna send this letter breaking up. I'm gonna send David Hefner a letter telling him that I'm breaking up with her and could he maybe just talk to her, take her out, let her vent, whatever." And I said, "They'll be married in six months." Jim said, "No way." I said, "Fifty bucks."

So we made the bet. So I wrote this letter, sent it off to her, got in touch with David Hefner, said "Help her get through this if you can. She may need a shoulder to cry on."

So I didn't hear from anybody for about four months. And then got a letter back, a joint letter from both of them, saying, "We don't know how to tell you this . . ." (Laughter) ". . . but we're getting married and we just wanted you to know."

So I won my fifty bucks from Kulczyk.

Rooftop Attack from the Cemetery

In Saigon, we had found -- Jim Kulczyk, me, Scotty McQueen, a couple of others, Dwight Huggins -- who was the only black member of that small detachment -- we had found this -- actually, Huggins had found this great little apartment a couple of blocks outside of Tan Son Nhut Airbase in what was called then Soul Alley. There was a reason it was called Soul Alley, because it was the enclave of black American soldiers who were working at Tan Son Nhut. And all of a sudden there were these few white guys. And we anticipated lots of problems with that, but we had no problems whatsoever. First of all, you know, we weren't racist. And second of all, Huggins was among us and vouched for us.

We were in this kind of cement, concrete kind of apartments that had four or five floors and little balconies on each floor. And then there was a rooftop. And the rooftop was sort of where we gathered every night, those of us who were in that group. We'd sit there and we'd look out -- you know, drink beer, those that drank beer, or those that smoked a joint, or whatever. Or those that just wanted to sit and watch the war from afar, because we could see out to where bombs were being dropped, where mortars and rockets were coming in. But they were in the distance.

On one side of the apartment building was this old, old Vietnamese cemetery. And it was nice -- it gave us kind of a little buffer zone there, and we enjoyed just kind of looking at the night. And one night we were sitting up there and all of a sudden we started taking fire from the cemetery. Charlie -- as the Viet Cong were called -- had made a foray into the city, as they often did, on a regular basis, and they were shooting at us on the rooftop from the cemetery. It wasn't real smart, because, while they had a good line of fire, we had a good vantage point.

But we were all sitting up there unarmed on the roof. So as soon as we started taking fire, we all scampered down to our various little rooms, and pulled out our weapons, and came back to the roof. And we had a lot of weapons! But, you know, we didn't use them in Saigon, they were -- and all of a sudden it's like, "Oh, we're under attack! We're in a firefight!"

So it's night time, it's dark, and every time there's a flash, you know, fire, from the cemetery, we're shooting down at the cemetery. And this goes on for about 20 minutes. I should mention we had a little wall, like a four-foot wall on the rooftop -- it wasn't just completely flat.

So this firefight goes on for a good 15 or 20 minutes, and none of us are hit. But we're just unloading on the cemetery, you know. And we don't know what's going on. But after about 15 or 20 minutes, there's no more shots coming from the cemetery. Either they've been hit, or they've all just scampered away, as Charlie does.

It wasn't like a jungle firefight. I mean, the jungle fire fights I was in were deadly, deadly, deadly, because it was them and us on level ground, you know, ten feet, twenty feet, a hundred feet away from each other. This was a whole different little ballgame. And it was kind of -- we were taking it kind of jokingly. This was almost fun. (Laughter) It was, "Oh, this is an interesting night! We didn't see this coming!"

So the next morning, after all this, we go down to the cemetery, because we're looking for bodies. And we don't see any bodies, but we see blood on tombstones. If we'd found bodies, we would have had to make a big report. No bodies, but blood being -- you could see where bodies had been dragged away.

So that was one firefight in Saigon, and it was inconclusive. (Laughter)

First Sergeant Nearly Cuts His Hand Off

So if we scroll back to Fort Eustis, Virginia, when I was basically kidnapped and put into the 166th Aviation unit -- the first sergeant in the unit was this really, at the time, when I first got there, this sort of really, what we called in the Army "strack" kind of guy -- straight-laced all the way, policies and procedures, and so on. By the time we'd been in Vietnam for awhile, he glommed onto me. And when I was moving my cadre of friends to Soul Alley from Tan Son Nhut, he came along. He had one of the rooms in the building that we were in. But he also was -- I mean, he'd been in the Army forever. I don't know how long -- 15 or 20 years, I don't know. And really all he liked to do was to drink and whore.

One night, in his room -- that was next to the room next to my room -- I hear this horrible, horrible screaming, crazy stuff. And I go rushing in there, with a weapon, because I think that bad guys have come. But no. He's standing there. His hand and arm are bloody messes. He was drunk. He had stood up on the bed in his room, with this little chickadee that he had -- and for some reason, he had stuck his hand up in the hard, metal, fast blades of the ceiling fan, and his hand was almost cut off. These were old French fans from the 1940's.

So I'm putting tourniquets on him, I'm getting him -- and it's after curfew, when anybody can be shot on the streets if they're out after curfew. And I'm flying through the streets with this guy, trying to get him back to the hospital at Tan Son Nhut. And it was only, like, four or five minutes from where we were.

Got him there, and he was still drunk as a skunk. They saved his hand, they saved his arm. And they said that was due to me. But I said, "No, this was his idea, he knew exactly where to go. He's almost to retirement. The accident wasn't his fault."

But it was completely his fault. But I said it wasn't anything he did wrong. I knew the whore he was with. (Laughter) She probably told him to stand up and put his hands up. (Laughter)

But he survived and he was able to retire with full honors.

Kim Hoang Moves to Saigon

So it's probably two or three months after we left Vung Tau, and we're at Tan Son Nhut Airbase. One day, there was a -- Kim Hoang just showed up. Somehow she had flashed my name at the main gate, and they brought her to me at our little head-quarters building at the helipad at Tan Son Nhut. You know, the MP's. They said, "She says she knows you and you vouch for her." And I said, "I do."

And she told me what had happened. A couple people in her family that she had been living with had been killed by the Viet Cong. And there was no more work at -- they were winding stuff down at the airfield there. And I said, "Well, let me see what we can do."

And by that time, I already had this little apartment on Soul Alley. And I knew that there was this little storage room up on the rooftop. So I was able to ensconce her in that little rooftop storage building for her little sleeping place. And then during the -- and I said, "Look, here's the deal. I think I can get every-body in that unit to have you do all their laundry and stuff. And I'll just haul it back here in my Jeep, and you can do the laundry, and I'll haul it back." And my shoulder was still sensi-tive and healing at that point, so it was kind of a chore for me to do laundry.

But I ensconced her there. And remember we called her "Baby San." Because she just seemed like, almost like a child. But of course she did everything perfectly. And everybody loved her and loved how good she was with everything she did. And then she started cleaning some of the apartments there.

So that's how she came to be up in Saigon, and came to live on the roof. Until later, as things progressed, I just moved her down -- after the rooftop shooting. And by that time, in my mind, I had adopted her. I was responsible for her. And she was gonna be under my protection for the rest of the time.

Marijuana Experiments

My experience with marijuana, ganja, weed, whatever, was during 1969 and 1970, in Vietnam. I'd never had any before then. But Vietnam was a place where marijuana was the most minor of drugs that could have ever been imagined. Although, much of the marijuana that came in from Cambodia was cut with opium, which made it pretty powerful stuff.

So I'd smoked a couple of times down in the Delta, but it didn't do anything for me. And I was in this mode where I wanted -- I didn't drink a lot and I didn't want to do anything that was gonna mess up my perception, because that was what was keeping me alive.

But then when we went up to Saigon in the beginning of 1970, it was a little different. We would hang out on the rooftop, and people would smoke. I'd be sitting there listening to all this, and it was just nonsense -- all marijuana smoke talk.

But I started thinking, "I wonder if this is good or bad for the mind and for thinking?" So at that point, I sent off to the University of Texas to apply for two undergraduate correspondence courses, because I was trying to accumulate credits along the way. So I had an algebra course and an English course. And my experiment was this: I was gonna do one of them only after smoking marijuana and the other one straight.

So the algebra course was the one I did while smoking marijuana. And nobody else knew what I was doing except for maybe Jim Kulczyk. Well, here's the upshot of it all. The English course I did with no marijuana, and I made an A or A+. But with algebra, I got stuck. I got stuck on a number. I don't remember if it was 7 or 9. But every time that number came up -- I mean, it was involved in everything. And I spent the entire semester -- and I never got through the first assignment (laughter) because I was so fascinated and enthralled by that number. So I thought -- that was a clue to me, that, yeah, this was bad for schoolwork. On the other hand, I thought, maybe this is how -- if people start obsessing about this stuff, maybe that's how they come to the bottom of what 7 or 9 is. So that was that experiment.

Then, when I was done with that, I had -- I don't even remember how I got them, but I had two pet ducks. Little tiny chicks. Ducklings. They were the same size. And I started raising them. And then I decided, I would raise one of them on regular duck food and the other just on marijuana.

The one that I fed with regular duck feed kept growing like a regular duck. The other duck didn't grow well. Or, I think I got that backwards. The one that I fed marijuana grew like crazy, and the other duckling was growing normally.

And one day, the duck that was on marijuana -- and we had these little balconies -- it kept trying to fly off the balcony. And it flew down and hit the ground. I went down and got it, it had broken a leg, and I patched him up the best I could. And he started recovering.

And then I switched it around, and started feeding them differently. And the upshot of all of that, as I can remember it now, is -- oh, and I named them, Dinky Dau and Dinky Duie. Those are Vietnamese expressions for crazy and even crazier. But at any rate, the one who was raised mostly on marijuana, who always just wanted to fly -- and I can understand that, who wouldn't, if you were a duck, and were high? After about two wrecks, four stories down, one time I came home and that duck was dinner. Kim Hoang had found him on the ground, brought him up, and cooked him.

So those were the two experiments with marijuana. I'm still trying to completely unravel them.

Pack of Feral Dogs in Saigon

So this was in Saigon, and this was actually in 1970 at some point, I don't remember when. But I was up in Saigon at that time. And there was a curfew in Saigon. Sometimes it was 10:00 at night, sometimes 11:00. But anybody out on the streets after that was subject to being shot dead on sight. Because they assumed anybody out after curfew was an enemy.

So I don't remember where I'd been or what I was doing, but it was late at night, it was like 11:00 or 11:30 at night, and I was trying to get back from somewhere. And I'm making my way through the streets of Saigon -- actually, in the suburbs, kind of, of Saigon. But all of these buildings in Saigon -- everything had -- you've seen them, I'm sure -- you know, at night, where they can pull down these metal doors for security purposes, so people can't break in and stuff like that.

And the streets are deserted because it's after curfew. But I'm being really careful to stay in the shadows and not get found or shot, and all of a sudden -- I'm on this long alleyway -- there's only one way in and one way out of this alleyway -- and all of a sudden I hear this pack of wild, feral dogs, who were the bane of the night time in the big cities, because they were killers. And I hear them coming, and all of a sudden I see them coming.

And there's a little tiny bit of dim light from one of the buildings, and I don't have any place to go. They were coming down one side, and I was running, trying to get out away to the other side, but they were a lot faster than I was. So I'm getting kind of, like, "I don't think I'm gonna get out of this." And I see that one of these buildings that has the metal door down on it, but also, some of these buildings had, beyond, outside, the metal door, a space of about 14 inches or so, and then another gate that came down, a wire mesh gate that you could see through. And I saw one of these buildings where the metal door was down but the mesh gate was up about a foot. It wasn't closed all the way.

And just as these dogs were getting to me -- and there were probably 30 or 40 of them, they ran in huge, huge, vicious packs -- I was able to get underneath, into the gap, underneath the thing, pull that down, and I'm stuck there for about 45 minutes as they are just jumping up against the wire mesh. They're coming at me, bouncing off of it and everything. And I'm there for 45 minutes.

And I'm thinking -- at first I thought I was gonna die. But once I got up under there, I thought, "Well, I'm not going to die, but I don't know how many days I'm gonna have to be here." Mainly I wasn't concerned about being out past curfew, I was concerned about the dogs. I mean, they were vicious. They were biting at the wire mesh, their mouths were bleeding. And after a few minutes, it was like, "Okay, I'm really not scared anymore now, because I think I am safe. But when are they ever gonna leave, if ever? Are they just gonna wait until I have to come out?"

But after about 30 or 45 minutes, all of a sudden some noise down the way caught their attention, and off this 30-dog pack ran. And I waited there, and waited there, and waited there. And I could hear their barks and growls and everything receding way down the alley. So at some point I finally came out, went back down to the other end of the alley, and finally made my way back to my apartment.

A Cyclo-mai Accident

So in Vietnam, in Saigon, and maybe the other cities, there were what were called *cyclo-mais* and *cyclo-daps*. *Cyclo-daps* were kind of like rickshaws that were peddled. *Cyclo-mais* were (laughter) motorcycles, but on the front of the motorcycle was a seat that would hold two people. They were, like, death traps. (Laughter)

And *cyclo-mai* drivers, as opposed to *cyclo-dap* drivers -- *cyclo-dap* drivers were, like, you know, the rickshaw drivers that just peddled their bicycles and you were sitting in the front seat. But *cyclo-mais* were the next gen. And these (laughter) crazed "Papa Sans" -- to us, they were all Papa Sans -- that were driving these things were freaking maniacs. And they drove like absolute crazy.

And of course, when you got onto one of these, they were like -- they were like taxis. You had to negotiate what the fee was gonna be and everything like that, to, you know, wherever you were trying to go to.

And I could probably tell 100 of those stories. But probably the worst of those stories was when -- and remember, the passengers, which would be me, are sitting in the front of the motorcycle. And he crashes into this taxicab at probably about 35 miles an hour. It throws me over the fucking taxicab. I land on a sidewalk on the other side. Papa San that was driving it is killed. And the taxicab driver is standing there yelling at Papa San, who's already dead, threatening to kill him for driving like a maniac.

And that was -- the whole gravamen of this story is, that was not an unusual happenstance in Vietnam.

Sapper Attack on a Soup Stand

There were hundreds, I don't know, thousands, of little restaurants and soup stands and beer stands and everything, on sidewalks, and everywhere, in Saigon. It was just wonderfully crazy in that sense. But there was this one little soup/beer stand where a group of about five or six or seven of us would gather together to get lunch or beer or whatever somebody wanted.

And we're at this soup stand -- it's on the sidewalk, it's not inside -- and Jim Kulczyk and I were there together with a few other people, and I don't remember who the other people were. I didn't know some of them. But at any rate, we're just sitting there eating soup, and Jim Kulczyk looks at me and says, "What?" And I said, "We gotta get out of here." And he didn't even blink. He stood up and said, "Let's go."

And we left. And this was only about two or three blocks away from our apartment in Soul Alley. And we just about get back, and we hear this enormous explosion. And what had happened was, sappers had driven by there on motorcycles and tossed hand grenades, one after the other, at the stand where all the Americans were sitting. Sappers were Viet Cong whose sole purpose was to create terror -- you know, go through a city or countryside or whatever, and toss grenades or throw explosives at civilians or military, whoever was in the way. It was just terrorism. They were terrorists.

And everybody left there was killed. Every single one of them.

And the only thing I remember as I sit here today was -- when we got back, when we found out what happened, when we started kind of grieving and mourning for the dead, Jim looked at me and said, "How the fuck do you do that?!" And you know, we kept each other alive. But if I had any influence in keeping us alive, it was from this gut level intuition.

Cheap Charlie's Restaurant

Saigon was full of restaurants. But there was an old restaurant, very near the Continental Palace Hotel, which was an old French hotel that was kind of a gathering place for -- they had a large kind of veranda where people would meet to talk. These people who would meet to talk were people like me and intelligence people, intelligence operatives, different intelligence agencies, and then just random whoever it was.

But about a block or two from the Continental Palace was Cheap Charlie's Restaurant. It had another name in Vietnamese but I actually don't remember that name now. But everybody called it Cheap Charlie's. And it was some of the best Vietnamese food you could ever imagine in your whole life.

But, it wasn't like it was super popular. It was only by word of mouth that people found it. And when I finally found my way there, it was like, oh, yeah, this is absolutely excellent pho or Vietnamese food, whatever the dishes were. So I would hole up there sometimes to eat and read and work on whatever I was working on. And this was for a long, long time. And I made friends with the people in Cheap Charlie's.

And one day I was sitting in there eating a bowl of pho, and one of the waiters came up and said, "G.I., you need to leave. We all leave now." And what was going on was, word had gotten around to them that there was a Viet Cong sapper heading towards there. So just as I was making my way out of a back door that this waiter was showing me, all of a sudden gunfire everywhere erupted, because bad guy sapper came in the front door and just started firing indiscriminately.

And the interesting thing about that was that nobody was killed. Because I was one of the last people out of there. Everybody else had gotten out okay. But the sapper -- people that had gone out and around the building and had come back around dusted the sapper.

But all that notwithstanding, it still was my favorite downtown restaurant in Vietnam, even long, long after that.

Jim and I Capture Some Viet Cong

The closest, dearest friend and comrade-in-arms that I had, and the person that I trusted most, in my first year or two of the military, was Jim Kulczyk. He was -- at least from an Army standpoint -- a helicopter mechanic, crew chief, and door gunner.

And Jim knew that I was -- because they flew me out to different places and dropped me off. And there was one time when Jim said, "You know, I don't know what the fuck you do, but I want to be with you on this deal." And I said, "I think that will work out. Yeah."

So we were flown out and dropped off. And this was down in the Mekong Delta, but closer to the Cambodian border. And we're moving around, and we come to this little village. And we've got to get through this village, because I had serious concerns, because I knew for a fact that the Viet Cong were in control of this area. So I didn't want to walk off of regular pathways, and go back and forth through the back of the jungle, because I had a feeling that they were boobytrapped and mined.

So we walk into this little village -- well, it wasn't even a little village. It was probably seven little huts and a little, tiny structure that was basically a Vietnamese beer joint. By the way, the Vietnamese beer of choice, which was actually pretty good, was called "Beer 33" in English. But in Vietnamese it was "Ba Mi Ba." So Jim said, "I'd really like a beer." And I said, "Let's get one!" I didn't like beer very much, but I was up for one.

So we walk into this little -- and it wasn't -- the little place was about the size of our bedroom, like 10 feet by 20 or 25 feet. We walk in, and of course we're armed to the teeth because we're out alone in the boonies. And we walk in, and in the very back of this place, there were four guys sitting at a table. And we walked in, out of the bright light into the dimmer light, and all of a sudden, I saw the four guys starting to rise. And I drew down on them. And Jim drew down on them when he saw what I was doing. And they all dropped their weapons and held up their hands. They were Viet Cong.

There was no fight. There was nothing. We took them into custody, and we marched them to a pickup point where we called in a chopper. We had caught these four Viet Cong that were in this village.

And the funny thing about all of this is, that while we had them in our custody, at gunpoint, I ordered two beers -- one for me and one for Jim. And we each had a beer while we were standing there. (Laughter)

So we marched them to where the pickup point was. The chopper landed and we all got in. But the saddest thing about all of that was -- there were CIA people on the chopper. And I regret this to my dying day. But they were trying to interrogate these guys and get information. And they had Vietnamese translators on the chopper. And before they got the information they needed, they kicked two of the four out of the chopper. And I thought, "You know, this war is so, so . . ." -- I mean, it wasn't the first time I ever said it, I was against the war before I went to the war. But I thought, "No. I will never forget this. This is how bad it can get."

So two of the four went out the chopper door because they wouldn't answer questions. The other two sang like little canaries. And from, I guess, a practical war standpoint, that might be kind of valuable, but from where I was sitting, from a moral standpoint, I thought, "I wish I hadn't put them on the chopper."

Sensei Watanabi

In the beginning of 1971, my official billets were moved to the St. George Hotel in Cholon. That was when I left the 166th. Cholon was a separate district of Saigon. And it was a pretty interesting area, because it was mostly Chinese or some other Asian foreigners.

And while I was there, I found this little restaurant down this little side alley that was the most marvelous secret place in the whole world. It was a Japanese restaurant. It had Japanese gardens. It had wonderful ponds with fish of various kinds. And the food was absolutely excellent. And there were no Americans there -- I never saw another American there.

It became my favorite restaurant. Cheap Charlie's was way far away, but this Japanese restaurant was close and had some of the best Japanese fare that I've ever had in my life. And there was this garden back behind the restaurant, that was attached to the restaurant. And I would go out there to look at the pond, and I would see this older guy. I thought of him as an old man; he was probably in his 50's maybe. But he was out there doing exercises, and they were aikido exercises. And I didn't know how to make -- you know, you never know how to approach somebody on all of this. I saw him two or three times, and he was always out there at certain times.

So one day, while I was there having lunch or dinner, I don't remember which, he walks up to my table, and he says -- and he's got really broken English -- "I see you looking at me." And I said, "I thought you were doing aikido." And he looked at me, and he said, "You know aikido?" And I said, "Not enough." And he said, "Come with me."

Well it turns out -- and I don't remember his first name, but his last name was Watanabi, I called him Watanabi-san -- he studied aikido -- he was one of the first students of Morihei Ueshiba, who was the founder of aikido during or just after World War II. And he had come to Vietnam, and he was teaching aikido at some French Vietnamese school downtown. And he looked at me and he said, "I want to know how much aikido you know." And he came at me. Fast! And I blocked him.

I didn't put him down, I just was able to block him. And he said, "You know enough for me to teach you."

So for the next -- my last couple of years in Vietnam, I was his student. And that's where the primary, major part of my aikido training occurred. And when it came time for me to leave, I told him I was leaving, and he said, "No, you're not leaving. You're taking all of this with you. And it will be with you for the rest of your life." It was a little more broken English than that, but that was the gist of it.

And sure enough, I mean, my aikido training, during the military, and in my police work, and even up until the time I was first practicing law in Austin, I was still going to a dojo and practicing aikido. And I will tell you, there have been many things in my life that have been lucky happenstances that kept me alive. But aikido has kept me alive many, many times, that were not just circumstance. And I will tell you, that it was that training that prevented me, especially in my police work, from having to do serious bodily injury to subdue bad guys. And in my law practice, the spiritual aspect of aikido -- the tenet of aikido is basically to try to transform your attacker into an ally -- and from my litigation practice and even to this day in my mediation practice, I still practice that aspect of aikido.

A Solo Firefight with Sappers

When my billets were at the St. George Hotel, the only people living in that hotel were people in MAC-V. The military had just taken over the hotel. But I had a house by that time in Saigon, with Kim Hoang. So I was never there, except very occasionally, every couple or three months, there was a rotation of who had guard duty at the hotel.

So one night I had guard duty, and there was supposed to be two guards, but whoever the other person was who was supposed to be there wasn't there that night, so I had it by myself. And, you know, I was armed to the teeth. But I wasn't concerned. I thought it would be fun, a little quiet time in the nighttime. Because things had been quiet for a while.

So I'm walking guard duty around this hotel -- it had alleys on three sides and then a main street. And the main street actually had a little bunker and guard shack where there was a guard for the entrance to the hotel. So I thought this would be easy.

So it's probably around 2:00 in the morning -- I think I'd started at midnight or something like that. I'm just kind of strolling around, and all of a sudden I hear a little noise somewhere back towards the back of the hotel in the side alley. And I'm thinking, animals. And then I'm hearing whispering. So all of a sudden, I'm thinking something's not right. So I unsling my weapon. And the next thing I know, the night lights up. There's -- I don't know how many, but they're all shooting, and they're all shooting at me.

And I'm kind of ensconced in a little doorway, a service door or something, and all this fire's coming at me. And I'm reaching around and I'm firing like crazy, and I'm unloading magazines and firing again. And pretty soon, their firing stopped. And I waited. And I threw a lighted match out in the alley, to see if anybody else was gonna shoot. Nobody did.

So by this time, it was, like, about 2:45. And people started coming down finally -- the front guard had raised an alarm. And I told them I needed lights, and they started popping flares up and turning on all the lights on the exterior of the building. I get the whole place lighted up with spotlights and flares.

And we all went back to see what was back there. Well, there were no bodies. There was blood all over the place back there, and you could see where people had been drug away. But, yeah, that was my little single-person firefight against, like, who knows, four or five or six Viet Cong sappers.

And it was scary. Because I really thought that this was a
little walk in the park. I mean, we were in the city. And that's
not to say -- I mean, there was all kinds of bad shit going on in
the city. But you know, when you're out in the boonies, you're
kind of expecting it. But when everything's quiet and calm and
looks like you've got control over everything, you're not really
expecting that kind of stuff. But that's the time when you really need to be on your guard.

The Cambodia Incursion

I still don't talk about some of the top secret classified stuff
that I don't know for a fact has been declassified. And there's
some of those stories that I'm just not gonna talk about. But
one of the "top secret" stories that I know is not classified anymore because the world knows about it was our -- let's call it
"clandestine," or some would say, "illegal," incursion into Cambodia.

Part of my job was going into Cambodia in what was called
the Parrot's Beak area. And the reason that we were going in
there was that North Vietnam, on the Ho Chi Minh Trail --
that went kind of straight down to South Vietnam from North
Vietnam -- it was being bombed so heavily and whatever --
but that was how the North Vietnamese were getting all of
their troops and weapons, and armaments, smuggled down
into South Vietnam for the North Vietnamese regular army
and the Viet Cong to use and to keep fighting, and that sort of
thing. So there was this secret deal afoot where we would start
identifying the paths that they were diverting through Cambodia to circumvent Vietnam, through all the jungles and down
the rivers, and through the mountains, to get stuff into Vietnam, which would come into various places in Vietnam, including the Mekong Delta.

So part of my task was to be assigned to a one-man drop off in there. I'd be flown in in a chopper and dropped in the jungles and I would be left there for three days, five days, I think, never more than five days, maybe a week. But never longer than that. It wasn't like I was out there permanently. But I was on my own. I'd live off what I had or off the land.

And what I was, was eyes and ears. And that was in my role as "combat journalist," which -- I carried a press pass. But that was while I was a MAC-V advisor. And I would make contact with various other elements of the American military that had intruded into Cambodia, or I would pop out of Cambodia to make my reports. And it was to identify where the troops were at any given time. My job then was to -- quite frankly, as my job was the whole time I was in Vietnam -- my personal job -- forget about my mission -- but my personal job was, no matter what I was doing, was to try to not get found. And that was one of the dicier "not get found" arenas that I was in.

But that was all sort of off limits at the time. And at the time, it was super top secret. And it took many years for that to come out.

And I had many close calls with both North Vietnamese regulars that almost found me and Viet Cong that almost found me. I was in no firefights. I was able to camouflage, move, get away. I never engaged them and was able to escape from wherever they were, and, you know, hide myself or move myself, but still get the information.

Probably I made eight or ten of those insertions and retractions in the span of a few months.

Teaching English at the Language School

At this point, I was really lucky. I mean, I was back in Saigon and teaching English to Vietnamese officers. And that was the golden gig that I had towards the end of my last -- periodically,

during the last half of the time when I was there in Vietnam.
When I wasn't doing other stuff, I would teach a half day at the
Armed Forces Language School attached to MAC-V.

And in that language school, the instructors were -- there
were only eight Army instructors in the whole school. I always
joked that they could only find eight people in the Army in-
telligent enough to put in as teachers. But the Air Force had
100 and something people, and the Navy had 80 or 90 instructors. They had been trained in the States and that was gonna
be their task. But they had never been out in the bush. But
they inserted a few Army guys who came and went, in terms
of, they had dual missions, and the language school was kind
of a cover.

But the Air Force and Navy guys used to complain terribly
about the accommodations in the St. George Hotel. You know,
the beds were horrible, this is bad, this is bad, the food's terrible. And one day, one of these Air Force guys was going on and
on about it, and I said, "You've never been out in the boonies
have you? Tomorrow I'm heading back out there, I'm gonna
take you with me."

And we did. And it was dicey. Nobody got killed, but he saw
how we lived in the boonies. And I mean, in the jungles -- not
in barracks or anything. And then, by the time we got back, he
was so rattled. And after that, he said to me, "Okay, you win. I'll
never complain about the St. George Hotel ever again." (Laughter)

My Mother Driving into a Breakfast Nook

I didn't know about this until I came back from Vietnam, but
this happened in about 1970. My young mother was brilliant
and had all kinds of potential. She went to hell and a handbasket -- alcohol, drugs -- and she became quite a mess. And even
long before I left for Vietnam, she was a mess.

So I'm gone, I'm really kind of disconnected from everything that's going on in the States, because all I would ever get was -- you couldn't get telephone calls. Occasionally, you would get some letter that would take three or four months to get to you from your APO -- Army Post Office Box.

But at some point, I get back from Vietnam, in late 1971. And all of a sudden I find out that, not only is she living in squalor and has lost the house that, actually, my father had given her in the divorce -- or was about to lose it. But I found out that part of all of that had to do with her driving through the neighborhood, and she was drunk, and she ran up through this person's yard, somehow came in through the back fence of this house, and crashed through the breakfast nook, and ran over this woman who was in a wheelchair sitting and trying to eat breakfast.

And I didn't really quite understand what it was all about, because I was getting little bits and pieces, but then, at some point, I was able to -- many, many years later, when things showed up on the internet, I saw the news clip of her at this woman's house while the news people and the police were interviewing her. And she said, "I don't know what happened, but don't worry, my husband" -- and they were divorced by this time -- "my husband owns all of the Cunningham Pharmacies, and he will take care of everything."

And that was sort of the last, I don't know, nail in the coffin, for my father. Because he disengaged from everything at that point, I think understandably. And the woman that she ran over in the wheelchair didn't die -- that was a good thing. And somehow, whatever insurance there was kind of wound up taking care of everything. But he, at that point, stopped paying anything towards her house, the house that she was living in.

And I came back faced with how to move her out of the old family place and into an apartment somewhere. And I don't think she ever, ever, ever spoke of that, because I don't think

she ever, ever remembered that situation. And that created
kind of a weird little dynamic when I came back from Vietnam,
because I was renting her a two-bedroom apartment, and Kim
Hoang and Sam and I were going to live in the other bedroom.
That did not go well, but that's another story.

Al Divicek

So Al Divicek was tough, sensitive, smart as a whip, and, you
know, like most of the guys I was in OCS with, they had all
finished college. I hadn't. But Divicek was probably my closest
compadre in OCS. And of course, I resigned from OCS at the
end, and he was toying with it, but he didn't. But we were both
opposed to the war. So that was it for Divicek. Once I left OCS,
I didn't ever know what happened to him.

But many years later, after the internet came about, I
Googled him. I wanted to know if he made it through the war
alive. And thank goodness, it turns out, he did. Of course, we
were in Infantry OCS. These were all people who were becoming lieutenants in infantry platoons.

So I tracked him down. I located him in New York City. And
on one of my trips to New York City, for my writing stuff and
whatever, I made contact with him. Talked to him a little bit.
He said he was a banker. And we got together.

He didn't want to meet anywhere else but where he was. So
he gave me his home address. And it was like a five-story walk-
up. And I make my way up to his apartment -- and this was not
a fancy building.

And I knock on the door, and I hear this, "WHO?" And I call
out my name. And I hear lock after lock after lock after lock
undone, and he opens the door. And I'm facing him again, for
the first time in years, since OCS. And he's a total mess.

He's hyper, he's hyper vigilant, he's locking all the doors as
soon as I get inside the apartment. It's a small apartment -- a

one-bedroom, a little tiny sitting room, and a bathroom. I go to the bathroom, and I see four guns in the bathroom. One on the toilet, one on the side of the toilet, and so on. And I notice that, all through the apartment, there are weapons.

And his eyes are weird. And we start talking and talking, and it turns out, he lost almost every man in his unit that he was responsible for. Because a platoon leader is responsible for the platoon, right? There were, like, only one or two out of his whole damn platoon that made it back. And he was a total, total wreck.

I started trying to talk to him. I said, "You know, nobody's trying to get you here." He said, "They won't! They won't get me here." He said, "Look out that window." Across the street was a mortuary. He said, "I've got a deal with them. Anybody trying to crawl up this building, they call me. I know. They're dead." And his eyes were crazy wild. And I spent some time with him. And I was, like, "Boy. He's gone."

So that was my visit with him. And not long after that visit, I was checking on him again, on the internet, and I saw that he had died. He had committed suicide in that apartment. And he was -- when I first met him in OCS, when he was recently out of college, he was so happy and so gung ho. And we were such good friends. And I thought, "This war has killed yet another one of us. And it won't stop killing." It's the war that keeps on killing.

Sam's Birth

By the mid part of 1970, Kim and I were together. We became a couple. And at some point, around October of 1970, she got pregnant. So we moved into this little house away from Soul Alley. It was a nice little place. And we had a live-in maid, and a cook that would come in. Because everything was dirt cheap.

And one of the things I liked about it was, there was a South Korean Colonel who lived in the next little unit, and he had his Jeep parked there every night with his guard in the Jeep. And nobody wanted to fuck with the South Koreans. I mean, if you think Viet Cong were brutal, the South Koreans were -- they gave no quarter to anybody. So I thought, "This is good, I've got myself my own bodyguard out there! He'll alert me if anything goes on."

So at any rate, it's getting closer to her due date. And on July 25, 1971, she's standing in the kitchen, talking to the cook, and all of a sudden, I'm looking at her, and she's got this puzzled look on her face. And I look down, and there's a puddle of water. Her water had broken.

And this is late at night. It's after curfew. But we have to get her to the hospital. And the problem with getting her to the hospital was, number one, it was after curfew. And number two, anybody who was out on the streets was subject to being shot, because nobody was supposed to be on the streets except for South Vietnamese police and military.

And another problem was, we didn't want to go in the same vehicle, because if they saw an American with a Vietnamese, out after curfew, that would just make us bigger targets. So I got her into a -- I paid a *cyclo-dap* driver -- a *cyclo-dap* instead of a *cyclo-mai*, because I didn't want any noise. I put her in there and he hauls her off towards the hospital, which is about three miles away. I go and talk to the South Korean Colonel, and he says, "Take my driver, and go, and stay right behind her."

So we're making our way through the streets. There's gunfire -- not everywhere, but sporadic heavy gunfire here and there. And there was also a rocket attack that night. So we had bombs bursting in air, we had gunfire everywhere, and we're trying to make it to the hospital.

We finally got to the hospital by about midnight, and it wasn't until about 10 or 11 the next morning when Sam was born. And it was a little Chinese hospital. It was called a *nha bao sanh*. It was a birthing hospital, and that's all they did there. It was just a little maternity hospital. But it was Chinese, so it had all these Chinese and Vietnamese midwives in there. And there was one old Chinese doctor, but he only came around about 6:00 every night, just to check and see if there were any problems.

And when they were delivering Sam, it was the weirdest thing I ever saw. Because, I mean, they had her on this bed that had this big hole in the bed. And after Sam was born and he was okay, these midwives started getting up on Kim's stomach and pushing, pushing, pushing. And what they were doing was, they were getting rid of the afterbirth. And they had a big bucket underneath there.

So somehow or another, we survived getting to the hospital and somehow, Sam survived his birth. And all's well that ends well.

Testing My Brain

Towards the end, I was a short-timer. I didn't have much time left in the military. It's an interesting place to be, because all of a sudden, you've been in war for two years, and now you've got to somehow become a civilian again. But it was worse than that. I was pretty well convinced that my years, my three years and some odd months, in the Army, had really rotted my brain. I was pretty sure that whatever brain I had to begin with was not the same brain I had now.

So I thought -- empirical sort of guy that I am at some level -- I thought, "I'm gonna be getting out of the Army, my plan is to go back to college, but I don't even know if I'm smart

enough to go to college anymore. I don't even know if I can
take a test."

So I walked into the MAC-V headquarters in Saigon and
went to the Army Education office. I asked them if they could
give me a test. They had all kinds of tests, and they started
talking about this thing or that thing. And they said, "We've
got CLEP." College level educational program, or something
like that. They said, "It's a series of five different tests over a
couple of days, and if you pass any of them, you will get three
hours' college credit for the class." So I said, "Okay, let's do it."

So I sat down there for three different days, a few hours
per test. And when the results came back, I passed four of the
five tests. One was -- probably had to do with mathematics or
something. But all the others I nailed -- history, English, whatever.

So that translated into 12 hours of college credit. And the
nice thing about it was, I walked out of there thinking, "Okay,
the Army didn't leave me more stupid than it found me."

Chapter 5

Vietnam After the Army: Ages 22-23

Hong Kong, Discharge, TV's, and Platform Shoes

Right before I got out of the Army, I found out that I had an R&R available. And I had this great thought that I would go to Hong Kong and buy TV sets. Because I didn't know how long it was gonna take me, once I got back to the States, to get back to Vietnam. Because it wasn't a matter of just going there and flying back; I had to get all this paperwork done. And I wanted to make sure Kim Hoang and Sam were taken care of. So the idea was that Kim could sell these TV's on the black market, while I was gone, to make money. So I figured out how many TV sets -- I think it was ten or eleven -- would carry her through for a whole year, selling them on the black market.

And somebody told me before I left, "Oh, if you're going to Hong Kong, you've really got to go to this tailor. He knows everything. He's fast. He can get you your clothes in 24 hours." And he gave me the guy's address and number.

I almost didn't make it to Hong Kong. We were flying on Air Vietnam, which was sketchy to begin with. (Laughter) Not the best reputation of airlines in the whole world at that time. So we're on this flight, and about an hour or so before we got to Hong Kong, we ran into this terrible, terrible weather. It was horrible. I mean, lightning was hitting the plane, and sparks were going all through. And everything was being tossed and turned in every different direction. And the overhead bin things, or lids, or whatever they are, were falling off. And things were falling off of the airplane. And the airplane would take these thousands of feet dives, and then try to straighten out.

And everybody on the airplane thought we were gone. But nobody was going batshit crazy. Because they knew. Everybody knew, "this is out of our control, there's nothing we can do. And God only knows what's gonna happen."

So finally, all of a sudden, we're coming down in this long -- and the plane was being shaken to smithereens -- and we're coming down, and I'm looking out the window. The weather clears a tiny little bit, and we can see the ocean. And we're coming straight down into the ocean, from what I could see.

But what I didn't know at the time was that at Taipei Airport in Hong Kong, the runways are built out into the water, out into the ocean. And we're coming down, and I think we're going into the ocean. But no, finally, we touched down.

And there had not been any kind of screaming or hollering or anything in the plane. But at that moment, when we touched down on the runway, the entire airplane burst into applause for the captain. It was some of the greatest flying, or avoiding disaster, that I've ever experienced.

So anyway, when I get to Hong Kong, the first thing I do is start buying TV sets and having them shipped back to Vietnam. Then I bought this fantastic pocket watch. It was, like, the biggest treasure I'd ever seen. It was about $50 or something like that.

And then I went to the tailor. And he's measuring me and doing all this, and he said, "I know exactly the style you need.

You're going to be going back to the United States dressed perfect for the country."

So then I spend time wandering around Hong Kong. But the next day, the pocket watch, when I picked it up to wind it, it literally, every piece of it, fell apart. And I could not remember where I'd gotten it, some side alley in Hong Kong. The whole thing -- it was just a pile of gears and screws.

So I go back to get the suit, after maybe two days, and it was this brown polyester suit that was cut like journalist coats, with the big pockets on the jacket. But it was a suit. And the pants were bell bottoms. And I'm trying it on, and the pants legs are about six inches too long. And I said, "The pants legs are too long." And he said, "No, no, no, no. Wait." And he comes and brings me the shoes that go with it. And they are these go-dawful-looking platform shoes that are about five or six inches high. Which all of a sudden shot me up to over six feet tall. And at first I thought it was pretty cool, because the whole world looked different, you know? And I said, "Are you *sure* this is the style?!" And he said, "Oh, yes, yes, yes."

So I bought that. And went back to Vietnam, and the TV sets started coming in. I had to make a deal with the Army post office to kind of smuggle them out of there, because this was not kosher really. So I would haul them back to the little house that we were living in, and Kim Hoang stashed them all.

So it came time to leave, and I had everything in order. She was going to be good to go for as long as it took. And I had a suit to wear after I got discharged.

So I left Vietnam and flew to Oakland Army Base. Got to Oakland and went through my discharge physical. And they called me back in and said, "We want to test your ears again. Something's off." They did the hearing test and they came and talked to me and they said, "Your hearing has, from the time you entered the Army, has diminished so much that we tested you twice. You have a serious, serious hearing problem. You will probably be deaf within two years." And I said, "Great, whatever." (Laughter)

So I turned in all my uniforms and stuff and I walked out a free man. It was like coming out of prison. And I look ridiculous in the suit and the platform shoes. And nobody's wearing anything like that. It's all hippie dippie stuff, jeans, whatever.

So I get on a flight to fly back to Houston, get to Houston, and I forget -- I think it was Rick Martinelli who came to pick me up from the airport, the same guy who dropped me off in the very beginning. And nobody recognized me because they were looking for somebody my size. They walked right past me, and I said, "Rick!" And he turned around and he's looking up. And it took me all of -- by the next day, that suit was gone and buried forever.

And I had to deal with family problems back in Houston, and family problems were in a state of high mess. But I was back maybe three or four weeks, and I get this call from this major friend of mine at MAC-V. Because I had given Kim Hoang his telephone number in case something happened. And something had happened. Apparently, like a week after I left, the Vietnamese police and the customs people descended upon the house, confiscated all of the TV's, took her into custody -- not in jail, but into custody -- and I was gonna have to figure out how to get back really, really quickly. And all of this was going on over the course of a week. I could not make any plans, flights to get back, anything. But I'm staying in touch with the major. And he was gonna pay for whatever. But it turns out, Kim Hoang, you know, street smart as she was, cut a deal with the customs people to give each one of them -- She said something like, "How about I give you and you and you two TV sets each, and I'll keep the rest." And they cut that deal. So by the time I got back to Vietnam, everything was okay. Everything was fine.

So yeah, the TV deal didn't work out exactly, but it turned out okay.

Teaching English

Before I got discharged, I knew I was gonna be coming back to Vietnam, but I didn't know how. You had to have some job lined up to come back to Vietnam.

I had all these great recommendations in terms of my teaching skills from MAC-V, because I was teaching and training South Vietnamese military. So I had those in hand. And before I left, I went over to the Japanese restaurant to talk to Watanabi, my sensei. And he mentioned to me a school -- two schools, actually -- that he thought I ought to talk to.

One of the schools was the London School. This is not related to the London School of Economics. The London School was a private English school, and the proprietors were the Contentos. They were Scottish missionaries who had spent, like, twenty-something years in China by that time, and had gotten imprisoned in China, and had made their way to Vietnam, and set up this school.

And I went to the school and talked to them. And they said, "Well, you know, we need, all of your resume and background." So I started gathering that stuff together and left it for them. And they went through it and they issued a letter that had to go to the Vietnamese Office of Education or whatever. So I knew I had a place when I came back, and that allowed me to travel and to come back in, because you had to have some reason for coming back in.

So I came back to Vietnam -- and I left a mother and sisters in a state of not great repair -- but I had to get back. And my plan was to teach to make a living. And this was basically on the local economy. I was making a lot compared to Vietnamese

people, but it was not a significant amount of money. But it
was enough to keep me afloat.

So I got back to Vietnam and I started teaching there. And
it was actually a really good experience. And I also -- I was
teaching maybe a half a day there. Then I also got a job teaching some classes at the University of Saigon. And more importantly, at the New Asia Institute, which was called Tri Tri
University. It was the only Chinese college in Vietnam. And
the London School and Tri Tri were in Cholon, the Chinese
section of Saigon. At Tri Tri, those were all college students.
But most of the students I had at the London School were basically high school students. And the London School was geared
towards preparing the students for the upper and lower Cam-
bridge examinations. These were the European equivalents of
the S.A.T.'s.

And it was enjoyable. I could ride my bike to work. I will
tell you -- there were many interesting little episodes teaching,
especially at the London School. But one of my favorites was
Mrs. Contento, who was this old, stern, missionary woman. My
classroom was next to her office, and the walls were paper thin.
And I was in the classroom one day, and one of the students
asked me, "Are angels male or female?"

And, you know, I'm sitting there thinking about the answer
to this. And I'm thinking, "There are archangels that are male,
and then a lot of angels are depicted as female, but, what difference does it make?" And I said to the class, "Well, you know,
my understanding, and all of this is -- there's no fact to all of
this -- but I think, in terms of the universe, that if there are angels, they could either be male or female, it doesn't make any
difference. Or a combination of both."

Mrs. Contento comes storming into the classroom! (Laughter) She starts lecturing for -- berating me -- but lecturing for
about twenty minutes on how "only males can be angels! That
is God's law! That is the way it is! And I will brook nobody

teaching anything different from that!" And I thought, "Well, I guess I'm gonna get fired."

So after that, I went to talk to her. And we started having this long discussion. I said, "I know you're about to fire me." She said, "Not at all. You're one of my best teachers for English. But you need to stay away from religion! Because you're in deep water." And I said, "Well, let's talk about it." And so we started talking about religion.

CIA Recruitment

I worked with various entities within the United States government during the time I was soldiering. I'll say this: Officially, the only time I ever had anything to do with the CIA was when I was hitching a ride on a CIA airplane and delivered a baby. That's all I'm saying.

After I was discharged, I get back to Vietnam, and I started my job at the London School. And at some point, probably a few weeks after I got back to Vietnam, I was coming out of our house, and the Korean major next door gave me a heads up that it looked like I was being followed by some Americans. And I thought, "That's interesting."

So I'm making my way to catch a ride on a *cyclo-mai*, and I've already spotted two guys. And they start walking up to me, and I turn around and look at them and say, "What?" They said, "You got a few minutes?" And I said, "Why?" They said, "We want to talk. We've got a car." And a car pulls up. I said, "Do I have to get in?" They said, "No." I said, "Where are we going?" They said, "We're going to go to the Continental Palace Hotel, and we're just gonna chat." I said, "Okay."

So we go to the hotel. We're sitting kind of outside on the terrace around the bottom floor. And they say, "You know why we're here." And I said, "Well, I'm guessing." They said, "Who are we?" I said, "The Company." They said, "Okay. We didn't

meet you before, but you worked, did some stuff, and we'd like
to offer you a job. We know that you're teaching at this school
for the last few weeks. We know that they pay on a local Vietnamese economy. You can keep that job, if you want to. But
what we're offering you is to work with us and --"

And I forget the amount. It was either $22,500 or $24,500
a year. Which was a veritable fortune in Vietnam. I mean, the
average Vietnamese person made maybe $100 a year at that
time. And I was making, with the language school, the equiva-
lent of $200 a year. It wasn't much.

I said, "Well, what would be my task?" They said, "Well, we
don't know. But you'd be on for it." And I said, "You know,
here's the deal, guys. I've got a wife. I've got a brand new baby.
I think I've done my time. And I don't think you want me, because it would be too easy for somebody to co-opt my relationship. Because I would protect my family first."

And they listened, they talked, they smiled. They said, "We
get it. But if you change your mind, let us know." And I said,
"Sure."

And that was the end of that. So that's why I never went
to work for the CIA. Other than the fact that I still was a huge
anti-Vietnam War person, but I didn't bring all of that up.

Mahatma Gandhi

During my first month or two of teaching at the London
School, I had a bicycle that I rode to work. I kind of liked hav-
ing the freedom of riding a bicycle in a very crazed traffic city.
It was a challenge!

On my way to the London School every day, from where
I lived, I would pass by this place that was this old colonial
building called the Mahatma Gandhi Memorial Association.
And everyday, I would ride past this and think, "I wonder
what's that all about." I knew of Mahatma Gandhi, but what I

knew at that time was a couple of little odd things. One is, the year he died was the year I was born. Somehow, to me, that, I don't know, was interesting. But the other thing was that, I knew, I thought, that, at some level, he was some kind of god, in India. And I thought the building must be a very religious shrine to him.

After I don't know how many times of riding past there, I was at school, and I was talking to Malani Srinivasan, who was one of my fellow colleagues there, who was Indian. And I said, "Do you know anything about the Mahatma Gandhi Memorial Association?" And she said, "No, not really at all. Why do you ask?" And I said, "Well, I've been drawn to Gandhi, but I don't know anything really about him. I'm just drawn to something about him." And I told her I was trying to figure out whether I could walk in there or whether there were certain things I needed to know about protocol or something.

She said, "I have no idea. But my husband Victor knows all about Gandhi. He worked with Gandhi. When he was in the military in India, he was one of Gandhi's bodyguards." And she said, "Let's ask him."

So she set up a meeting for me to come to their house and meet Victor, which I did. And he said, "I would be happy to take you over there, and you are way off base in terms of think-ing you might offend somebody. This will not be offensive to anybody." Because I didn't even know, do I have to take my shoes off? You know, I didn't know.

So we went to the Mahatma Gandhi Memorial Association. And it was basically a little museum of Gandhi in Vietnam. And I was totally, totally impressed. Gandhi -- and I don't know if everybody knows this, but -- when he was growing up in colonial India, he went to London and became a London barris-ter. He was an attorney. He wore the top hats and the suits and everything. And that was not a Gandhi that I had ever imagined had existed, that he was a lawyer.

So we're in there, and he takes me on this little tour. Nobody's paying any attention to us. It's just, welcome, welcome, welcome. And after all of that was over, and we were back at Victor's house, he said, "You seem smitten with Gandhi." And I said, "Well, I don't know about smitten, but I certainly have a really, really high respect for the man." And Victor said, "I did, too. And I guarded him with my life. But I'm not a follower of Gandhi, I'm a Christian." And I said, "Does that make a difference?" And he said, "In some ways, yes, but in the big way, no."

And then he said, "I have something for you." And he went to his bookcase and he pulled off a copy of Mahatma Gandhi's autobiography, which was given to him by Mahatma Gandhi. And he said, "I want you to have this."

And I read it. And I've re-read it. And I will probably re-read it again. Because it is probably one of the most honest -- not necessarily laudable in all cases -- but probably the most honest autobiography I've ever read in my life.

And I was also drawn to him because my actions and objections and my approach to a non-violent resistance of the Vietnam War were all captured in there as well. And of course in my younger kind of mystical woo-woo state, I thought, "Something of Gandhi, when he died in 1948, came floating into me, in 1948." I'm not going to say as we sit here tonight that I think any differently, even though the rational part of me thinks, no, of course, that was just a weird coincidence. But that was my closest connection to Mahatma Gandhi.

Pearl Buck and the Vietnamese American Children's Fund

Anyone who doesn't know the history of Pearl Buck should try to understand the history. I'm not gonna go into all that. But I had read her stories and books before. And I was in Vietnam, barely out of the Army, and was working with the London School where I met Malani and Victor Srinivasan.

And I learned that Victor was trying to save these children. He had a little tiny operation of taking in Amer-Asian children and trying to help their mothers and trying to keep these little families together.

And he had said to me, "We need help." And I thought, "I'm nobody. I don't know how to put people together for all of this." I was way, way out of my league. I had nothing I could do. And the only thing that popped into my mind with respect to Asia, and children, was Pearl Buck, who I had read about before. So I wrote her a letter. And I didn't think I'd ever hear anything back, but I got a letter back from her. And we had, I don't know, two or three correspondences. And nothing ever came of it because she finally died.

And I don't know whatever happened to that correspondence. I've looked for it. It may be buried somewhere in her correspondences, it could be buried somewhere in all these random little boxes that I have. But what's important is that I was then pulled in, then committed, not by any promises, but by what needed to happen. And this was a small project that needed to be.

But I never forgot how encouraging she was, how interested she was, in this situation -- the Amer-Asian children abandoned by the American G.I. fathers, the women left behind to deal with all of this. She was so supportive of what I was trying to do, and the connections that I was trying to make, and what we were trying to accomplish in Vietnam. And then she died. And I thought, that's the end of it. But that was not the case.

Thank You Note from a Chinese Student

When I was teaching at Tri Tri, or Chee Chee, University -- the Chinese university in Vietnam -- these were all college students and they were all -- I mean, I've never seen better students in my entire life than Asian students. They revered their teachers, they were there to learn, and they really put their heart into it. And I would occasionally get some little notes or cards of thanks or something from some of the students. But the one that I kept, and the one that I thought was so beautiful, from both a naive standpoint and from a sort of crush, loving crush, standpoint, was this one particular note I got from a student, that I thought, "This is a keeper. I will keep this forever. This is just too classic." And this is it:

MY TEACHER

In this school, there is a teacher I think he must be a most handsome one. He teach us the subject of Mastering Modern English.

How can I believe that he is the handsome one. It was because:

My teacher has a standard length, and very smart of his dressing. He has a brown hair his eyes was blue, a tall nose and a sweet mouse, that makes him looking like a ripping apple that girls would fall in love with him very quickly.

Do you know who his is He is Mr. Cunningham, the most clever, and great teacher that I have never meet.

By Lam Juc Can

Chapter 6

The Film Years: Ages 23-30

David Saving Sam's Life, and Homelessness

I finally got my little boy Sam and Kim Hoang out of Vietnam, and we came back in 1972. For a few years before that, I had been paying for my mother to have an apartment, because during the divorce stuff, my mother drunkenly sold the house that she was given in the divorce so that she could have more money to buy liquor. So anyway, she had to have a place to stay -- I didn't want her homeless. I put her in a two-bedroom apartment off of T.C. Jester in Houston. It was a nice enough apartment.

And I was thinking this was the perfect arrangement -- there's two bedrooms, we could stay in one bedroom -- Sam, Kim Hoang, and I -- and she'd have her own bedroom. And life would go on until we could figure out where we wanted to go and what we wanted to do.

Well, even sooner than immediately, Kim Hoang and my mother were complete enemies. My mother treated her like absolute crap. I was trying to go out to find work, and she'd be stuck there. And apparently, the battles were royal. And it was getting bad.

But before it got too bad, there was a birthday party for Sam. It would have been his second birthday. So there was a party. And David Hefner came over, and some other folks, I don't even remember who. And the apartment complex had a nice little pool.

And they were all out playing in the pool, around the pool, or whatever. And I got tagged to go out and buy another bag of ice or something. And so I'm gone, and by the time I get back, Sam had fallen into the pool, and was drowning, and David Hefner dove into the pool and pulled him up and saved him. And of course, that's the way David Hefner and I always rolled. Sam is here as much because of David Hefner as because of me.

But things were going really south, real fast, and it got so bad that I had to get them out of there. Oh, and one of the things that was really kind of funny was, my mother had a boyfriend, a drunken alcoholic boyfriend, at that time, who was staying with her. And he did something -- hit her, knocked her down, something like that -- and I marched in and told him, "Get your ass up and get out of here, you're gone." And he said, "Can't." I said, "Do it, or I'm coming after you." He said, "Okay, okay, okay. Would you hand me my leg?" He had only one leg; his prosthetic leg was leaning against the wall. (Laughter) And I said, "No. You want your leg, you go get your fucking leg." He crawled out of bed, crawled across the floor, got his leg, put it on, and left. And that may not sound funny, but to me, that was funny to me, a big bully crawling to get his leg.

But at any rate, I wound up pulling Sam and Kim Hoang out of there, and we had no place to go. And we became homeless for about a week or two. I had already re-enrolled back in the University of Houston by that time, so I'm trying to make classes, and so on. So we're homeless -- sleeping in the car in parking lots, on Galveston Beach, and so on. It was a little Japanese station wagon of some kind.

And then, for a tiny little bit, we stayed with Uncle Max and Aunt Tata. But Kim Hoang made war with them. So again, we left. And then we stayed for a couple of weeks at Rick Martinelli's house, until she made war with them.

Finally, I found this little apartment over near the University of Houston for, like, $110 a month, or something like that, and I got that. So finally I got all of that situated.

Meanwhile, during all that period of time, I was not only dealing with that stuff, but also school stuff -- trying to get back into the University gear -- and also starting to have to deal with the issues in Vietnam, that I was getting news about.

So the first homecoming stuff for the first month or two was pretty challenging. But somehow I leveled it all out and for a while it was okay, once we got that apartment.

The Vietnamese American Children's Fund

This is 1972, not long after I was back from the war. And my head was in all different kinds of places. This was a bad war. I was grappling with all of that. I was grappling with the insanity and alcoholism of my mother. I was grappling with the huge war and complete disconnect between my mother and Kim Hoang. I was grappling with trying to earn just a tiny little bit of money. I was still waiting for my G.I. Bill to go through so I would have, you know, $300 a month coming in. I was throwing newspapers -- I would go in at midnight, wrap newspapers until 2 or 2:30 in the morning -- 400 of them -- and go throw newspapers until about 6:30 in the morning. And then I would go to the parking lot at the University of Houston and sleep until somebody would come, I would have designated, to come and wake me up, you know, before class started. And then go to classes all day. It was a pretty hectic time.

And during the course of all of that, sometime in 1972, I started getting these letters from Malani and Victor on their school and safe space for Vietnamese mothers who had children who the fathers had either abandoned them or never knew that they had a child. So they were getting in desperate straits money-wise, and they were asking me for money. It was like, "We're drowning here. We're dying. Children are dying. We need your help."

I had no money, but I couldn't let it go. And that altered everything I was doing in terms of what I thought I was gonna be doing, going to undergraduate school. So I got together with Peter Williamson. He was a volunteer lawyer for students at the University of Houston at the time. I told him I needed to set up a nonprofit organization to start raising money for this project, and he helped set that up and sat on the Board of Directors. And I talked to people at the University and was given office space for this organization, and it was the Vietnamese American Children's Fund.

It was by the seat of our pants. It was as basic as it could possibly get. And I think the first thing -- first I started kind of gathering up volunteers who would work on stuff. And we started setting up things like these sponsored bicycle races, you know, so much for every mile or whatever. And there were articles about that in the various papers and whatnot. And we started bringing in a little money. And I funneled the money in that direction.

And one of the volunteers was Leslie Weinstein, who -- the organization needed kind of a full-time person to be fielding telephone calls and doing all this stuff. Basically an administrative assistant. So I hired her for that. Her boyfriend was Mickey Leland, who was a U.S. representative at the time. And she was terrific, she was great.

So we were getting lots of local support. And then there was this -- I started getting requests to go speak on radio and television stations, and all of a sudden it was around the country. And I was getting called to testify in Teddy Kennedy's Senate subcommittee on refugees. It became -- I hardly had time for anything. I was still trying to keep up in school, but I was going in every single different direction. I was on NBC television with Barbara Walters -- actually stayed with her at her apartment during that time when I was in New York. I was going to ABC, and, I don't know -- I can't even remember all of the -- across the country, from the west coast to the east coast -- how many television and radio spots and newspaper stories there were about the VACF. It was doing some good.

And I would be speaking in churches, mainly I would get invitations from Unitarian churches and Lutheran churches. Maybe somewhere along the line, some random other kind of church. But that was when I was first introduced to Unitarianism, and I knew at that moment, "Here is the philosophical-spiritual place for me."

I had also engaged, by that time, Pearl Buck's auxiliary program Welcome House, which dealt mostly at that time with the same situation in Korea, from the Korean War. And I got in touch with them, and I was trying to get them to put funds in, and they were putting funds in.

So that's how the VACF came into being.

Jim Jones, Mickey Leland, Leo Ryan, and Denton Cooley

So everybody in the world knows about the Jim Jones story. He took his whole entire cult down with him to South America. And he was in absolute control of all of them.

Leo Ryan was in the House of Representatives and was one of the public sponsors of the VACF, and so was Mickey Leland. And they went down there. And Leo Ryan was killed in the massacre. Mickey Leland -- my memory's a little fuzzy on this

-- he wasn't killed by Jim Jones and his group, but he died on the airplane flight down there. So the body count for Jim Jones just kept growing.

But some of the other volunteers in the VACF entered into the Texas Legislature. So yeah, for its little, tiny moment in time, the VACF was a pretty huge deal.

Denton Cooley, the world-famous heart surgeon from Houston -- I met with him and talked him into taking this child of ours, if we could get the child out of Vietnam, to bring the child to Houston for heart surgery. And he said, "Bring her on." And it happened, and she survived. She was an orphan, and we placed her with a family in Houston.

Death Threat at My Grandpa's Funeral

In 1973, my Grandpa died, and I went to the funeral. And I was gonna be one of the pall bearers. And my crazy cousin Butch was gonna be a pall bearer. He was standing behind me as we're carrying the casket. And he leans forward and says, "You're never going to leave Gonzales County alive. You are dead."

And I stopped. I held the whole casket procession up. And I let go of the casket, and people were, like, trying to hold it up. And I turned around and I said, "Try it now, asshole." And he said, "We gotta get him buried first."

And so we buried my Grandpa. And I thought -- I mean, he was waiting to come after me. But for some reason, he didn't. And I think the reason he didn't was, he was in the Army and tried to make himself seem like a badass for being in the Army, but he was stationed in Germany the whole time. And he thought that maybe I was not the same little kid that he could bully around before, and he backed off.

Saving a Drowning Woman in Galveston

This was probably in 1973, in the winter time. There was an opportunity to bring Victor and Malani to Texas. So we brought them to Texas. And as part of that little trip, we took a jaunt to Galveston. Before that, they went to Welcome House, part of the Pearl Buck Foundation, that I had set up a connection with.

So we took them to Galveston. And, you know, Galveston has these jetties going out. And I think this was the 34th Street jetty, I'm not quite sure. So we were out on the end of the jetty, and it was a chilly, blustery day. Sam was on my back in a backpack.

So we're walking out to the end of the jetty to look at the water and the splashing and everything. Well, we get out there, and all of a sudden we hear these screams from the other side of the jetty. Now on each side of these jetties, as anybody who knows the waters of Galveston knows, there are all these cross-currents and undercurrents. It is dangerous to be anywhere near the jetties in the water. Two women -- teenagers, twentyish, I don't know how old -- got sucked out. And they were struggling for their lives.

And people were standing on the end of the jetty -- there were probably 15 or 20 people out there on the end of the jetty -- and they're screaming for help. The boyfriends of these two women were up on the jetty, saying "Swim! Swim! Swim!" And these girls are drowning.

And this was just military training, muscle memory. I took my backpack with Sam off, handed it to Kim Hoang. She's going batshit crazy, screaming at me, "Don't! Don't! Don't!" Victor and Malani are trying to figure out what all this craziness is all about.

And there was one other person on that jetty, and I'll never forget him, although I never met him. Don't know his name.

But he was a Hispanic guy. And he did the same thing. And we both went in the water.

And we were struggling and fighting. But each one of us got to a different girl, and we grabbed them. And they were fighting, because they were drowning, and drowning people often fight. It was a struggle. We were probably fifty or sixty yards off the beach. And it seemed to take forever. I was pretty sure that because of the fighting this woman was doing, we were going to both drown. And I think the Hispanic guy was having the same problems.

It took us more than 30 minutes in waters that were in the 30's to get these women to shore. We finally got them on the beach, and people started pulling everybody up. And they were calling ambulances. People were standing around me, and I was really out of it by that time, and they were saying, "We need to get you in an ambulance." And I said, "No, no, no, just get me somewhere warm." Because I was, I mean, everybody was freezing. We were trembling and freezing.

So I left. They hauled me away. I said, "Get me some warm brandy, something." So we left. It took me three or four hours -- it was hypothermia. I mean, everybody was suffering from hypothermia. But they took everybody else to the hospital, but I didn't want to go. It took three or four hours for me to get back to something like a semblance of normalcy.

And that was one of a number of episodes that Kim Hoang railed and screamed and forever -- and validly, in that sense -- harped and harped and harped on, how could I take such a chance, what if I had died? Of course, she was afraid she would have been left all alone with a kid. And so I completely understood that, but that wasn't any part of my calculus when I went into the water.

And I will tell you, 30 minutes in freezing water with fighting drowners is not something that I would recommend that anyone ever do if they can avoid it. (Laughter)

Stopping Potential Abuse

So there was another time at my Grandpa's farm, and some interlopers had been spotted down by Sandy Fork Creek, near the pecan bottom. I was back from the war and it was after my Grandpa had died. And everybody was armed to the teeth on our side, because of course, we all carried weapons on the ranch. And we got down there and certain people in the group started shooting randomly at all these people scattering in all these different directions.

And it was mostly black kids. And then there's this white guy, who's hollering, "Please stop! Don't kill us!" And I was able to get all the local family to stop shooting long enough so I could go and talk to whoever this was. It turned out he was a high school teacher from Waelder, who had his high school kids out there with him. But mainly, I could tell, that it wasn't just kids; it was one or two black girls that he was grooming, and had them out there for nefarious purposes.

So I had to broker this weird peace, where the black girls would come with us, and he would head back to Waelder, and either we would shoot him on the spot, or we would report him to the police. Which did he prefer? And of course his choice was pretty easy, it was, "Don't shoot me." So we got the girls back -- and some of the people on my family's side of the thing were not real black-friendly -- that's not quite the right word, there was a complex relationship between blacks and whites. But once they figured out that these black girls, these teenage black girls, were perhaps going to be abused, then it wasn't a matter of black and white, it was a matter of right and wrong.

So I took the white guy into custody and my cousins, who would shoot at or kill black people for trespassing on the property, at my direction took these girls back to town to their homes in Waelder, which was only about four or five miles away. And I had the county sheriff come out and arrest the high school teacher. And the weird thing about it was that the high school teacher and one black girl, they both testified that they were in love, and it created kind of a really ambiguous, ultimately ambiguous situation. By that time I was gone and back to Houston, I don't know how that worked out, but I do know that nobody got shot that day, and so that was a good day.

Hollywood (David Seltzer) Calls

In addition to all the other VACF stuff, one of the things I did was I was a consultant on a documentary called *The Sins of the Fathers*. I think it was on NBC, and I think the producer or the director was Shad Northshield. So he was in contact with me, and I happily just kept feeding people whatever knowledge I had of the situation, which was vast.

And then one day, in 1974, I get a call out of the blue from a guy who called himself David Seltzer. He said he was a screenwriter for ABC and Lorimar Productions, and he was working on a story about Vietnamese American children fathered and abandoned in Vietnam. He said, "If you have a few minutes, could I pick your brain? Alan Alda has seen you before, heard you, read about you, and he said that you were the go-to guy for some information. Can I have 30 or 40 minutes of your time so I can piece this all together?"

And I laughed. I said, "Whatever it is that you're doing, it's not gonna be pieced together in 30 or 40 minutes." I started talking to him for a few minutes. After about 15 minutes, he said, "Can we meet?" I said, "Sure, come to Houston."

So he came to Houston. We met up. I was living in a tiny two-bedroom house on Sunnyside Street. We sat and talked -- I think we went to a restaurant or a coffee shop. We talked for about four hours. And by the time it was done -- and I told him, "You're never going to be able to write the screenplay for this movie if you haven't been there, seen it, and done it." And he said, "Could you take me?" And I said, "Yeah, I'll do that."

And I had a couple of reasons. One is, it sounded like an important movie. And two, I really needed to get back to Vietnam, because I was getting weird reports about Victor -- that he had started sending stuff directly to Welcome House saying that I was not getting the funds to him, and he needed funds directly.

And I also needed to get a sense of what the military and political situation was, because the one thing I needed to do was to make sure that I could get all my people out if the end was near. And I didn't know the answer to that at that time.

So we made plans to go to Vietnam, and we did. Lorimar Productions and ABC sprung for our trip. We went in the late fall, I'd say November or so, of 1974. And we were there for about a month. And we just barely survived.

Sean's Birth

So in June of 1974, Sean was born. I was struggling my way through the University of Houston still, and I was head of the VACF. I will say that some of my professors were very good with cutting me some slack when I was having to go and deal with, you know, testifying before Congress, or going on some of these jaunts to raise money. Yeah, I appreciate that a lot, them cutting me some slack.

And I was accumulating my college hours during that time. And then of course, Sean was born. And it was -- there was nothing dangerous or horrible about the birth, it was perfect. He was perfect.

But of course, when I left to go to Vietnam with David Seltzer, I was leaving Kim and Sam and Sean behind. But I had gotten situated by that time to where we were about a block away from a big grocery store and, like, a K-Mart or something like that. She didn't drive. But she had access to places. And I had people that I had checking on her and the kids.

Green Eyes, Randy Newman, and Genevieve Bujold

This was in 1974ish. I had to go out to California to work for a few months. Lorimar Productions wanted to hire me to start working on this film, which was *Green Eyes*. It was a made-for-television movie, Lorimar Productions and ABC. It won a Humanitas Prize. It also won a Peabody Award. It probably would have won an Emmy had it not been for the fact that we were up against *Roots* (laughter) that year. It was tough competition.

But at any rate, I was supposed to come out to California and meet up with Seltzer and some other people from ABC and Lorimar.

They put me up in a beach house in Malibu Colony, Malibu Beach. And it turns out that my next door neighbor, who was, like, about five or six feet away, from window to window, was Randy Newman. And I'd sit there working during the course of the day on, you know, writing stuff, and he'd be plinking on his piano, all day long!

And it goes without saying that it was beautiful and there was great scenery and beachwalking and everything. And also, one of the little daily routines that I did was to sit with a cup of coffee on the porch on the beach, where Geneviève Bujold, who was a very famous actress at one time, would always come strolling down the beach topless! And I thought, "Yeah, this is the life!" (Laughter) "Randy Newman playing music for me all day, and now this! Yeah!" (Laughter)

And, you know, there were all these little -- I'd venture out to all these little sandwich shops and whatnot, and run into various celebrities, I don't remember who because I was never starstruck. But yeah, that was a pretty good gig.

Thwarting Our Murder

That fall, David Seltzer and I headed to Vietnam. And part of what I was doing there was to show him what everything was like. And part of what I was doing there was checking on the situation with the VACF. I was getting reports from these women that, not only was Victor approaching them, but they were also concerned with how familiar he was with the children. And Victor somehow sensed all of this, that something was going on. And the third thing I was doing was making contact with people I had known in Vietnam before then.

And I had to leave Kim Hoang and Sam and Sean. Sean was just a baby. I had to leave them.

So I'm taking David Seltzer around the entire city, to orphanages, and our facilities, and all these other kind of things. And he meets the street kid, that became Trung in the film, when we were at a park in downtown Saigon. That part of the movie was kind of, pretty, true.

But one of the things that was going on was, Victor had set up this thing, this trip from Saigon down to the coast, to the beaches, to take the children on a bus to the beaches down on the South China Sea. And what I did not know at the time was that everything was so bad already in Vietnam by then that all Americans were restricted to Saigon. We couldn't leave Saigon because the countryside was too dangerous. But I didn't know that.

So David and I joined them on the beach trip. We ride down there on the bus. And there was this Cambodian driver for a separate vehicle that was Victor's.

We get down there, and we're letting the kids swim and so on. And one of the teachers, female teachers, asked, "Can I tell you truth?" And I said, "I always want to hear truth." And she said, "He is beating the children and I think he is touching the children in places that he shouldn't be touching them."

And when it came time to leave the beach and go back to Saigon, Victor said we didn't need to ride on the bus, we should go back with the Cambodian driver in the little pickup truck. She was in front and we were in the bed of the truck. So we're riding back to Saigon, and I -- I knew that country. I mean, I knew where we were, down on the coast. I had been, crawled, all over that country. And we're going and going, and the bus is gone, nowhere around. And I said to David, "Listen, I don't want to alarm you, but I think we've got a little problem." And he was already scared anyway, being over there, because he'd never been in a war zone before. And he said, "What do you mean?" I said, "I don't know exactly. I can't figure it out, I'm still trying to figure it out. But we're not going in the right direction. Something is wrong here. We're not following the bus. This is not the way back to Saigon. This is the way out to the rice paddies and jungles, and I know this is not where we're supposed to be going."

So we're going and going, and we reached a certain point, and I'm really concerned. I'm yelling through the little back window at the Cambodian driver. And I didn't trust her as far as I could throw her. And I told her to stop the truck.

She stops the truck, she pulls a pistol and she's got it pointed in my face. I pull a pistol, and point it in her face. And I said, "One of us dies. It's either you or me. But we're not riding in this truck anymore. We're getting out."

And she laid her pistol down. We got out of the truck. And she hauls ass.

So we're out in the middle of fucking nowhere in North Vietnamese and Viet Cong controlled territory, and David Seltzer is just about to shit himself. And I said, "Don't worry, we'll figure this out. We need to get back on a main highway, and it's about three miles back."

So we're trudging all these three miles back, and we get to this highway that I know is headed towards Saigon. And there's a bus coming. I wave the bus down, and we get on the bus.

And the next thing I know, about a mile or two farther, the bus gets stopped by the Viet Cong. And they get on the bus. And they're coming along and talking to people on the bus. And they get to me, and they're speaking to me in Vietnamese, asking me if I'm an American. I said, in Vietnamese, that we're American civilians, we're not military. And they got all antsy and told us to get off the bus. And I said, "No. We're not. We're going to Saigon." And there was this discussion between them, and they finally said, "You speak Vietnamese, we let you go." And that's what got us back to Saigon.

And by the time I got to Saigon, which was another few hours later, I had figured it out. Victor knew that people were on to him. And he had engaged his driver to kill us out in the middle of nowhere and dump us in a rice paddy. And we had somehow made it back to Saigon. And things were very tense after that.

There were a number of things that still happened in Vietnam after the debacle at the beach. A lot of trust was damaged. And we had already met Trung, the street urchin. And David Seltzer ultimately adopted him along with another little half-crippled girl that was in one of our orphanages. And the deal, between David Seltzer and I, was, if you don't adopt them, I will. And David knew he was in a much better financial position than I was, but I was ready.

The Fall of Saigon

So I got back from the trip with David Seltzer sometime, I think, in late December 1974, before Christmas. And I was frantically trying to finish up school. But I could see, during the trip, that Vietnam was on the verge of collapse. The circle

was tightening. So when I got back, the first thing I did was, I
made arrangements with a commercial airline company out of
Seattle, I think it was, for a 727, or something like that. I put
a deposit down on it of multi thousands of dollars. Because I
knew the end was coming. And they were just waiting for the
word.

And then at some point, during -- as things were starting to
unravel after the first of the year -- I was making all these calls
back and forth to Vietnam, and they were very, very expensive
telephone calls. And all of a sudden, my telephone bill was a
little over a thousand dollars, and that was a lot of money back
in the 70's!

And then as things started getting really bad, Southwestern
Bell cut my phone service off. The bill wasn't due yet, but they
cut it because -- I called them and started talking to them, and
they said, "It looked like this was getting way too high, so we
had to cut it off." And I just raised holy hell with Southwestern
Bell, started threatening lawsuits against them and everything.
I said, "You can't do this, this is an international relief agency,
the bill's not due for another two weeks," or whatever it was.
"You better have that phone back on because lives are at stake
with this." And I kept going up the chain there and finally got
someone who said, "Oh my God, yes, right, the phone's back
on." And it was kind of a race to see, were we gonna get in
enough money that month for me to cover the phone bill? But
it was absolutely critical. So I made a loan to pay the phone bill
off, just to make sure it was covered.

So finally, in the spring of 1975, yes, the place was going
to hell in a handbasket. I went out there to get things set up
as a staging center in case something went wrong. That was
gonna be in Ojai, California, and it was in a Jewish Center. And
so we had this arrangement with this big Jewish Community
Center that had plenty of facilities and everything, and it was
a lot of negotiation because it was a kosher place. And we had

all these children maybe coming in from Vietnam that were non-kosher. They jumped through all these hoops to get some, you know, blessing, to allow non-kosher stuff in one particular area. Everything was a negotiation.

So it came time. I went out and headed back into Vietnam on this 727. We got there at the very last minute on the last day that planes were getting out of there. I frantically ran into town and -- I had told Victor to get a staging area of all the children and everything, but I went back in to try to find everybody that I could find, that I knew, that I could get to the plane.

Well, the plane was absolutely jam-packed full. People sitting in the aisles, in the seats, everywhere. And we were the last civilian aircraft to make it off the runway at Tan Son Nhut Airport. The plane behind us got hit. Because rocket mortar fire was coming in, the whole city was under attack. To get a sense of the chaos of that, just look at the film of what it was like at the U.S. Embassy in those last couple of days.

But we got off, we got back, we got to California. And then the children that we had -- some of them went on to Welcome House in Pennsylvania, and David Seltzer adopted two of the children in all of that.

So yeah, that was the end of the war. And that was the end of the VACF.

Hell's Angels in L.A.

When I had gone to California to get things set up, I had this Dodge station wagon, of all things. I decided to make it a family trip. I packed everyone into it and we headed out to California. This would have been, like, January of 1975, or something.

So we drive to California. We got to L.A. And I need gas, so we pull into this service station. And all of a sudden about 50 or 60 or more Hell's Angels motorcycles pull into this gas station. They have me completely surrounded and they're revving their engines and talking their trash and so on. Kim Hoang is going absolutely crazy because she thinks we're all gonna die. I'm a little concerned, but it's, like, well, I mean, here we are.

So I tell Kim and the kids to stay in the car and lock the doors. I get out and walk over to one of the Hell's Angels, and he's glaring at me. He says, "What in the hell do you want?" And I said, "I want to talk to whoever's in charge." And he laughed. And he said, "Okay."

So he takes me over to the leader of the pack. And the leader says, "What?" And I said, "You know, here's the deal. I got a wife sitting in that car, just freaking out, scared shitless of you guys. I'm not scared of you, I don't care. You can do whatever you want to do to me. But I got two little kids in that car, and they're scared shitless. And here's what I'd like for you to do. You don't have to do it; we can do it a different way. But what I'd like for you to do is call all your troops off and let us just get the hell out of here, and you go on with your life."

And he looked at me, he stared at me, and he said, "You got guts." And I said, "Nah, I'm just trying to keep my family safe." And so, he calls all his people off. They all part ways -- it's like the parting of the Red Sea -- and we drive out of there and there we go. (Laughter)

H. Ross Perot

In 1975, after the fall of Saigon, I was back in school at the University of Houston. There were maybe, in those days, 15 Vietnamese people in Houston. There's now hundreds of thousands of Vietnamese people in Houston. But in 1975, before all the refugees started coming in, there were about 15 to 20. A few of them were students from overseas, and a few of them were the wives of guys who'd been in Vietnam.

One of these guys -- and we had kind of made contact, because the women, the wives, were so isolated. We wanted to find a little community for them at some level. Which we did. But it was more like a group rather than a crowd.

But one of the guys was not a former soldier. He was a black guy and had been a contractor over there -- worked for one of the defense contractors over there. And I liked him a lot. He was fun. We kind of became friends. And we started talking about this problem with all the boat people that were gonna be coming out, and were starting to come out. People were still trying to escape.

And we started kicking things around, and we came up with this idea. What if there was an island between Vietnam and somewhere else, that we could create a kind of refuge place? And that's sort of how it started out. So that they didn't all drown at sea and everything.

But then we thought, "Well, what could we do with all of this?" So then we thought, "Well, we can build a little --," in his mind, in my friend's mind, it was like, "build a little kingdom." And I thought, "Well, let's think beyond that a little bit. What if --" And this went on for a while, these discussions back and forth. I don't know how long, a month or two or three.

But then I came up with this notion, "Wait a minute." I think I had read something around that time about H. Ross Perot. I said, "Wait a minute. What if we created not really a little kingdom, but a kind of refuge that was, not only just refuge, but people who landed there, if we moved a computer-making business there that would sponsor all of this, then they'd have workers they could train and put in. And we could build little houses, have a little company town, and everything like that."

So we got all jazzed up on that. And then I thought, "Well, how does one get in touch with H. Ross Perot?" And I had no idea how to get in touch with him. But there were some computers in those days, and I had access to one. Or somehow, I found something somewhere that had a telephone number for him. As it turns out, it wasn't just a business phone. It was his home phone number I had unearthed somehow.

So one day I called that number, and he picks up. And I said, "I'm calling for H. Ross Perot." And he said, "This is he." And I introduced myself, and I started laying out this idea of buying an island. And I told him, "We've been working on this for quite some time, putting plans together and everything. But to make it all work, we're going to need the capital, and the business opportunity that you would have, by putting a company there to do chips or whatever it is you do, basically -- assembly, anything."

And he said, "Well, that's interesting. Do you have some stuff you can send me on it?" And I said, "We're putting it together now." And he said, "How much do you think you'd need for startup on all this?" And I said, "Well, the whole thing is probably a ten million dollar deal." And he started laughing. He said, "No, I don't think this can be done for less than twenty or thirty million." And I said, "Okay." (Laughter)

And so then, for a period of time after that -- little did I know how scattered Ross Perot was -- we were going back and forth on all this. I was sending him these elaborate business plans and everything that we had done. And at some point, about, I don't know, a month or two later, he gets back in touch with me, and he says, "Well, I've been pouring over this. I've got so many irons in the fire right now. I don't think I'm interested in this. But I'm interested in you."

And I said, "What do you mean?" And he said, "I know your background. I've had you completely checked out. I want to put together a team of ex-military to go into Vietnam and rescue American prisoners of war." And I said, "Well, what's the plan?" And he said, "Let me get back to you on that."

So he gets back to me, and he says, "Well, the plan's pretty simple. We're gonna drop you off in Thailand -- you and about eight to ten others. And you're gonna go into Vietnam, and you're gonna find the prisoner of war camp, and you're gonna get the guys out." (Laughter)

And I said, "Well, Ross, I gotta tell you, from a military perspective, that's not a plan. That's, like, a suicide mission." (Laughter) And he got all bowed up a little bit and said, "Well, if you're not interested, just tell me!" I said, "You don't have a plan yet." And he said, "Well, do you want to do a plan?"

And I said, "Quite frankly, I can't think of any plan to go into Vietnam at this moment, from Thailand, or even Laos or Cambodia, that -- if you don't know exactly where the camp is, and you don't know exactly what's going on on the ground, and you don't know exactly how you can get extracted, and how you can extract the other people -- I don't know how this could work." And he said, "All right. I'm gonna look elsewhere."

So that was the end of the island business. And it was also my great missed opportunity to haul my ass back into Vietnam on a suicide mission. And it turned out that it was pretty much a suicide mission. He actually put a team together later on and -- I don't remember exactly, I could look it up, there's stories about that -- but they went in -- all I can remember is, it was an entire fiasco. I'm not sure they all made it back out. But they never even found any prisoners of war.

Binh and Family Come to Houston

1975 -- the entire year -- was pretty scattered, hectic, discombobulated. Sometimes in my thinking, I used to think that, when I went back into Vietnam during the fall of Saigon, that Binh and his family got on the plane and they were some of the last few on the plane, and we got them out. That might be correct, but I'm not sure it is correct, because so many things were swirling in so many different directions. And I believe that, in fact, they got out a little later than that, that I was not able to find them on that trip.

But they got out, and they made their way to Fort Chaffee, Arkansas, and made contact with me. And this would have been in, I think, late 1975. There was a program where you could sponsor refugees, so I immediately jumped into that and sponsored them. And I got them to Houston.

I lived on West Sunnyside. It was a tiny little three-bedroom house, and I moved them in. Binh, his wife Kim, and Tao -- she was a baby, maybe 18 months old, something like that. And I could see immediately, as I had seen before with Kim Hoang, that tension was growing. And I was spending time dealing with that. But I made it clear that they were going to stay with us as long as they needed to stay with us until we could get them on their feet.

While they were there, I was also working on *Green Eyes*. David Seltzer and I were talking back and forth about that. And I think I was back in school.

Then I got word that Lorimar wanted me to come on board as an assistant producer and writer for *Green Eyes*. And we were making plans to start filming, so I had to go out to Los Angeles to help interview potential actors, especially for the main character, Dubeck. And that wasn't going so well. I was jettisoning people right and left.

Finally, we got some actors lined up. And then we had to figure out where we were going to shoot the movie, because at that time, of course, we couldn't go back into Vietnam. So I was sent off to scout Thailand, the Philippines, and maybe somewhere else in southeast Asia. But first I came back to Houston and made sure that Kim Hoang and everybody were situated. I thought everything looked okay, so I headed out to Thailand.

Near Death in a Bangkok Sauna

So I went to Thailand and stayed in, I forget, a snazzy, fancy hotel in Bangkok. And shortly after I got there, I'd gone out walking around the city for awhile, to see if there were streets, or things that would translate into what Vietnam looked like. And I was finding some of that, but Bangkok was a big mess of a city. It was very crazy. But I hadn't dismissed it, I just thought I needed to see everything and everywhere.

I think I was there for about two weeks. And sometime during the course of the first week, I discovered they had this sauna and spa and massage thing in the basement of the hotel. So I thought, "That sounds cool. I've never done any of that. Never had a massage or been in a sauna." So I signed up for that. Because I was on an expense account! (Laughter)

So I get there, and the first thing that happens is, I took a shower. Then I went into this sauna, which was about four or five little layers of benches. So I was gonna stay in there, and they were gonna come get me.

And I'm in there, and at first it was very nice. But after a little time went by, I'm getting a little too hot. And I'm thinking, "Well, I thought they were gonna come get me." So I go and try to open the door, and it's locked. It won't open. So I'm thinking, "Well, they've got to come any second now."

And so it starts getting warmer and warmer. And I think, "Well, the heat's at the bottom." So I keep going up a level and up a level, but then at some point, I'm getting really foggy, but I can still think, "Wait a minute, all this heat is rising. So the higher I get, the hotter it's gonna get." But there was no good place to be.

And I was just at the point of completely passing out, when all of a sudden, the door opened, and a bunch of people came in and got me and took me out. And it turns out, there had been some glitch, and they had forgotten that I was in there. And I was in there for a long fucking time!

So they brought doctors down there and everything. And they said, "It's a miracle you're still alive, nobody's lasted that long in that kind of heat!"

And the funniest part of it was, one of the massage people said, "Well, would you like to take a cold shower and get a massage?" And I'm, like, just completely out of it! (Laughter) But I laughed anyway, and said, "No, I think I'll pass, I've skirted death, I can go to bed now." (Laughter)

Encounter with a Serial Killer

One day, during the time in Bangkok, I'm just walking, walking, walking through the city. And you have to understand, Bangkok is a city of canals. It's like Venice. They've got canals going every which way. It's part of how the public transportation stuff works.

So I ran into this old cemetery. But the walls were about eight to ten feet high all the way around it. And I was standing there at a gate that I could kind of peer through, and I could kind of see the cemetery. And I thought, "This would make a nice shot at some point. I don't know how we'd use it, but there were old French cemeteries in Saigon."

So I'm peering through the little bars of the gate, and all of a sudden from above me, I hear this voice. And it was, "Hi!" And I looked up, and there's this guy sitting up there, on top of the wall. He says, "You American, right?"

I said, "Yeah." I'm always suspicious overseas, with anybody that comes and approaches me, because there are so many scams. So he jumps down off the wall, and I start walking away, because I'm thinking he's on the hustle and gonna ask me for money or whatever.

But he follows me and he says, "Hey, look, I'm not trying to ask you for money or anything." And of course he's saying this in kind of broken English. "I just feel so lucky when I find somebody that I can practice my English with a little bit."

So we start walking and talking, and he's telling me all about his family and so on. And then he said, "Please, it would honor me to pay you back for all of this, if you could come to my house and have a meal with us."

Well, that's a pretty important thing in that part of the world. And I thought it over and said, "Well, where do you live?" And he said, "We just have to get on the canal and get a boat, it'll take us there." And I said, "Well, I've got some time commitments this evening, I really need to be back for that. How long do you think this will take?" And he said, "We can probably get there and back and eat within an hour." So I said okay.

And so we get on this boat, and there's a guy driving the boat, a little motor boat. There's a bow, and a seat in the middle, and a seat at the back. I sit at the back, of course, so I can see what's ahead of me.

And we're going up the river, and we're going, and we're going. And I see him talking to the guy. And thirty minutes pass or so. So I ask him, "We're not there yet?" And he says, "It's just right up here! It's just right up here!"

So we get going a little bit more, and I'm already getting bad vibes. We go about 10 more minutes and I said, "Look, we need to turn around and go back." And he said, "No, no! We're here! We're here!"

So the guy pulls over to the bank, and he gets out and says, "Just wait here for a few minutes, I just have to tell them that we're here, and then I'll come back and get you, and we'll go have dinner." Well, I knew things were screwy at that point. And I watched him going up, and I see him up on the side of -- they're, like, hills up there. And I see him on one of these

terraced levels, and he's going house to house to house. And I
said, "This is bullshit."

So he comes back and says, "Okay, come on!" And I said,
"No. Not coming on. I told you I had to get back. We're getting
back. I'm going back. You can stay here with your family. Quote
family."

So he jumps back in the boat, and says, "No, no, I'll go back
with you, make sure you get back okay." So we're chugging
down the river, and I know. He knows that I know. And I know
that he knows that I know.

So we're making our way back, and it's starting to get dusk.
The light's getting dim. And I'm sitting on the middle thing, so
I can watch him, and he's sitting on that back thing. Well, there
was a paddle back there. And I look down for a minute, and
all of a sudden, boom! I get hit flat in the head, and it knocks
me semi-out. I'm semi-unconscious, I'm not fully unconscious.
And I'm trying to make sense of what it is.

And he says, "Oh! Bat hit you! Bat! Bird!" And I just laid
there for a minute. And then I opened my eyes, and I said,
"Back! Sit down over there. You come this direction again,
you're going out of the boat. Period." And then I tell the driver,
"Pull over as soon as we get close to the city."

So he sits there, and I'm sitting there watching him. And the
driver finally pulls up to one of these little docks. And the guy
says, "Let me come with you to make sure you get back to your
hotel okay." I said, "No. You stay in this boat. If I see you get
off this boat, you're a dead man."

And I've got a knot on my forehead. So I go up. I'm watching
him. I get up to the top of the stairs, to where the streets are.
And I had told the driver, "As soon as I'm out of the boat, go."
And I could see the guy still talking to the driver. And the driver's shaking his head. So I yell down, and said, "Go!" So the
driver takes off with this guy.

And for the rest of the trip and for years after that, I wondered what the hell was really going on. And one day, when I was out working in California, I met a guy named Tommy Thompson. He used to be a journalist in Houston, with the *Houston Press*, and he had written a book called *Serpentine*. And he was telling me about the book. And this was in about 1978 or 1979.

And so a few months later, I remembered about the book, and I got it and started reading it. And I'm thinking, "Boy, this sounds like a familiar M.O. to me. This sounds like a familiar story to me." And the more I read, all of a sudden he was killing people in Bangkok, and stealing passports and money, and he was getting all over the world on these different passports and everything. And then I turned the page, to where they've got pictures of him, and it was him. It was Charles Sobhraj, the mass serial killer of southeast Asia. And I thought, "Oh, now I get it. I skated. I was one of the lucky ones."

The Philippines

I could see that Thailand was going to be a logistical nightmare to try to shoot anything in, especially within the city. Although it had possibilities.

But then I went to the Philippines. I spent probably two weeks there on the scouting mission. I started making contacts with some of the Filipino military and government people, stuff like that.

And one of the things I could see, just walking in the streets, and going around with some of the military people, was, "Yeah, I could make this street work. I could make this street work." And the Filipino authorities were on board with helping to clear the streets and everything.

And then I found out there was a huge refugee population of Vietnamese, boat people that had landed in the Philippines. And I thought, "Okay, I think I've got everything here we need."

So I went back, and we were still in the process of interviewing people for the movie. And I was part of that. It was me, and the director John Erman, and sometimes David Seltzer. So we started picking the cast. We decided on Paul Winfield, who played the main lead. And Rita Tushingham. And a couple of other minor players.

And we interviewed lots and lots of potential kids to play the street kid, but we didn't find anybody. And I said, "We'll find somebody."

So after that, I went to the Philippines first, to start doing all the groundwork. And that was probably a month or so. I was making notes on scenes for this and that.

And then John Erman came. We were staying in the Manila Hilton Hotel. He'd been there, like, two or three days. And he knocked on my door and wanted to talk. And he just broke down in tears. And basically he was saying, "I've never shot on location before. This seems crazy to me. I don't know what I'm doing. I don't know how I'm gonna handle any of this stuff."

And I said, "John, it'll work. I'll be here with you. Don't worry about it." And he cried and cried. And he made me promise that *I* would make it work. And I said, "Okay!" (Laughter)

And then after that, Jonathan Lippe came -- who was later known as Jonathan Goldsmith and then as the Most Interesting Man in the World. He was in his probably mid-thirties. I was probably about 28 or 29. He played sort of the comic weird sidekick character.

So he comes to my room, and he's all hyper. He's really hyped up on something. And he said, "I'm trying to figure out how to do all this stuff. And I'm really trying to figure out how to deal with this country. I've never been in this country before. And all I want to do is get laid. I want to get laid! I want to get laid! These are the most beautiful women I've ever seen!"

And I said, "Well, I suggest that you lay in a good supply of condoms." (Laughter) And he said, "Oh! No! Check this out! I've been wearing a condom since I left the United States!" And he drops his fucking drawers, and he's got this flaccid penis with a droopy condom hanging off of it. (Laughter) And I said, "Okay, well, I probably didn't need to see that, but okay. You're on the right track."

And that's how crazy everything was. And everything was just absolutely crazy. But then the weird thing was, we had to start auditioning for locals to play certain Vietnamese parts, especially the kid. The kid was going to be the lynchpin of that whole movie. And after I had left the States and gone to start setting everything up in the Philippines, they had kept interviewing kid after kid after kid, and nothing was working.

And I kept telling John Erman -- I mean he was just dazed. And everybody was dazed and confused. Because this was not your first world country. And I said, "Look, we've still got time before we have to start shooting. We've got time."

But he said, "Can you go to Hong Kong and see if you can find anybody?!" And I said, "Well, John, I could, but I don't know that -- I think we probably just haven't found the right one here yet." He said, "No, no! Go to Hong Kong! They've got lots of talent there!" I said, "Okay." So I went to Hong Kong.

Eating Live Monkey Brains in Hong Kong

So I'm in Hong Kong at the Peninsula Hotel, which is probably -- then, I don't know, probably still now -- the greatest hotel in Hong Kong. And I really don't know what I'm doing. I don't know how I'm going to start finding people. I mean, I had contacts and stuff in the Philippines, but I had no contacts in Hong Kong.

So I started making some contacts, and I started interviewing kids for the part. And these were all Chinese kids. Which was fine, we could make that work.

So I'm there for, I don't know, maybe a couple of weeks. And I'm tied into some Chinese production people in Hong Kong. And we had a great big dinner at this very, very sort of secret place in Hong Kong. It was this Chinese restaurant, and they invited me to this big dinner, a welcoming kind of dinner.

I'm a fan of Chinese food, of course, and Asian food. But all of a sudden they were doing this weird thing that I didn't understand. It was this huge table, and there was this hole in the middle of the table. And they're saying, "You will have the treat of your life. This is one of the most honored things that we can give to anybody."

And all of a sudden, they bring this live monkey out. And somebody goes under the table and straps the monkey in, and the top half of its head is sticking up through the hole. And somebody comes along with this machete-like knife, and goes whack! And chops off the top of the monkey's head. The monkey at this point is still alive. It's not screaming, but the head is pulsating.

And then they get all these glass straws that they stick into the monkey's brain, and everybody starts slurping monkey brain out of these straws. And I thought, "Am I up for this? I can't say no." It was one of these things where -- there are things you don't do, that you could do, to offend people. And I wasn't going to offend my host. So I slurp some monkey brain. It's supposed to be eaten before the monkey dies, so it has to be done very quickly.

This was one of the delicacies of China. And I didn't know this at the time -- I learned it later on -- but one of the biggest dangers of eating raw monkey brains is getting spongiform encephalitis. I didn't know anything about that at the time.

So I'm not gonna say that was the highlight of my Hong Kong trip (laughter), but it's certainly the most memorable part of the trip. And it became clear to me, while I was there, "Nope, I'm not gonna find what I'm looking for here." So I left and flew back to the Philippines.

Finding Lemi

So the big pressure on me at that stage of the game in the movie production was finding the child that could be cast as Trung. He was a key character, the little street kid. And back in L.A., they had been interviewing kid after kid after kid. And they had sent me to Hong Kong. And nothing worked.

I got back from Hong Kong to Manila, and John Erman was melting down. I said, "John, stop it. We've got a little time here. We've got a week or two." And he said, "We've been looking for almost six or eight months!" And I said, "You never know. Let's put out a new little blurb in one of the Filipino papers for interviews."

So we did that, and we started getting these kids coming through. And what was interesting about the kids was, they were not little kids necessarily. Mostly they were, like, teenagers. But out of that group of people, we were able to plug in other characters -- teenager-type kids. So it looked like we were making a little progress.

And one day, this kid showed up who was about four feet tall, and he spoke English, he spoke Tagalog, and he was so bright that he could pick up and remember Vietnamese. And we're interviewing him, or auditioning him, and we get about 30 minutes in, and I said, "I think we've got it."

So we picked him. His name was Lemi. I never knew another name for him. And Lemi and I connected. I found out stuff about Lemi that nobody else knew. One was that he was not 8 or 9 years old, he was, like, 16 or 18 years old. And he had this condition. He also had a thyroid condition, and if you ever watch the movie, you'll see I always put a bandana around his neck so you couldn't see his thyroid condition. His neck was fat and lumpy.

But I knew he was the one. And John Erman said, "I don't know, I don't know." I said, "Trust me on this, John. This is our guy." And he was a centerpiece of the movie. And this was, like, three or four days before we had to start shooting. And we had him.

So that was how we got Lemi. And the strange thing about Lemi was that -- he was almost grown, he was an older adolescent -- and he was super horny. He just wanted to get laid all the time! Well, we had to assign him a nurse as a kind of guardian to keep him from, like, (laughter) going off the rails. And he was a challenge.

But Lemi glommed onto me and would listen to anything I said and would do anything I said. So I became sort of his guardian, but I had an *ad litem* appointed to him (laughter) -- a nurse *ad litem*! And there were some other little episodes that involved Lemi during the course of the filming that I had to step into -- one, when he was trying to, you know, talk the nurse into having sex with him. And other things.

But he was the right one at the right time, and we found him. And he's a centerpiece of the movie.

Mila

So we are on very, very tight deadlines from Los Angeles to get things done in this movie. And it's crazy. It's mostly undoable. But this is the kind of pressure, in the film industry, that people put on everybody. And you've got, you know, these people dealing with talent, you've got these people dealing with logistics, you've got these people dealing with, you know, trying to get situated for filming. And then you've got the money people, pushing, pushing, pushing, because every single day is dollars and cents to them. And that's not the way that creative people normally are viewing everything. That's why they have the business people in there, pushing everything full speed ahead. And everybody is freaked out about it, from the directors, to the writers, everybody.

So I'm just plugging along. I'm getting the people we need, bringing them in. And my philosophy is, bring them in, we'll cull them, and it's pretty easy to do, and doesn't take long.

And then one day, Mila walked in. She was this wraith of a Filipino woman. But there was something that immediately connected with us. And she was there auditioning for anything that might be available, and really, there wasn't anything available for her. I didn't see it, nobody else saw it.

But after the interview, I said, "You know, I want to keep you in mind for something. There's something special in there. Let's just stay in touch." So of course I had her information and everything, and I gave her my information.

So we actually connected. And of course, this was when -- the beginning of the end of when my marriage was falling apart back in Texas. But we had this thing. And we were trying to spend as much time as we could together, because maybe I had, like, an hour a day, in the course of, like, 15 to 20 hour days, when there was just a smidgen of time.

So in one of these little smidgens of time, we were traipsing through Manila, walking, going to eat or do something, and I noticed that we were being followed. I noticed that we had two or three different guys following us. And I mentioned it to her. And she said, "Yes, but please pay no attention." And I said, "Well, I can't help but pay attention." And she said, "No, no, you do not know who you're dealing with here. These people are government and they don't play nice." And I said, "Really! Okay. Let me see how nice they play or don't play."

I was being too -- I was out of my element but, being what I am, I decide I'm going to go up and confront one of these people that's been shadowing us for, like, an hour or two. And she begs me not to. And I go up there.

I get up to him and I said, "You're following me. What do you want?" He says, "Get out of my face." This is a Filipino guy. I said, "No, you get out of my face." And the next thing I know, I've got a knife up to my throat and a hand on a gun on his hip. And he said, "You will die."

And Mila comes up and starts talking in Tagalog, and after a very long -- probably only about 50 seconds or so -- he pulls the knife away, puts it up, and says something to her. And she says something back. And they leave.

And I thought, "You know, I keep thinking I'm in my depth. But I'm not always in my depth here. And that was a close call. And I should have listened to her."

They were following me because I was a foreigner dealing with Filipinos, creating a movie, doing stuff with the military. I was high on their radar screen.

She, at the time, by the way, had just come back from about a year or so of living in, I think it was Italy. She had done her master's degree work in Italy, in art or something. So there wasn't any official thing I could hire her for, that fit into anything, without me being just really, really, you know, the kind of Hollywood person that hires somebody for whatever. But I kind of made her the unofficial -- I mean, she got paid for it, a little bit -- photographer. Because she also had a lot of photography experience. So she was there kind of chronicling some of all that.

And you know, when it was all over, when all the filming was over and everything, we were both pretty smitten. And I was torn. Because I came back to the States and there was all this stuff going back and forth between us. And I just couldn't.

I had these kids, I had Kim Hoang. I couldn't do it. So that was the end of it.

But I kind of kept track of her. She went to work as a muckety-muck for one of the airlines, and finally retired. And then one time, when I was out in California on a case, when I was a lawyer, I made contact with her. And this was probably when both of us were in our fifties. We were gonna get together. But she had already married somebody else, and I was married to Andi by then. We talked on the phone and decided, no, we're not gonna get together.

But that was a -- it was a good but very crazy period of my life. And I don't think, even if we'd ever gotten together -- it would never have been permanently. It never would have worked.

Filming and Bluffing some Pirates

Green Eyes was the first -- well, the only real production, from beginning to end, that I ever worked on. And it was -- I thought it was hard in the beginning, you know, timewise, lots of work. But once we started shooting, I was working 20 hours a day. I got four hours a night of sleep on a good night. And the problem was that I had been assigned so many hats, and I was too stupid to realize that people were assigning me these hats because they needed a little rest. I was doing second director work -- shooting all these things that weren't with the main characters but with other people, like, establishing shots, and all of that kind of stuff. And I was having to deal with all of the interactions and crises and disputes between the actors, which were a lot more numerous than I ever thought they would be. And I had to be dealing with still locating additional locations that hadn't been decided on. And dealing with the Filipino government, because they kept saying, "No, you can't do this, you can't do that," and I'd have to be negotiating all of that.

So I was getting pretty worn to a frazzle. Of course, I'd spent years in a war. I knew what being worn to a frazzle was. I knew, yeah, if I have to go 18 or 20 hours a day, I can do that. Or I can do 24 hours a day if I have to. But the problem was that there was never any down time. In all the months we were there filming, I don't think I ever had any real down time. Down time was measured in an hour here or three hours there. That was down time. So that was the grueling part of it.

And it wasn't just grueling for me, it was grueling for a lot of the other people -- because it was -- the emphasis from ABC Television and Lorimar Productions was, get this done and get it on schedule. And the schedule wasn't as long as a regular movie. A regular movie, we would have had a year, maybe a year and a half or something. But this was a made-for-TV movie, and it was all dollars and cents from the accountants that were weighing in every single day from the United States. So we only had about five or six months once shooting started.

So that was -- I could see it was affecting me, in terms of health. I was starting to feel -- I mean I was just dead tired. The actors would -- whatever their problems were, I had to go deal with. And their problems sometimes were penny-ante and sometimes they were just meltdowns. And the director of course had never shot anything on location before, it had always been in Hollywood. Or not overseas, anyway. And the Philippines was a tough place to shoot. So that was wearing everybody down.

And then there was the actual logistics of everything. We were going out to shoot about 50 or 60, 70 miles out of Manila, in the jungles. And we'd gotten the -- I'd made arrangements with the Filipino government to get us all these military vehicles and whatnot, everything from Jeeps to Deusenhalfs -- those are a certain kind of truck that carry troops -- and some armored vehicles and that sort of thing. And I had arrangements for everybody to have M-16's, but not with live ammunition. They had blank rounds.

And we're heading out one day -- I'm in a Jeep in front of this convoy, going out into the jungles -- and we get accosted by a wall of Filipino pirate bandidos. And they're all pointing their weapons at us, and I'm there at the head of the convoy. I had already -- because of Vietnam, I had already told everybody in the convoy, "We've got to be ready for anything. We don't have live ammo, but we've got the bluff of live ammo."

So here's like 50ish people blocking us. And they're not in tanks or big trucks or anything, they're all in Jeeps and motorcycles and motor scooters and everything like that. And they're saying, "We're taking everything." And I said, "No. Don't think so."

And I motioned to everyone behind me with my left hand, and all of a sudden, every extra -- every Filipino extra, every American extra, every production extra -- jumped out of all of these various trucks and Jeeps and everything, with all of their weapons -- M-16's, rocket launchers, all of these things -- pointed right at these guys. And none of it worked, nothing was live ammo. And they surrendered.

So then we had this whole group that had surrendered to me! We had Filipino regulars and soldiers that we were paying for off duty stuff. They called and had the Filipino Army come out and haul all these people away and arrest them. And what they said to me was, "This is the biggest single arrest we've ever seen!" (Laughter) And it was all bluff. But you know, whatever works.

The Embassy Party Scene

This was one of the more difficult shoots of the entire movie. Not as difficult, but in many ways, as difficult, as some of the jungle scenes that we had to shoot. And my job was to find

every single location, get it set up, and get everybody ready for
it. And part of this -- I don't remember if this was a combination of me and John Erman, or even if it was in the original
screenplay, I don't remember now -- but there was going to be
a segment of the movie that had to do with the American Embassy throwing a party. And the juxtaposition was going to be
between the American presence and the Vietnamese presence,
and this party going on.

So I found this great place to host the party. And I knew a
lot about Embassy parties because I had been involved with
the American Embassy when I was in Vietnam in the Army,
and after I got out of the Army, with the VACF. And I knew how
extravagant those things were in juxtaposition with the out-
side-the-party people that were witnessing this from afar. So
that was how I designed this whole thing.

And it was gonna be a night shoot, which are difficult. And
we had to have, like, a hundred Vietnamese or Asian children
involved in this scene. And I was sick during that period of
time. I was really worn to a complete frazzle. I was just barely
able to function because of the exhaustion and whatnot. But I
was there and got it all set up. And it was this great Embassy
party where all the high muckety-mucks were in the party. And
there was this big balcony. And then beyond the balcony, down
below, there were all the *hoi polloi* that were down there. And
it was a great scene of the movie, I thought.

And getting it set up and getting it shot was a nightmare.
But we did. But the upshot of the scene was, all of this food
and everything that was there, every kind of delicacy in the
world -- Paul Winfield and Rita Tushingham were at the party.
And I had all these children down below the balcony where
they were. And my suggestion was, "Guys, we've got all this
food, they're so hungry -- give it to them!"

So that's what happened in the scene. And, a lot of these
children that were there were Filipino urchins, you know. And

Vietnamese -- it was a mixture. So yeah, everybody got into it. But they got into it more than just, "Oh, this is a good idea." Paul Winfield and Rita Tushingham took this as, "Yes, this is how we need to save the children. And this is what we need to take away from these rich people." Because the characters played by Paul Winfield and Rita Tushingham were not the high muckety-mucks, of course. Rita Tushingham was a social worker there and ran an orphanage, and of course Paul Winfield was this ex-soldier looking for his child that he'd fathered in Vietnam. And all of the high glitz and muckety-muckedness of the elites got to them, both from the standpoint of direction and from the standpoint of their own moral sense of stuff. And so then all of this food stuff was being thrown over the wall to the children, who were eating it. And I think that was one of the better scenes in the movie.

The Final Scene

We're getting close to finishing up the movie. We were over time and over budget. Pressure was being brought to bear to get it all wrapped up.

A major seminal scene in this movie is -- Dubeck realized at some point that, yes, his child was dead, but he had glommed onto Trung, the street kid. And Trung ran away. So one of the last scenes in the movie was Dubeck trying to find Trung.

But the director, John Erman, had to go back to the States. Everybody went back to the States except for me, Paul Winfield, Lemi, and some cameramen. So I was appointed Assistant Director at that point, and I had to direct the next, like, five days of filming, which I'd never done before in my life.

And the deal was supposed to be that Dubeck ran around looking for Trung and then found him sitting outside on a street corner somewhere. And I thought, "No, that's not right." So I was doing all this second assistant filming stuff, and doing all these stock photo shots, and going up and down the streets looking for everything, and I thought, "Ah! There's a great bridge in this town that reminds me of a bridge in Vietnam. We'll have him sitting on the bridge, on the ledge of the bridge -- not suicidal, just sitting there."

So we shot one scene of that, and everybody thought it was great. And I said, "It's not great. It's missing something." And they said, "What?" And I said, "Balloons."

So we got these elongated balloons, and I built this thing around Lemi's head -- you know, put one of these elongated balloons around his head, which just looked ridiculous. And then we re-shot it. So Rita Tushingham and Paul Winfield are going down the street, and he says, "Stop! Stop!" And there's Trung, sitting there on the bridge, on the top of the bridge, on the ledge of the bridge, with this balloon built around his head. And it became one of the most significant shots in the whole movie, because it was so ridiculous but poignant all at the same time.

Apocalypse Now

Everybody else had left the Philippines, but I had to stay to wrap up some stuff with the Filipino government and everything. So I was wrapping that stuff up, and I was still at the Manila Hilton Hotel. And I get this call at the hotel from Francis Ford Coppola's people, who want to meet with me.

So we met at one of the restaurants in the hotel, and they're going on and on about how Francis Ford Coppola is doing this movie *Apocalypse Now*, and it's gonna be a really big production filmed in the Philippines, and they wanted to know if I would work with them on that production. They said they were very impressed with my work. And they were telling me that they had, like, a six-month schedule on this.

And I said, "It ain't gonna happen. Whatever you're planning on shooting, it's not gonna be done in six months." Because they had told me all about how the story was gonna unfold and everything.

And they said, "What do you mean?" I said, "The logistics, the travails of filming on location in the Philippines, filming in the jungles, filming in the mountains, the monsoons, getting the cooperation of the Filipino government -- I'd be shocked if this film could be done in two years in the Philippines."

And they sort of laughed and scoffed and said, "Well, no, it will be done in six months." And basically came down to, "Are you on board or not?"

And I said, "Well, here's the deal. If I'm going to work on the movie, you have to move my family here. I'm not gonna spend another minute away from my kiddos. They're gonna have to be here. And here's what I want in terms of money. And you're gonna have to let it soak in that this is not gonna be done in six months."

After I told them how much I wanted them to pay me, they said, "No, no, you don't understand. People would pay us for the opportunity to work with Francis Ford Coppola." And my response to that was, "No, you don't understand. Francis Ford Coppola should really be anxious to pay me for the opportunity to work with me." (Laughter) And that was kind of what turned them completely off. (Laughter)

So they said, "Well, it will be done in six months. And we're stunned at what you're asking for. And we're not gonna bring your family over." And I said, "Okay. Good luck. And goodbye." So that was the end of that.

I came back to the States, and they moved forward. It took them over four years to film in the Philippines. One of their major stars, Martin Sheen, had a heart attack during the filming. And the monsoons hit. And the Filipino government was not responsive. And it took them about four-and-a-half years to get that film in the can.

Meanwhile, I was on with my life back in the States, but I was kind of keeping tabs on it. I was still working in the film industry. And I was in New York, meeting with my literary agent -- novel agent -- on a novel that I was working on, and while I was there, I got a call from my film agent in Los Angeles, who said, "You've got to get to Los Angeles immediately! Somebody wants to buy your screenplay! You have to get here tomorrow, time is of the essence, we've got to strike while the iron is hot!"

So on that last day in New York, *Apocalypse Now* was premiering in New York. So I went to see it, mainly so I could sit there and gloat, because in my mind, I had a vision of what the story would look like, and I thought, "They'll never be able to do this well without me." I was riding high at that time. So I go and watch the movie, waiting to see how screwed up it all is, and how much they got wrong, and I thought, "Jesus. It took them five times longer than they thought it would -- I was right about that -- but they made a great, great movie."

So I walked out of there and the next day I flew to Los Angeles. I get to my agent's office, and she said, "They decided not to buy the screenplay." And I had spent my own money, like a thousand dollars, to get from New York to Los Angeles and back to Houston. But that's how snarky and nefarious and capricious the film industry is. So it was at that point that I almost decided I was out of the game.

Charles Grodin, Sammy Davis Jr., and Neil Diamond

When it was time for *Green Eyes* to come out -- it was a made-for-TV movie, but they had a movie version of it to be premiered in Los Angeles. And it was kind of a big deal. And of course I was invited out there to be part of it. And people were giving me great credit for all of this stuff, even though "credit" wise, movie wise, I didn't get all that credit.

So I was going to be staying at John Erman's house. He lived in Brentwood, just right outside of UCLA. It was a great neighborhood. He had a house, and the house had a little garage apartment that was connected to it, you know, upstairs. So I was going to be staying in that garage apartment.

So I get into the room and start getting settled in. And I'm looking around the room. And in the little drawer on the nightstand, there was a big tube of KY jelly. And I thought, "Hmmm. Well, this tells me a little bit, I think." And he had said something about his "friend" who had been staying there for awhile but was not there anymore.

And one day, I was there by myself at the house, and John was running late from some other meeting at some studio or whatever. Knocks come on the door, and one of the people who came in was Charles Grodin. And he started out as a complete and total asshole. And I have a way of dealing with assholes, and he wasn't happy with the way I was dealing with him. I basically told him, "I get it. You're a complete and total asshole. You're waiting for John. Have a seat. Don't expect to see me again, because I don't like you."

And he said, "How dare you?! Everybody likes me!" I said, "Nope. Obviously, everybody doesn't." So that was my one interaction with Charles Grodin. He tried to make up for it a little later, but it was all fatuous and phony. And fatuous and phony really describes a lot of Hollywood.

Then, Sammy Davis, Jr., was there for the premiere. And he made a special trip over to me to talk to me about the movie. And one of the things I remember about him is that he was so small and so delicate. I mean, his little hands -- and I thought -- because all I had seen was Sammy Davis, Jr., playing these parts where he was blown up bigger than he really was. And I was really impressed with him. I thought, "Yeah, he's genuine."

And it's hard to find a genuine person out in Hollywood. Most of the people I ran across were not genuine.

Then, on another night while I was there at John Erman's house, I go to bed, and I'm laying in bed, and all of a sudden the door opens and in comes John. And he tries to crawl into bed and touch me. And I said, "John, crawl out of this bed really quick, before you force me to do something I don't want to do." And I made him sit in a chair across from the bed, and I explained to him, "John, I understand all of this. I get it. But I'm not a homosexual. I love you to pieces. I think we'll always be friends. But please do not ever, ever try this again." And he didn't. He understood. But that was kind of the end of our contact.

And -- I can't recall quite exactly how and where it was, but at some point out in Hollywood, I ran into Neil Diamond. And he was telling this story about how he just gets all this flood of gifts and letters and everything from fans. And on his birthday one year, he received this cake. And he cut into the cake, started eating it, and it was filled with pubic hair. His female fans were sending him pubic hair inside of cakes. And God only knows, I don't know what else he ever got. But that stuck in my mind, because that was, like, "Yeah, that's a bad day at the office." (Laughter)

The Pharmacy and M. David Lowe

After *Green Eyes* was wrapped, I came back to Texas. I was done with that. There were feelers -- people putting feelers out to me -- but nothing was really coming through.

And around 1976 or 1977ish, my father was going through some medical stuff, my grandfather was going through some medical stuff, and the pharmacies were in dicey business situations. And they prevailed upon me to come in and kind of just fill the gap for a little bit, until they got better. So I did, and I started looking at everything. And there were things that needed to be fixed, and I started fixing things.

But I was really at a low ebb, because it was, like, "My career that I was building has now collapsed, and I've been dragged back into this thing that I never wanted to get dragged back into." But I dug into it with, you know, a mission to get it all squared away.

So for quite a bit of time, I was working on that. And I started getting things back on an even keel. I had to -- my sister Susan had been brought into the organization, and that wasn't working out real well. So I assigned her to be sort of an assistant manager at the old first Cunningham Pharmacy. And there were problems, and I wound up having to kind of remove her from that situation.

But things got back on an even keel, and about a year later, in around 1977 or 1978, I thought, "Okay, good. I can exit gracefully now." And I told everybody, "I'm leaving."

But then I didn't have anything to do. I needed to find something. I could have stayed at the pharmacy -- I was making money -- but it was just dragging me deeper into the abyss. So I went to M. David Lowe Personnel Agency, who placed people in different jobs. And I took all these little tests and whatnot that they had. And at the end of that, they interviewed me, and they said, "Look, we think you're extremely well suited for working for us." So they said they would give me a salary for the first, whatever it was, three months or something. And the salary was acceptable. And they emphasized that the program was based on everybody being dressed like I.B.M. employees. Which meant a suit and a tie. But I took the job, because I needed it. I had bills to pay and kids to raise.

So I'm working for them. And it was like a big room where everybody was in little cubicles. And there was a big bell in the middle of the room. And every time somebody made a placement -- because, eventually, when you were off of salary, you were getting a commission based on every person you placed -- they would go ring the bell. And everyone would be yelling and screaming. And I thought, "God, this is just so horrible."

And I wouldn't wear the kind of clothes they wanted me to wear. I mean, everybody had, like, the best suits and everything. I wore whatever I had. And the shoes I had at the time -- I remember this because there were many comments on them -- but I was wearing Roots. These were these reverse negative heel shoes. They were weird. And I was weird. And my hair was long and weird. And I thought, "They're never gonna keep me around here for a month." But they did. They liked me for some reason.

But they also noticed that I was more interested in people who really needed jobs rather than the easy placements. So they started giving me all the people with thin resumes and people who were just trying to make it. So we'd spend our days making calls to different businesses, trying to sell these people, basically. I was there for about a month, and I thought, "I would rather be back in the war." But I'm pressing through, because I'm trying to distance myself from the pharmacy operation. And this was paying the rent and stuff.

Then one day, I get a call from Random House, Ballentine Books. They wanted to know if I would be willing to do the novelization of *Green Eyes*. And they said there would be an advance. It wasn't a huge advance, but it was like, I don't know, $10,000 or $15,000, which was *a lot* in those days. And I said, "Okay." So as soon as I hung up the phone, I went into the manager and quit.

But then, I got dragged back into the pharmacy business for a bit. So I would work there during the day, and during the nights, I would write the *Green Eyes* novel. And I did that for four or five months.

Shane's Birth

The deal was, the reason that we kept having kids, is because Kim Hoang wanted a girl. So we were gonna give it another shot. And the deal was -- because I had talked to her doctor, a Chinese doctor in Houston, an OB/GYN, named Dr. Chiu -- and we all came to the conclusion that, yes, after this birth, no matter what it was going to be, there was gonna be a tubal ligation after the birth. Little did I know that Dr. Chiu and Kim Hoang weren't planning on going through with that at all. (Laughter)

So, I don't remember much about the pregnancy except that I don't think there was anything terrible going wrong. I think there might have been some times where she had to be off her feet for a while. The usual kind of stuff.

So we get to the hospital, and I think it was Memorial Northwest Hospital that he was born in. And I'm in the waiting room. I wanted to be back there, but Dr. Chiu said, "No, absolutely not, you're not going to be in there." And I thought it was some weird Asian thing, but then I later realized it was because I would have seen that a tubal ligation was not happening. (Laughter)

So I'm cooling my heels in the waiting room. And Shane was born. And Dr. Chiu comes out and she's beaming. And she says, "It's a boy!" And I'm thinking, "Okay, great, I'm gonna have three boys!" But then they did say that he seemed -- and this was true for all of them, Sam and Sean and Kristy -- that he seemed to have a touch of jaundice or something. I didn't know what to think about that because it was like, "Really? I mean I think that's probably connected to the Asian thing." But I didn't know.

But it was fine, everything was fine. Perfect. And I thought we were done with having children! I would later be glad that we weren't! I had finally finished undergraduate school and I think at that time I was going through the Sheriff's Department Academy. So I thought I could see daylight.

And before he was born, I had decided to name him Shane. There was Sam, then there was Sean, and then there was Shane. I liked the alliteration and adding one letter to the name each time. And of course, I loved the movie Shane, too. You probably didn't know that Shane is one of my favorite movies. (Laughter)

The Omen

So David Seltzer's main home, his family home, was in Ojai, California. And I had stayed there many, many times, and for some lengthy periods of time while I was out there working. And then actually during the evacuation of Saigon and everything, that was home base.

And his wife was there. And they had this goofy-ass, kind of weird handyman, that took care of the little animals. It was a couple of acres of property or so. Had a guest house on it; that's where I usually stayed, was the guest house.

And the kid that worked there -- he seemed kind of slow, and was odd, very odd. He was about 17 years old or so. But he seemed like he was kind of part of the family.

And also it was there in Ojai where I met Krishnamurti. He's a famous philosopher. He actually started out being raised to become kind of the head of Theosophy. And he broke away from it. He was sort of a guru. He had his own little compound there in Ojai, and people flocked from all over the world to hear him. I've got some books by him. Very smart guy.

So anyway, later on, after I came back to Houston, shortly before I joined the Sheriff's Department, I was still scrambling around doing work for the pharmacy, trying to do this and that and just cobble together a living. And I knew David was working on a new movie, called *The Omen*. He was the screenwriter for it.

At some point, after the movie had wrapped but before it came out, when it was in post-production, he called me up one day. He was frantic. And he said, "I'm writing the novelization for *The Omen*, and I've never written a novel -- just screenplays. I don't get the feel, the rhythm." He said, "Can you do me a favor? Can you just write, like, the first two chapters so I can get a sense of the rhythm and everything?" And he said, "If you do, I'm gonna gift you the guest house in Ojai."

And I thought, "Well, that's not a bad gig." So I sat down and started writing and sent him two or three chapters. Spent, I don't know, a month or so writing. He got it and he was profusely thankful. And so he went on and finished up the novel. And he said he would put a good word in with his publisher for me. All that kind of stuff. People say stuff like that all the time in Hollywood. Sometimes it's lies, sometimes it just never pans out.

So the movie comes out, the book comes out. And I didn't hear anything from David for a long time after that. And one day he calls me up and says, "I've got bad news for you. I can't give you the guest house. I was gonna carve out the property and give you the guest house on the property, but my wife ran off with the yard boy," -- the 17-year-old -- "and she instituted divorce proceedings, and she got the house and the property. So, sorry." (Laughter)

But he said, "The good news is, the book was a hit! Thank you very much! I made $1.6 million off of it!" And there was nothing about giving me a cut. And I had been listening to his crap for years by that time. And I hung up and I remember, as I was hanging up, I was kind of both shaking my head and chuckling to myself and saying, "I am so done with Hollywood."

Candice Bergen and Louis Malle

Candice Bergen is a beautiful, wonderful actress, still, even in her 70's or 80's or whatever she is. She was married to Louis Malle, the French director.

And I got a call one day, just out of the blue -- because I had been around a bit. I wasn't, like, a well-known quantity, but I was a niche quantity, and the niche seemed to be, if it was Vietnam, my name came up. So I get this call one day. It was from one of their, I don't know, minions. And they said, "Would you be available for a call with Louis Malle?"

So we set up the call, and he calls me. And he's describing to me that they're trying to do this movie -- I don't know if it was -- I think it was more a documentary. And actually, ultimately, it got done. I think it did. But it was going to be about Vietnamese boat people who made it to the coast of Texas and became shrimp boat operators. And all of the hardships and everything involved in all of that. And actually, at that moment, I was kind of tied up in other things. But it sounded kind of interesting. So I said I would be interested. So he said he would have Candice call me.

So Candice Bergen called me at some point. And we talked at length, and we yucked it up. And then she decided she wanted to meet up. So we met up, in Houston, and we talked for a long time. We really kind of hit it off. There were some sparks flying.

But we both agreed, in talking all through this, that no -- in my opinion, they had everybody they needed. And she said, "I can't believe you would say something like that. Because anybody else would say, no, no, you desperately need me." And I said something like, "Well, I said that to Francis Ford Coppola's people one time, and it didn't go over very well." (Laughter) "So if I see everything's going to be okay, I'll just say everything's going to be okay."

So I did not take that job. It was not offered, and I did not take it. And I don't think I've ever seen the movie or the documentary. But I did give both of them a number of tips and ideas.

So that was my run-in with Louis Malle and Candice Bergen. And it was yet another -- and this is the way it is in the movie industry. People will go to -- actors, for example -- they'll go to forty auditions and maybe one out of forty, or one out of a hundred, they may get a little part. That's just the way that world works. And it was not how my world was at that time. Actually, I think at that time -- I'm not quite sure exactly when it was -- but there were other things swirling in my world at that time, and I was not going to go down to the Gulf Coast and wrangle something. I think I already had something going at that point that was at least keeping me surviving.

Chapter 7

The Sheriff's Department: Ages 30-37

Application and Academy

After the very end of Vietnam in 1975, I was kind of stuck trying to help wrangle the pharmacies. Which was just horrible to me. I did it well, but it wasn't what I wanted to be doing.

And the pharmacy was open 24 hours a day, and so was the little cafe. And there were various police officers and sheriff's department people who would stop by there at night, because we gave them half price on food and free coffee. And I got to know some of these people. And one of them was a detective named Ray Davis, who actually worked on one of the big serial murder cases that crossed the United States. And he took me aside one night and said, "You'd make a good cop."

I'd never really thought about it, but I told him I had a dear friend who was a cop, which was David Hefner. And it was just a conversation. But I started thinking about it. I started thinking about how I was getting pulled more and more into the pharmacy business as I was trying to extract myself from it. And one day, I thought, "Huh. Maybe I'll go for this."

So I made an application and went through all the extraordinary paperwork. And they interviewed me. And the next step was, they wanted to have a sit down conference with my wife, Kim Hoang. It was at my house, and I was there. And one of the questions they asked her was, "You do know that, if he's a law enforcement officer, that he could walk out the door one morning and be killed and never come back."

And I thought, "This is the end of my application." But her response was, "I met him in the middle of a war. Everyday he walked out, I knew he might not come back. This is no different." She could have sunk that whole boat then. But she didn't.

So I got accepted for the Sheriff's Department Academy, which was out at Atascocita. There were two major instructors there, and one of them was Carl Loker, who was an ex-Marine drill sergeant. He was about my size and he was a hardass, you could tell. He was up in everybody's faces real quick, laying down the law and everything.

It was supposed to be sort of set up kind of like Army basic training or boot camp or whatever. It's kind of like the military. But it was like Army basic training lite.

So at one point, we were going to have our hand-to-hand, close combat training. And we were all in this circle and Carl Loker was in the middle of the circle holding court. And he said, "I want to know who the man is out there who thinks he can take my ass." And nobody raised their hand. So he was going to pick someone. So he's walking around the circle, and he points at me.

And I said, "Sergeant, you don't want to pick me." And he said, "Oh now I *really* want to pick you!" So we get out there, and we're going at it, and it took me about 40 seconds to lay him out on the ground. And he's sitting there looking at me like, "What the hell just happened?"

So he reaches up his hand, and I pull him up, and he pulls me close and says, "What branch of the service were you in?" And I said, "Army, Sergeant." And he said, "Where did you learn those moves? Where does that come from?" And I said, "Aikido, Sergeant." And he said, "I've heard of it. It works." (Laughter)

And after the Academy was over, after the graduation, I got called into the office, and Carl Loker and the other instructor were there. And they said, "Look, we don't report this, we don't post it. But we wanted you to know that you were number one in this Academy."

So, yeah, that was my entrance to the Harris County Sheriff's Department.

First Day in the Jail

At the Harris County Sheriff's Department -- and I think almost every other sheriff's department in the world -- they do not assign people from the Academy to the streets. That's what police departments do. The Sheriff's Departments put people in the jail system. And what they kind of explained to me was, "You will be in the jail system for one, two, three years, or forever, depending on the needs of the Sheriff's Department." Which translates to, they're assessing you all this time.

The first day I ever showed up for duty as a fully-sworn deputy, I was assigned to the psychiatric ward, or floor, of the Harris County downtown jail. And I got there and there was nobody, no other deputy there. Although one deputy came in, as I was there for about ten or fifteen minutes, trying to figure out -- I don't know what I'm doing. And he said, "The deputy who was going to be here to supervise you today is out ill," or whatever. "So good luck." (Laughter)

So I'm sitting there, and I've got a huge notebook that is there about procedures and whatnot for that particular floor. And I'm kind of flipping through that. Then all of a sudden I feel a presence next to me. And I turn around and look. And there's this six foot, four or five inch, black inmate standing next to me, in his jail clothes.

And I said, "What are you doing here?" And he said, "Hey boss, I'm a trustee up here. I'm here to help you out." And I said, "Okay, all right. So, show me where your cell is." So he takes me back to his cell, and I said "Step in there." And he said, "But boss, I'm on your side." I said, "We'll find that out later." So I put him in there and I lock the cell.

Oh, and in those days, we had these giant, like -- imagine the old key chains with the giant keys on them, for the cells -- that's what we had in those days! So I locked him in his cell, and he went along with that fine, which I thought, "That speaks okay of him." But I had no idea whether he was a good guy or a bad guy or whether he was gonna slit my throat or whatever.

I made a call or two, but I couldn't get anybody who would answer my question. So I'm sitting there, and I thought, "Okay. One of the things I've figured out from all this is, I've got to make rounds and make sure that everybody is okay and no-body's committed suicide and all that stuff." So I start walking through the psychiatric section, and some of these people are yelling and screaming at me, and some are saying "Hey, boss!" And of course, you don't know anything, right?

So I get to this one cell, and somebody's throwing feces and urine out at me. And I stopped and went back and said, "Step back to the back of the cell." And he did. And I said, "Listen. I've only got two uniforms. If you fuck this uniform up, I'm coming in there, and it ain't gonna be pretty." And he says, "Okay, boss! Okay, boss!" So he stands back.

And there's another inmate, like, two cells down, that is yelling, "Hey, boss, if you need any help with anybody, you just let me out, and I'll back you up!" (Laughter) This is how crazy it was.

So I finally get a call back from somebody in the system that says, "Yeah, he" -- the big black guy -- "yes, he's a good guy. He's a trustee." I said, "Okay." So I go and let the trustee out, and I'm talking to him. And he's a great guy. He's wonderful. We hit it off. He's telling me everything. He knows the drill. He knows what I need to, who I need to check on. He's basically training me. (Laughter)

And we're going along, and you know, somebody starts to throw some more, a bucket of feces at me, and the trustee is going, "Stop it! Stop it! This guy will kill you!" (Laughter) And they went, "Oh! Okay!" (Laughter)

So that was my whole day. But by the time I was done with that eight-hour shift, I learned more about the population of people that I was gonna be dealing with in jail, in the worst possible way, than I had learned in the Sheriff's Academy. But I made it through that day. And I was probably assigned to that section for a number of weeks -- I don't remember how long. But then I was assigned to the Capital Litigation section.

Charles Harrelson

In the Capital Litigation section, there were two major, at least, in my mind, two major prisoners: Markum Duff-Smith, who was -- nicest guy in the world you'd ever want to meet -- convicted of, and sentenced to death for, killing his sister and her husband and either one or two infant children, I don't remember if it was one or two. Professional guy. He'd done it for the insurance. And then there was also Charles Harrelson, Woody Harrelson's father. And they were on my floor, and they were next door neighbors.

And Harrelson -- who of course had been convicted for the assassination of Judge Wood, out of San Antonio, a federal judge -- went on a hunger strike. And somebody warned me -- the deputy that had been in charge of him before I was on duty that day had said, "Harrelson's on a hunger strike. He's been on a hunger strike for two days. And we're holding him for the FBI, so we've got to treat him with kid gloves." And I said, "Okay." And it was big news in the Houston Chronicle or the Post -- Harrelson's on a hunger strike.

So I'm making my little rounds, and I get to his cell and ask how he's doing, and he says, "Don't talk to me, I'm on a hunger strike." I said, "Oh! Okay. So I don't need to order you anything for breakfast? What about lunch?" And he said, "Nope, I'm not eating anymore, I'm on a hunger strike."

So I finish my rounds and get back to my desk, and I'm thinking, "This guy's full of shit. This is all gamesmanship." So I started asking around a little bit, and one of the other prisoners said, "You know, boss, Duff-Smith is sharing his food with Harrelson." And I said, "Really? Okay, that's good to know." Because everybody's always looking for an angle, you know, wanting to catch a little, you know, "I did you a favor" kind of thing.

So I walked into Harrelson's cell, put him up against the wall, cuffed him, and said, "I'm moving you to another cell." And he said, "You can't do that!" And I said, "Yeah, I can do anything I want to do. You're on a hunger strike. My job is to protect the prisoners up here. I am not going to allow you to die by hunger-strike suicide in front of the other prisoners; it could damage them at some psychic level. So I'm going to put you at the end of the hallway."

And he starts raising Cain, saying I can't do that. But I put him down in this cell, at the very end of this hallway. And he's going batshit crazy, he's yelling and screaming, "I want to talk

to your supervisor! I want to talk to the FBI!" I said, "I'll pass
that along."

So I call my supervisor, I tell him what's going on. And
(laughter) he says, "Jesus, what are you doing?!" And I said,
"You know, this is a scam. I'm not gonna put up with it." And
he said, "Well, yeah, but this is the FBI's prisoner." I said, "I understand that. But Duff-Smith is feeding him, and I don't think
this is right." And he said, "I hear you. I think I agree with you.
But I've got to report this to the FBI." And I said, "Do whatever
you need to do."

So the next thing I know, the FBI shows up on my floor.
And they said, "What do you think you're doing?! You can't
do this, this is our prisoner, and he's on a hunger strike, and
you're moving him into isolation." So I said, "Okay, well here's
the deal. You go rent a hotel room. We're holding him for you --
he's not our prisoner. You go sit on him in a hotel room." And
they said, "We can't do that, that's why we've got him in the
Harris County jail."

And I said, "Okay. Well, if he's in the Harris County jail, he's
under the Harris County jail rules. And my sense of this is, he's
not on any kind of hunger strike. He's playing you. He's playing a game. And if you want to take him out, I'll sign him out.
Otherwise, you give me until 5:00 this afternoon, and if he's
not eating again, then I'll put him back where he was."

So by 4:00 that afternoon, Harrelson was begging for food.
(Laughter) And so I sent somebody back there with food, and
he was chowing down, and his hunger strike was over.

Humble Substation

I got reassigned to the Humble Substation, which was basically
at Highway 59 and FM 1960. It was a relatively small substation, but it was our farthest north substation.

So I showed up there to start working the booking desk. And the way this station was set up was, it had maybe four, maybe five, cells. Basically it was a holding spot, and it would have other units or transport vehicles take people down to the downtown jail from there. So it basically was just a small little jail, but a very, very busy one.

So I showed up and the main desk deputy was this enormous guy. He was a thumper -- boom, with his fist, on top of people's heads, if they fucked up. His hand was as big as a horse's hoof. Just boom. Nobody messed with him.

But I was the little guy. And he said, "I don't think you're gonna last here a week. We've got mean, rough people here." I said, "Maybe *si*, maybe no. Who knows?"

And I cannot even count over those months the number of fights that we got into, and how many fights that I pulled people off of big guy. Because big guy had a way of picking these people up and yanking them over the desk onto the floor behind, right? And then he was trapped with them. No, no, no. I went over the desk, out into the melee.

And it got to be that I had the reputation out there of, "He's not gonna let anybody fuck with him." But that wasn't what I was trying to do, I was just trying to protect myself and keep these prisoners arrested and not harmed too bad. And the fights were too numerous to name. And I mean, these were people who were drunk, these were people who were felons that were gonna be going back to prison, and this little bitty jail was their opportunity to try to escape. And on my watch, and on big guy's watch, nobody ever got free.

So, a few weeks after I started out there, the big guy said, "I might just want to keep you here forever." But other people apparently were looking at me, too.

Collecting Weapons at Atascocita

When I was working the jail system, sometimes I worked the Atascocita jail or facility, which is more like a small prison. It's kind of like Del Valle in Travis County.

On the first day I got assigned there -- there was this section of the facility that I was in, and I was in this little round, center thing, and all around it circularly there were cells. And then outside the cells was the day area where people could come out of their cell during the course of the day.

So I'm working this that first day, or maybe it was my second day. But one of the prisoners came up to me and said, "Hey Boss, I really need to call my lawyer." And in my little round space, I had a telephone. And I said, "Well, look, nothing's for free. You bring me some kind of weapon, and you can make your telephone call." So within about three minutes, he brings me back a weapon. And I put it on my little desk and gave him five minutes on the phone.

Then all of a sudden, the word had gotten around, right? So somebody else comes and another weapon came in. And then all of a sudden there was this whole damn line of, like, I don't know, 40, 50, 60 people standing in line, bringing weapons. (Laughter) I got about maybe 20 calls into all of that, and I had this whole pile of knives, shivs, screwdrivers, home-made blades, and one really old .32 caliber handgun. I've got this whole pile of weapons! And at a certain point, I just stopped everything and told everyone to go back to their cells.

But it was such a spectacular haul that it did not escape the Sheriff's Department. I had called my supervisor and said, "Look, here's what happened." And he said, "This is insane!" So they sent in a whole team to scour that entire section for weapons.

So that was one of the little things -- and of course, all the prisoners were giving me all these reindeer games. And I wasn't even paying attention to their reindeer games. I was just pay-ing attention to, "Wow, I'm getting a lot of damn weapons off my floor that could come at me at some point," right?

So apparently that made some impression on the Sheriff's Department as well. Which wasn't intended -- it was just me doing what I want to do.

Prisoner Escape at Ben Taub Hospital

Ben Taub Hospital was kind of like Brackenridge here in Austin -- it was a public hospital. It was busy, busy. A big trauma cen-ter in Houston.

So I was assigned for, I don't know, two or three or four weeks, there. And this was where prisoners that had been shot, or shot up, or injured, or whatever, were taken. The charity hospital.

So I had this prisoner. He was a holy mess. He was shot all to hell. He had broken bones, he had a jaw half shot off, and so on. And he was my charge on my shift. And my shift was a morning shift.

So I finished up my shift one day. And during the course of that night, while I was home, the prisoner somehow gained control over the deputy that was watching him at night. Clunked the hell out of the deputy, or something. And right before early morning, the prisoner got up and made his way out of the hospital.

So I'm driving to Ben Taub Hospital that morning. I park in the parking lot, and all of a sudden, I see this guy, my prisoner, walking through the parking lot. (Laughter) He was just all -- he still had stuff on -- you know, like, splints and casts. Just hob-bling through the parking lot like Quasi Modo.

And I thought, "This is interesting. This is my guy, and he's making a run for it." So I get out of my car -- I wasn't in a patrol car, I was in my personal car. I get out of my car and I'm fol-

lowing along behind him for a couple of minutes. And finally
I say, "Hey." I said his name. I don't remember what the name
was now. I said, "Do you want me to just finish you off now, or
do you want to go back into the hospital?" And he said, "I just
needed to get a breath of fresh air." And I said, "Yeah, okay."

So we're going back inside. I put him in handcuffs and
march him back into the hospital. The deputy -- nobody even
knew in the hospital that he was gone. The deputy was
knocked cold senseless, but not killed, which was a good thing.
So I march this guy back in through the emergency room, and
they're going, "What the hell is going on here?!" (Laughter) So
anybody that ever says that working in the jail system is never
fraught with strange situations has never worked in a jail system.

So yeah, put him back in his bed. The deputy had a slight
concussion from whatever the guy did to him.

But it was one of those really fortuitous things that went on
to my record -- here's the guy who caught him before he got
away. (Laughter) And it was like, I'll take it! (Laughter) But it was
pure serendipity.

First Night on Patrol

At some point, a few months in, the Sheriff's Department, in
their, whatever -- whoever decides all these things and picks
people to move to patrol -- all of a sudden I was notified that I
was going to be moved into patrol. And I was gonna be in District 2.

District 2 was generally my district for all the years that I
was in the Sheriff's Department. It was a great district. Maybe
everybody thinks their district is a great district. But also, because of some of the things that happened along the way, I was
pulled into other districts sometimes. At that time, the Harris
County Sheriff's Department had four, I think, districts. Maybe

five. But at least four. District 2 was from downtown Houston all the way out I-45 to FM 1960, then over all the way to Highway 59 and a little bit beyond to Atoscacita and Lake Houston, out in that direction, and then back up 59 all the way to downtown, into the fourth and fifth wards of downtown Houston. So, I mean, it was an enormous district. And Dimmitt Johnson and I ultimately partnered up in that district.

But the first night I was on patrol, I was put with a deputy who had been in the Sheriff's Department a few years at that time named Monte Heron. And we're patrolling, we're answering calls, and all of a sudden there's a chase going on from, I don't know, Huntsville or Conroe or somewhere like that, chasing a bad guy towards Houston.

So we're on I-45, and bad guy flies past us, so we get in on the chase. Of course, I'm riding shotgun; he's the driver. And I'm already kind of squinky about this guy, because he talks like he's on drugs or something, I don't know. You know, he says, "We're gonna catch him. We're gonna kill him. We're gonna skin him." (Laughter)

So bad guy is coming down I-45, and then he jumps off I-45 and shoots over to Highway 59. And he starts heading back north again. And we're chasing behind him. And all of a sudden he jumps off the highway, turns around, comes back and gets on the highway the wrong way, and starts heading toward us, going the wrong way! And we're going the right way, and every time we go over one of these overpasses, with limited view, I'm thinking, "We're dead. We're going to slam into him head on."

And I'm saying -- and I'm nobody, I'm just a brand new guy, right? And I'm saying, "You know, I don't think this is how it's supposed to be. I don't think we're supposed to be doing this." And Monte Heron said, "Forget everything you ever learned. This is the way it is. Get used to it."

So anyway, the bad guy jumps off of 59 at, like, Jensen Drive, or somewhere like that, and we chase him down and catch him. And in that big chase, there were, like, six different accidents, but we never hit anything. And I thought Monte Heron was either a genius or the craziest guy I'd ever met.

So that was the first arrest I ever made, and my first night on patrol. And somehow I survived it.

Time for a New Flashlight

This was probably still in my first week of being on patrol. We got a call -- there was this grungy beer joint out north, on Hardy Road. And there was a shooting. It wasn't a fatality, but somebody opened fire in the beer joint, and we got a call.

I don't remember -- I think I was still with a training partner, but I don't remember who it was now. So we get out there and everybody at the beer joint said that the shooter had fled across the street into the woods. And that was a heavily wooded area out there.

So we've got a boatload of units that show up for this thing. And we're moving through the woods looking for the shooter.

There was an officer nearby me. We were about, like, eight feet, ten feet apart. And I've got my flashlight out, everybody's got their flashlights out. And I've got my flashlight shining ahead of me, and this guy walks up next to me, the other deputy, that was experienced, and he says, "You can't see shit with that flashlight. It's no good." And he flipped his flashlight on, and there was the shooter, forty feet away, aiming at me with a rifle.

And we took him down, arrested him, took him to jail. And I thought, "Okay, lesson learned. I do not have the right flashlight for this job." (Laughter) So the first thing I did after that was to go get the highest beam/tech flashlight in existence.

A Sniper at NASA

Some of these stories are a little out of sequence. And also, I will mention that, in between all of these stories are the usual stories of domestic disputes, assaults, chasing down people who are running from the cops, some traffic stops. I'm not really going into all of those kinds of stories.

But this particular story was kind of interesting. It was when George Bush, Sr. -- George H. W. Bush -- was Vice President. He was going to be in Houston and also out at NASA, doing something at NASA. And I was put on a joint task force between the Sheriff's Department and the Secret Service.

So I was out at NASA, and I was in charge of a particular building -- to clear the building, check it out, make sure no bad guys were there. So I'm starting to check the building out, and I'm walking up the stairs in this -- I think it was, like, a four-story building. And I get up towards the second floor, and all of a sudden I see this guy in blue jeans with a sniper rifle, or M-16 like rifle, coming down the stairs.

I draw down on him and start hollering at him, "Drop the weapon! Drop the weapon! Sheriff's Department!" and so on. And he's not doing it fast enough. And I said, "I mean NOW!" And he holds everything up above his head and says, "I'm gonna put the weapon down. I'm Secret Service. Let me put the weapon down."

So he puts the weapon down. And I say, "Let me see some I.D." And he pulls out something, but I can't see it because we're probably 12 feet away from each other. And I say, "Take one step at a time. Do not touch that weapon. Pull your jacket open so I can see if you have any other weapons." He had another weapon. I said, "Put it down."

So he makes his way down the stairs, and when he's about four steps away from me, I said, "Stop." And sure enough, he was a Secret Service sniper. But nobody -- the communications were so bad between the two agencies -- nobody had told me there was gonna be a sniper in *my building*.

And at the end, once we got all straight away, he said, "I just want to thank you for not shooting me dead." (Laughter) And I said, "Well, I'm glad I didn't have to." (Laughter)

A Bad Guy Heading to my House

Also when Bush was in town -- after the NASA incident, I was back on patrol. I was sent to a call about somebody threatening to kill the Vice President.

So I make this call. And the guy made it very clear to me when I arrested him that, "Nothing will stop me from doing this. You won't stop me, nobody will stop me." And I said, "Well, we'll see about that."

So I took him to the Harris County jail downtown to book him -- he also had an outstanding warrant. And I'm booking him in, and one of the booking sergeants says, "We can't book him. You have to turn him over to the Secret Service. And when they're done with him, they will ship him back to us, and we will process him on the outstanding warrant." So I turn him over to the Secret Service and go on about my business.

A couple of weeks later, I'm just doing what I do at home. I lived on a cul-de-sac in North Harris County, out pretty close to where the airport is now -- it wasn't there then. And there was a long road from the end of the cul-de-sac. And on this day, my kids and the neighbor kids are all out in the front of my house playing basketball.

So I'm driving away -- I'm not on duty, I'm going to the store or something. And I'm driving down this long road. And it was, like, late May. It's pretty warm, hot outside. And I see this guy walking down the street, toward the cul-de-sac. And he's wearing a black trench coat. And as I drive past him, I'm thinking, "What's wrong with this picture?" And I thought, "There's something familiar about this guy." He was tall, he was lanky, he had a particular gait. And I thought, "Wait a minute. Could this be that guy, the one who threatened Bush?"

So I turn around, come up behind him, get out of the car, put him down on the ground. And underneath his trench coat, on one side, was a sawed-off 12-gauge shotgun. And on his other hip he had a 1911 Colt .45. And in one pocket, he had a pocketful of shotgun shells. And in another pocket, he had four or five magazines for the .45.

So I arrested him again. Even though I was in plain clothes, I had a gun and handcuffs. I always had cuffs and a gun. But I didn't have communication. We didn't have cell phones in those days. So a car came by, and I stopped them -- it was another neighbor that I kind of knew -- and told them to call HPD -- because this was actually in HPD territory -- and tell them that an officer needs assistance and give them the address. So it didn't take three minutes for an HPD unit to get there.

So they transported him. And -- there aren't many times in my life when I have been really, really angry, but this was one of those times. I went back to the house and called the jail and said, "What the hell happened?!" And they said, "We don't know. Apparently the Secret Service held him for a few days and then just cut him loose. They didn't send him back to us."

And I said, "I want to know the contact for the Secret Service." So he gave me the name and the number, and I called and I railed and I railed. And they were all apologetic and everything. And the end of that was, they said, "Well, it sounds like all's well that ends well!" And I said, "Fuck you."

Saving a Kidnapping Victim

Sometimes I was on patrol alone in marked cars. But one of the things I really loved was, one of the deputies that I had worked with early on, on patrol, named Dimmitt Johnson. He was a

World War II veteran and he'd been with the Sheriff's Department for over 20 years. And he had one of the, probably the only, one or two, unmarked vehicles in District 2. And District 2 was probably right up there with maybe one other district in terms of being the most horrible, deadly, crazy, criminal area of Houston. So we would work together, and we loved working the unmarked car business because we could creep up on a lot of stuff.

So one night we were on patrol, and there was a call that went out about a kidnapping of a female from a bar. So we were cruising in that general vicinity and identified the suspect vehicle. So we come up, hit the lights, bump the siren, and the car stops and everything.

We started getting out. I'm riding shotgun that night. And Dimmitt's calling in the stop. And I know there's weapons involved already, so I've got my weapon out. And I get out of the car. I've got the door open, and I'm standing behind the door, looking over the door. And on the speakers, I say, "Put your hands outside the windows! Open the door slowly! Exit the vehicle!" And so on. You know, all the usual stuff.

And the door opens on the passenger side, not the driver's side. The driver is probably thinking about bolting, right? But the passenger starts getting out of the car, and as he's coming out of the car, I see a pistol in his hand. And I'm on him. I'm hollering, "Drop the pistol! Drop the pistol! You're dead if you don't!" And he drops it.

So I pull him out, we pull the other guy out, get them both arrested. Free the kidnap victim. Put the bad guys in jail. And that was one of the times -- there were a number of times -- but that was one of the times that, clearly, clearly -- because he had the weapon in his hand as he was coming out of the car -- I could have shot him. But I didn't. And those are always the close calls.

The Kidnapper Tries to Rob the Pharmacy

About a year later, after the kidnapping incident, my father had called me to come take care of some kind of business at the pharmacy one night when he was unavailable or ill or whatever. Maybe I had to make a deposit for the pharmacy or something. And to see how everything was going.

So I'm there. And it was a huge pharmacy, and the office was on the second floor and overlooked the entire pharmacy. And all of a sudden, I'm hearing a commotion and getting a call on the telephone upstairs. It's a hysterical clerk saying, "He's trying to rob us! He's gonna kill us!"

I stand up and look through the window -- and I'm in plain clothes that night, I'm not working, I'm not on duty, but of course I have my gun and handcuffs with me -- and I look down and I see this guy with a pistol pointed at the pharmacist from a few feet away. And I could tell that he was trying to rob the pharmacy.

So I go tearing down the stairs, I go running over, I tackle the bastard. And we're fighting in the aisles of the pharmacy. And he's got a pistol, and I'm trying to keep it away from me. So I pull my pistol, which at that time was my little trusty backup pistol, and get it to his head, and get him under arrest. And I turn him over and look at him in the light. And it is *that same guy* who I arrested, who came out of the passenger side of the car with a gun that night a year before. So I put him under arrest and called HPD and they hauled him off to jail.

And the funny thing about that was, there were some people who worked in the pharmacy that didn't even know that I was with the Sheriff's Department! (Laughter) And they were just stunned! But I wasn't gonna let bad guy have anything to do with doing anything bad in that store that night. And this time, he went off for twenty or thirty years.

Deputy Constable Stops a Train

This is kind of an oddball little story. I got a call one night -- I was in a marked patrol car that night, just me -- and it was a train-motorcycle accident. There were train tracks that ran along Hardy Road. Hardy Road was a major artery in my district. So I was, like, two minutes away, and I took the call. So, you know, "4299, *en route*," and so on.

And I got to the scene of the event, and it was wild and woolly when I got there. The train had stopped mostly, but was just barely rolling. There was a deputy constable up on the train with his gun to the head of the engineer, yelling at him, "Stop it! Stop it! I'm gonna put a bullet in your head!"

And I'm looking at this, and I'm thinking, "What the hell?!" So the train's coming to a stop. And I said, "Constable, come down here!" And he says, "No, I'm putting this guy under arrest!" And I said, "Not yet. Come down here. And put your weapon away."

So he comes down off the train. And I'm trying to find out what in the hell's going on here, right? And it turns out that the deputy constable was leading a funeral procession, and he got up on the train tracks, and the train was down the tracks some ways, maybe a half a mile or so, and he puts his motorcycle on the tracks, he's sitting on the motorcycle, and he's holding his hand up, telling the train to stop.

Anybody knows that when a train's going full blast, it takes it a mile or more to stop. But no, he's sitting there on his motorcycle, throwing his hand up. And of course, the train puts the brakes on way back when, and it's just, like, screeching along. And he finally jumps off his motorcycle, it runs over his motorcycle, and he's on the side of the tracks. He runs to the train, jumps up and tries to to put the engineer under arrest for attempted murder or something.

So it's a total mess, right? And I said, "Look, here's the deal. You're not putting anybody under arrest here. If anybody gets arrested, it's gonna be you. And I'm going to be the one arresting you." And he said, "For what?" And I said, "Oh, I can think of a half a dozen things, but the top of the list is pure stupidity." (Laughter)

So I relieve him of his weapon and call my supervisor. And this is a dicey deal because it's interagency stuff. So I call my supervisor and told him what was going on. And he said, "Okay, I'm gonna get in touch with the constable in that precinct and I'm gonna bring him. Don't arrest him yet."

So they get there, after 10 minutes or so. And the constable is chewing out the deputy constable, saying, you know, "What the hell were you thinking?" As anybody would say. And the constable and my supervisor talked for a minute, and my supervisor came over to me and said, "Look, how about this? I talked to the constable. Rather than putting the deputy constable under arrest, would it be okay with you, Ben, if he was just fired?" And I said, "Okay. Nobody's been killed here. I can live with that."

So that was the resolution of that little mediation on the railroad tracks.

Naked Guy with a Sword

The north side of Houston, in my district, was mostly comprised of some pretty low rent, bad areas. I loved it, because there was always action. There's nothing worse than just sitting and waiting. But working the night shift, I don't remember ever sitting and waiting for anything longer than about three or four or five minutes. We would make anywhere between 10 and 15, or 18, calls every night. So it was a busy, busy place.

So one night, Dimmitt and I were together. We were in an unmarked car. And we're patrolling, and we get a call about somebody trying to kill people with a sword on the north side of Houston. We were only about three or four minutes away from there, so we took the call.

We get there, and another unit was there. And there's this naked guy in the middle of the street with a huge sword, like an enormous -- I don't remember. It was not a samurai sword. It was like a medieval sword! And he's yelling and screaming and jumping and dancing.

So I get out of the car and tell him to put the sword down. And he's hollering, you know, the usual stuff -- "Fuck you! Come and get me! I'll kill you!" That kind of stuff.

And there was another marked unit that had made the scene. So I had the marked unit get on one side of him, and our car was on the other side of him. And I said, "Okay, start moving forward." And we just both moved, the two cars forward until we had him pinned. He could have gone the other two directions, but he was so screwed up, he didn't realize it. So we just pulled the two cars together until we had him pinned between the two cars. (Laughter)

I took the sword away from him. He was high on PCP. And Dimmitt and I arrested him and hauled him off to jail. And he's in the backseat throwing tantrums and fits and everything. And Dimmitt turned around and said, "If you don't shut up, I'm gonna take your sword and I'm gonna cut your head off." And the guy shut up. (Laughter)

Extra Job at Bank on FM 1960

Working as a deputy sheriff, the only way you could really make it financially, working for county wages, was to be able to get extra jobs. So I had a number of extra jobs along the way. But this one was particularly sad.

I got a call from a deputy -- there was a bank on FM 1960, and it was a security job at the bank. And he said, "Hey, can you switch days with me? I can't do it tomorrow because I have a family thing." And I said, "Sure." So we switched days.

So the next day, he went to work there on what should have been my day. And on that day, a bank robber came walking into the bank, and the first thing he did was to shoot this deputy dead. And then he robbed the bank.

It should have been me. It was my day to work the bank. And I've never quite gotten over that.

A Disgusting Doughnut

Cops are known for wanting doughnuts. But I have to tell you, I actually enjoyed doughnuts a lot! (Laughter)

So I decided to stop by -- I think it was a Shipley's -- on my way in to work one day. And I grabbed two doughnuts and a cup of coffee.

So I'm driving along and eating these doughnuts, and all of a sudden I bite into something that makes me start to gag. And it turns out that somebody at the doughnut shop had put a bunch of -- I don't know if it was facial hair or pubic hair -- into the doughnuts. But whatever it was, it was enough to make me, of course, gag, and also stop along the side of the road and throw up.

So that put me off of doughnuts for a while. Because they knew that cops came in to get doughnuts, right? And I went to investigate who the hell did it, and they said, "Oh, yeah, he's already gone. He was an ex-con."

So, yeah, that's some of the little nitty-natty stuff you had to deal with as a cop sometimes.

Hostage Negotiation in a Trailer Park

On regular patrol, I had done what amounted to hostage negotiations just in my regular job. I became known, I became the point person for it. And then the supervisor of the district put together a special team for any kind of crisis situation, and I was on that team as the hostage negotiator.

And this night in particular had been a long night on patrol. I was alone, not with Dimmitt. I had gone to work around 9:30 p.m. and this call came in around 1 a.m. for a domestic disturbance that was apparently rapidly escalating. And the information I got was -- a unit had just arrived and I'm getting reports from that unit -- it was a trailer park -- and there was a guy in a trailer and he's threatening to kill the wife and the baby.

So I pull up about two or three minutes later. And I told the unit that had gotten there first, "Back away a little bit. Don't go doing anything cowboy."

By this time, the supervisor was in on the game. He said he was sending various units, "Where do you want them?" I said, "I want three units in front, I want two units not directly in back, but I want deputies back two or three rows watching to make sure that nobody comes crawling out of the house backwards. And I want somebody off to the side."

So I start talking to the guy and asking him, you know, what's going on. And he's yelling and screaming, "I'm gonna kill them if you don't back out of here!"

I said, "Well, you know, nobody needs to die. Especially your wife and, I'm guessing, a child in there. Oh, by the way, how old's the child?" Got him to start talking about the child a little bit. And starting to talk about what's going on, "How'd the bitch mess you up tonight?" you know, all that stuff. And he's still playing it really coy, but he's starting to talk a little bit.

And there's one particular deputy that I knew -- I had known him for a few years, I mean, even before I was in the Sheriff's Department. And I always thought he was kind of a little bit squirrelly, and a real gun nut. But he wanted to know where he was supposed to be, and I said, "Go back behind the trailer. Set yourself up. Just make sure he doesn't come out that way."

So then the guy inside the trailer tells me, "If you don't back off and get everybody out of here, I'm gonna blow both their heads off." And I said, "Well, what have you got to blow their heads off with?" And he said, "I've got a 12 gauge shotgun." I said, "Well that'll do it. You know, you've convinced me. Let me back everybody off." So I backed everybody off except for me.

And I was kind of positioned behind this tree stump. I had some cover there. And I said, "Look, here's the deal. How about -- I've got everybody backed off, I've done everything you needed, and given you everything you need. You probably need, what, a cigarette or something?" He said, "Yeah, a cigarette and a beer." I said, "Okay, let me see if I can get that for you."

So I bummed some cigarettes off somebody, and somebody brought a beer. And I said, "Okay, I'm coming up to the door." He says, "Not armed!" I said, "Hey, look out. You can see me. I'm standing here by this tree stump. I'm gonna put my gear on the tree stump, and I'm just gonna bring you cigarettes and a beer."

So I take off my utility belt. Of course, I've got my trusty little .38 in my back pocket, and I had my handcuffs, too.

So I'm holding the beer and the cigarettes, and I said, "Here, let me come up and talk to you. And mainly -- I'm gonna give you this -- but I want to be able to look at mama and baby, to make sure that they're okay. If that's okay with you." He said, "I ain't hurt them, I ain't hurt them." I said, "Okay, good. As long as that doesn't happen, everything's good, and I can help you get out of here."

So I walk up very slowly. I get up there, and he lets me stick my head in. The minute I stick my head in, I hand him a cigarette and a beer, and I jump him. I put him in handcuffs. I put him in custody. Bring the troops in to check on mama and baby.

And so then I go out to make sure where everybody is outside, that I put on perimeters. And that one particular deputy, the squirrelly one, was, like, four aisles down, curled up hiding under a trailer, scared out of his fucking mind. And I had to tell my supervisor about that. He wasn't where he was supposed to be, and he was hiding. That wasn't a good thing.

But yeah. Arrested papa. Got mama and baby out. Supervisor said, "You know, this is why I've got you where you are. Wrap it up." He didn't even come out.

That was kind of what hostage and crisis negotiation was all about, in terms of -- it wasn't anything like the movies. They were these little things -- I mean, these dramatic, big things, but were tiny things. And that was just one of a number.

Terms of Endearment

When I was working with the Sheriff's Department, I also was able to do extra jobs. And actually, those extra jobs were pretty lucrative.

So I got a call one day wanting to know if I would sit on this house for about, I don't know, two or three weeks. They were filming *Terms of Endearment* there. I think it was over in River Oaks.

So my job was to, you know, be there at night, to make sure that nobody broke in and started stealing equipment and doing all that other kind of stuff. Just making sure the house was safe. So it was kind of a really plum job.

I would get there at night around 8 p.m. or so and I'd spend all night there until the next morning. When people started showing up, then I would leave. So there really wasn't anything for me to do all night. But the interesting thing about it to me was I spent a lot of time getting to know the family that lived there, from, you know, just walking around, looking at the pictures and books and stuff. I'd poke through all this stuff that was just out. I really kind of got to know the family, even though I never met them.

So there wasn't anything that happened during the course of the time that I was there. I didn't have to arrest anybody. Nobody tried to break in. It was just another kind of milk run extra job. And I got paid well for it.

So a number of months later, I got a call from David Seltzer, the screenwriter that I worked with on *Green Eyes*. He called me up one day, kind of out of the blue, and he said, "So, it looks like *Terms of Endearment* is gonna be a huge hit! How did it go?"

And I said, "What do you mean?" And he said, "Well, you were there." And I said, "Well, sort of. I'm not quite getting where you're coming from."

And he said, "I had talked to the director a year ago about hiring you to work on the movie -- on the production end of the movie." And I said, "Well, I never got the call. But, I was there."

And he said, "Now I don't understand." And I said, "I was hired to guard the house that they were shooting at in River Oaks."

So I was supposed to have worked on the movie in a production capacity, and whatever, the wires got crossed. But I wound up being there anyway as security! (Laughter) And you know, it's kind of a shame, because that could have been a different arc, because that movie won something like five Academy Awards. But I never had any input on anything from a movie standpoint. My job was just some local cop that was providing night security at the location.

Butcher Knife Murder

This was on a Saturday night. Friday nights and Saturday nights were always pretty wild and woolly. We got a call, and the call was over in Northeast Houston. And the call was, "there's somebody lying on our front porch."

Dimmitt and I were together that night. I remember that clearly. So we pull up to the scene, we go to the front porch. And sure enough, there's an old man, 60-something years old, on the front porch of these people's little house. And this was not a good side of town, right? There were some Hispanics that lived in the house, and they were all hysterical. They didn't know what to do. They were a sweet little family.

The guy was dead. And he had a chest wound. So Dimmitt's trying to talk to the family, and I'm out there looking at the body. And I see a blood trail and start following it. I get about four houses down, and I see the blood trail leading up to the door of this house.

So I call for Dimmitt and he comes over. And I holler out to the house and ask whoever's in there to come to the door. And this old woman comes to the door, she's in her 60's.

And I said, "I need to talk to you." And I'm, like, standing behind a tree, because I don't know what's going on. She steps out and she says, "What?"

I said, "Where's your husband?"

"I don't have a husband."

"Okay, well, do you live with anybody?"

"I did," she said.

I said, "Okay. It looks like he's dead." And she said, "Good." And I said, "Will you please step out?" And she said, "I don't think I should." And I said, "You're not gonna have a choice."

So she steps out, and she's got this 12-inch butcher knife in her hand that's bloody. And I said, "You need to put the butcher knife down." And she says, "He deserved it."

I said, "Tell me why." And then she starts going into all the abuse that he had given her all these years. And I said, "I hear you. I understand. But you need to put the butcher knife down on the porch and then walk out to me and we'll talk."

So she put the butcher knife down on the porch, she walked down the steps, and I took her into custody. I actually put her in handcuffs. I said, "I hate to do this to you, but this is just procedure."

And it turns out that, for years, he had been -- it wasn't so much sexual or physical abuse as it just was constant emotional abuse. But then as things unfolded more, it wasn't just his direction towards her, it was her direction towards him, too. They were both completely abusing each other emotionally.

And she said, "I'm sorry. It had to happen. He needed to be dead." And I said, "Well, you accomplished that."

So we took her to jail. I don't even know what the ultimate resolution of that was. I never got called for the trial, so I think they cut a deal or something. So I don't know what ever happened to her.

Contempt of Court

I had apparently been subpoenaed as a cop to go testify in a criminal felony case. However, word never got down to me that I had been subpoenaed.

So one morning, I get a call from a supervisor saying, "You've got to get to the courthouse. The judge is infuriated. You're supposed to be testifying at trial!"

And this was, like, around 9:30 or something in the morning. It woke me up, because I'd been working all night, right?

But at any rate, I woke up and said, "What? No! I don't have any, I didn't get any notice of this." He said, "Get your ass down there."

So I suited up -- you know, got in my uniform. And I got down to the courthouse around 10:15 in the morning. Maybe a little later than that because I was out in far north Houston, and the courthouse was downtown.

And I get there and I walk into the courtroom, and the judge -- a female judge -- she just went ballistic on me. The minute I walk through the door, she's yelling at me. Calls me up to the bench and says, "You think you're above responding to a subpoena?! You were supposed to be here this morning by 9:00, and you weren't here! I'm holding you in contempt of this court!"

She didn't ask me why. She didn't ask me anything. And I said, "Okay."

She said, "Bailiff, take this deputy into custody!" And the bailiff doesn't know what to do. I mean, he's another deputy sheriff, right? The bailiffs were all deputy sheriffs.

So he comes over and says, "Where do I take him?" And she said, "Take him to the jury room!"

So we walk into the jury room, and the deputy that escorted me in there said, "What do I do about your gun?" I said, "Do whatever you want to. Take it, leave it, I don't care." He said, "I'm not gonna take your gun! Let's just sit here."

So we just sat there. We sat there and we sat there, for about 45 minutes. And finally, she sent somebody to knock on the door. The bailiff went out for a little bit, then came back in and said, "Okay. You're released, but she wants to see you at the bench."

So I get to the bench and she says, "Deputy Cunningham, have you learned your lesson?!" And I said, "Yes, Your Honor, I think so." And she said, "All right, then, let this trial proceed."

So that was when I was taken into custody. I'm guessing when the bailiff went out, he told the judge that I'd never gotten the subpoena. But I don't know that, I didn't hear any of that. And she never asked me. All I know is, I was technically under arrest for about 45 minutes. (Laughter)

Officer Needs Assistance

I was on patrol one night, and I actually vividly remember where I was. I was on Aldine Mail Route Road in Houston, and I had just finished up a call. And I'm back in my patrol car, and all of a sudden, an "officer needs assistance" call comes in. And it sounded really urgent.

What had happened was -- this Hispanic woman had called the Sheriff's Department. It was a burglary call. And the officer who had responded to that was a female officer named Virgie. We didn't have many female officers in those days. I mean, maybe we, in my district, maybe we had two or three. But Virgie I knew really well. And she was really good. Oftentimes when we would have female subjects that we needed to search or something, we would call for a female officer. So I knew her really well.

And Virgie had responded to this burglary, and she got there, and the burglars were gone. But the HIspanic woman said, "I recognized them. I know where they live. They're three blocks away. I'll show you the house."

So the Hispanic woman shows her the house, and Virgie goes up and knocks on the door. And all of a sudden, the door flies open, and the bad guys drag her into the house. And there's five or six of them.

And the Hispanic woman gets on Virgie's radio in her unit, and she's calling in, saying, "They're killing her! They're killing her1" So that was what got us moving that night.

And one of the weirdest parts of all of this was that the dispatcher was Virgie's husband. He was taking the call. And, you know, he's playing it straight. But you can hear -- you can hear the stress.

So got the address of where the call was, and I was, like, three or four minutes away from it. And I said, "I'm on it." And units were popping in one after the other. Because, if there's an "officer needs assistance" call, everybody jumps in. This was not just the Sheriff's Department. We had DPS calling in, we had HPD calling in, we had constables calling in, we had game wardens calling in. (Laughter) Anybody in law enforcement who was out that night was on their way to the call.

I got to the call about thirty or forty seconds after the first deputy got there. And this deputy was a big old boy. I didn't know him. But he was about six foot four, and about three or four feet wide. And he goes barreling into the door. And one of the bad guys is standing there with a baseball bat, and he swings and hits this deputy straight in the head, and he comes flying out just as I'm coming to the door. I have to jump across him.

They have already ripped Virgie's uniform shirt off of her. She's struggling to keep them from getting her gun. So I'm the second one in. And I start -- you know, I lay into everything. But right behind me, people are coming in.

So we wound up arresting, I don't know, five or six or seven of them. But I remember I arrested two of them. Put them in my patrol car. And some of them were being taken to the downtown jail. And I was gonna take my two to the Humble jail, which was closer. It was my substation.

Oh, and by the way, Virgie was beat up a little bit. Her uniform shirt was ripped off. She was wearing -- as we all did -- a bulletproof vest underneath. And I got her with another deputy, and reported in to dispatch, "She's okay. And we've got everybody under arrest."

So anyway, I got my prisoners to the Humble jail, and I put them in an interrogation room. And -- the emotions were running high on this. And I needed to go and get something from the desk sergeant to start doing the report. So I left a couple of deputies -- that weren't actually involved in the arrest -- I put them in there with these two guys to watch them until I got back. Because they were my prisoners.

So I come walking back in, and one of the deputies I see slam this guy over the head with one of these big industrial staplers. And the other deputy had his pistol out and was fixing to pistol-whip the other one. I had to stop them. I had to pull my pistol, because they were so -- they were saying, "Fuck you! Get out of here!" You know.

So I pulled my pistol, and I said, "Listen. Stop it. I am about to arrest both of you. These are my prisoners. I am responsible for their safety now. You are not going to touch them. And I want you to get out of this room and we'll deal with your situation later."

And so that's how wild and woolly it was that night. They both got some sort of discipline, I forget what now. And I got some little bit of commendation for it. I mean, not a formal commendation, but, you know, word from here and there, "You did the right thing."

But the good news is, Virgie wasn't severely injured. Her husband did a remarkable job of staying calm and professional during all of the response. And everything worked out okay. We got all the bad guys. The Hispanic lady got all of her stuff back. And a number of bad guys went to prison.

Someone Crashes into Dimmitt's Car

We were on patrol in an unmarked car, Dimmitt's car. That car was really his pride. I mean, he loved that car. He had taken it out and souped it up and gotten special suspensions on it himself. This was his pride and joy. He owned it, but we were allowed to use it because it was up to specifications. It was this high-powered Plymouth or something. We could cruise around and find all kinds of stuff, because nobody could tell -- all the

lights, you know, the red lights and flashing lights and everything were behind the grille. There were no lights -- it was a
great, great car.

So we're on patrol one night. We were in North Houston.
And we were on our way to a call. But we weren't rushing. It
was some minor call.

And we get to this intersection, a red light intersection. And
we've got the green light, and we're going through the intersection. And this car flies through the red light, rams us, spins us
around a couple of times, and knocks us into some barrier of
some kind. And he keeps going.

And Dimmitt is pissed. And we have no lights -- I mean, no
headlights. Nothing was working. So I said, "Follow him, Dimmitt!" And I pulled out a hand-held spotlight, plugged it into
the lighter. And we're following him. It's a chase. But the only
light we have is that spotlight!

So we're chasing him for about four, four-and-a-half miles,
something like that. And he finally runs into a ditch. I got out
of the car, went and put the guy under arrest. Had him under
arrest. And Dimmitt came over -- there was another unit that
had showed up, and I had put him in the back of the other unit.
And Dimmitt came storming over there, opened the door and
just knocked the shit out of the guy. And he was about to do
it again, and I grabbed his arm, and said, "No, no, no, Dimmitt.
No. Enough is enough." (Laughter)

That was the maddest and most upset I ever saw Dimmitt
Johnson get.

Raid on a Biker Joint

I need to preface this story with kind of an institutional reality
of the Sheriff's Department. A police department -- like the
Houston Police Department, had, I don't know, a thousand
plus officers on the street. Because in the Police Academy, you

go through the Academy, and then they put all the graduates out on the streets. The Sheriff's Department does it differently. The Sheriff's Department puts every graduate from the Academy into the jail system, so they can start learning all the ins and outs and reindeer tricks of all the bad guys and everything. But, even more importantly, I've always thought -- they pick and choose after watching the deputies in the jail system, who they want out on the streets. So I've always thought that was a little better system. But -- there were only 200 plus patrol deputies. Most sheriff's deputies -- at that time, I don't know how it is now, but it's probably not any different -- spend years, sometimes their entire career, working in the jail system. So that's the preface.

So we had a big raid planned on this biker drug joint out in North Harris County. It was notorious. So orders came down that we were supposed to go raid the place and snatch up all the bad guys that we needed to catch. Then I get a call from my supervisor, before the raid, and he said, "There's a major in the jail system who's never been out on the streets, and he really wants to see what it's all about. You're going to be his chaperone."

So the night of the raid comes, and we probably -- and we hit this joint in full force. We've got patrol cars, paddy wagons, you know, a dozen or more patrol cars and a couple paddy wagons. We're ready to rock and roll.

So we go into this bar and we start hauling people out. And I'm taking out some prisoner to put in my patrol car. And I get him ensconced in my patrol car and I'm walking back to go get some more. But then I see this major that I'm babysitting coming out with this guy who's about six foot four or five and umpteen hundred pounds. He's probably four-and-half feet or five feet wide. And the major is trying to hold him by the elbow, and I see the guy keep trying to pull away. And the major's got this weird look in his eye, like he doesn't know what the fuck to do.

So I walk up to him and I say, "We got a problem here?" And the major says, "Yeah, this guy says he's not going to jail." And I looked way up at the guy, and I said, "Is that a fact?" And he said, "Yeah. I ain't going back in the joint."

And he was standing about three-and-half feet away from the back of a pickup truck. So I said, "You can come with me easy, or you can go hard." He said, "You're nothing." So I went up under his throat with my hand, and I just pushed him back. And he's so big and so huge, he has no coordination or control. And he lands with his back in the backup truck, with his feet holding him up. And he can't move.

So I told the major -- and I'm looking at the guy's wrists, and his wrists were enormous, handcuffs wouldn't fit him -- so I told the major to go over to my patrol car and get the ankle shackles out. So he brought them out, and we used the ankle shackles for handcuffs on his wrists. And it took both of us pulling him up -- maybe we even had a helper -- to stand him straight up.

So we got him up, marched him to the paddy wagon. And I said, "But I want this guy at my substation in Humble." We had about 15 people dropped off in Humble, which is a very small substation. We only had maybe three or four cells out there. And thirty or forty more went downtown.

So I had all these people lined up along the wall, sitting on the floor, shackled. So now they're all in my custody. So I'm going down this line, just checking to make sure everybody is okay. Because that's your job, once you've got them in custody -- you've got to protect them.

So I'm going down the line, and I get to this guy, and I said, "Are you okay?" And he said, "No. I want to make a complaint." And I said, "Oh, really? What kind of complaint?" And he says, "I got choked almost to death by this little Mexican deputy." I said, "Well, that sounds like I need to get a supervisor over here to talk to you, and you need to make a full report."

So I pull a supervisor over who takes this report, and the guy describes this little Mexican deputy. He said, "He couldn't have been more than five feet tall. But he tricked me and did something to me and then choked me almost half to death."

And the supervisor -- the supervisor knew what had happened -- he said, "Okay, I think I've got it. I need the name of that deputy." "I don't know his name, I just know he's a little short Mexican guy." And the supervisor said, "Okay, little short Mexican guy." And of course, that was the end of that complaint, because there was no little short Mexican guy out there! (Laughter)

Undercover Drug Buy Goes Bad

This is kind of a sad story. I wasn't actually in the exact middle of it; I was in kind of the clean up of it.

But got a call out to Pasadena, which was outside my usual district, but I had jurisdiction in any district because of the position I had. So we get out there, and it was all just a confused mess.

Here's essentially what happened. There was a Harris County Sheriff's undercover officer out there at a club in Pasadena, working narcotics. And, as it turns out, there was a Houston Police Department undercover narcotics officer working the same club. And they had no idea about each other. There was no communication going on.

So they somehow hooked up with each other for a drug buy, each one thinking the other was a bad guy. And they go to the restroom in this club, and the deal takes place, and the Sheriff's deputy started to pull his gun to arrest the other guy. The other guy, the police officer, thought the other guy was about to shoot him. And the police officer won the shootout and killed the Sheriff's deputy.

In those days, we didn't have integrated communications between HPD and the Sheriff's Department. And that was the upshot of it. And I'm sure the HPD officer was just ready to put a bullet in his own head for that, because it was just such a horrible mistake and everything, and he had to live with that forever.

So, yeah, communications between and among law enforcement agencies has improved quite a bit since those days, but in those days, it was just yet another added potential disaster.

I was out there investigating, after the fact, so this wasn't anything that was a danger to me. It was just very, very sad.

Extra Job at Fiesta

Some of the extra jobs that I had -- there was the bank, and then of course the filming thing. Then I also had an extra job at a Knights of Columbus Hall, for weddings and birthdays and stuff. Those were a hoot, and some of those got a little rough because fights would break out and people would try to steal cars or puncture tires out in the parking lot, or something like that. So that was kind of interesting.

And then also Weiner's Department Store, which was probably the most boring extra job I ever had in my life. All I did was basically stand there. And I was in uniform, of course. So nobody ever tried to shoplift anything. Nobody got out of control. It was really boring, and that was a long eight hours, or whatever it was.

But one of the more interesting ones I had was at a Fiesta. I think Fiesta started in Houston, and I think this was the first Fiesta store in Houston. It was in East Houston, off of, I think, Fulton.

But my job was to -- and it was a big shopping center. There were other things in the shopping center. I was engaged by Fiesta, but sometimes I had to deal with stuff that was out in the general parking lot, which could have been any of the stores out there.

But one day I snatched up this kid who was about 12 years old, 11 or 12, who was shoplifting in the Fiesta. And I marched him outside, and I read him the riot act, and I said, "You know, I can put you away for a long time as a juvie, and then you're gonna be an adult criminal after that."

And he's like, "I'm so sorry! I'm so sorry!" And I said, "Look, here's the deal. I'm gonna cut you loose on this. I'm gonna be watching you always. But all I ask is, if you see anything going down --" Because he was there all the time. I mean, I don't know if his parents worked around there or whatever, but he was there all the time. I said, "If you see anything going down, you need to give me a heads up so I can step into it before it turns into a mess." And he said, "Okay! Okay! Just don't put me in jail!"

And so, for all the time that I worked there -- and it was many, many times. It wasn't every day of the week; it was usually one day a week or so. But boy, anything going down, he would come and give me the skinny. It was like, "there's two guys in the parking lot, and they've both got guns, and they're threatening to kill each other." So, boom -- I was there and snatched them up. So he was my best little helper I ever had in the whole world. And I kind of liked that job, because there was more going on -- there was more action going on than in some of the other extra jobs. So that was my Fiesta stuff.

And interestingly -- this doesn't have anything to do with police work -- but I noticed that -- you know, my father was looking to expand some of his pharmacy stuff. And this was when third-party stuff -- Medicare, Medicaid -- was starting to come in. And they didn't really have all the computers set up for it. But I mentioned to him, "Look, Fiesta Mart for some of this third-party stuff, might be a good place to put a little pharmacy. Nothing but a little drug store." And so that actually came to pass, although it was kind of a fizzle. But that's a different story.

But yeah, the Fiesta stuff, and that kid -- and I'll always -- I wish I could remember his name -- but he was such a cool little grifter. I was so impressed with him. And he was true to his word ever after I had that first conversation with him, when I snatched him up.

The L.A. Overpass Shooter

I got a call one night, and it was an aggravated assault with a knife at some little meaningless random convenience store out in the middle of North Houston somewhere. And I get there, and there was the bad guy, and he rabbitted. So I go chasing his ass down the side of these buildings, and he's trying his best to get away. He was small and wiry and fast. And I caught up with him. And I got up close enough to him to catch his head, and I slammed his head against the side of the building, and he went down. He was not completely out, but he was out enough for me to arrest him.

So I put him in my patrol car, and he's under arrest. And I'm driving him from far North Houston -- close to the upper Harris County line -- to the downtown jail, because at that time, for some reason, the Humble substation was full. So I'm driving him down I-45, and it's a long drive.

So at some point, he says, "You know, I gotta tell you, this was the best arrest I ever had." (Laughter) He said, "You could have done me a lot more damage than you did me. And not only that, but when you arrested me, you respected me." And I said, "Well, I have no reason to not respect somebody until they don't respect me. You rabbitted. I'll let that slide."

So then there was silence for another five or ten minutes. And then he said, "You know, I'm gonna tell you something. This is not in your jurisdiction, so you don't have any jurisdiction over it. But I've been waiting to get this off my chest for awhile, and there's nothing you can do about it because this happened in California, in L.A."

And I said, "You know, you don't need to be telling me anything. Let me reiterate that you have a right to remain silent and have an attorney," the whole Miranda thing.

And he said, "Yeah, yeah, yeah. But I want to tell you. I killed two or three people shooting at them off of overpasses in Los Angeles. I'm not sure if all three died, but I'm pretty sure two died." And I said, "Really? Huh. That's interesting."

He said, "Yeah, I know it sounds crazy, but I wanted to get it off my chest. And thank God it's in a place where it can't come back to haunt me." (Laughter)

So, we get to the downtown jail, and I book him in. And then I call L.A., the sheriff's department or the police department, I don't remember which. And they said, "You're kidding! You've got him?! We've been looking for him for two years! We'll come and get him!"

So they came and extracted him within about a week or two and took him back to L.A. And I never heard another word about it.

A Burglar at my House

I told a story, way back when, about Sergeant Flint, who was raping and sexually abusing the Vietnamese personnel who he was in charge of hiring when I was down in the Mekong Delta. And the secretary from my unit was highly vetted. She was a college graduate. Her name was Cuc. And she was just wonderful. And during the course of all of that business with the sexual abuse and whatnot, I pulled her in as the interpreter to take

down all of the statements of each one of these many young
women that had been abused.

I was not responsible for getting her out of Vietnam years
later, when it all collapsed. But somehow she got out. And
apparently she had married an American contractor who had
been working in Vietnam.

And somewhere along the way, we touched base again together, in the 70's, like 1977 or 1979, somewhere along that
line. And they were living in California. And she called, we
talked, we had a wonderful conversation. She said they were
looking to move away from California because California was
so riven with violence and gangs and all this stuff where they
were living. And they also had a severely disabled child who
had spina bifida. And they were thinking about wanting to
move to Texas, to Houston. So I invited them to come.

So we made arrangements, they came to Houston, and they
came to my house. So we were sitting in the kitchen. And the
door to the garage was in the kitchen. So we're sitting there and
chatting, and they're talking about all the horrendous violence
and how scared they are living in California. And they were
looking at where to move, Houston or somewhere in Florida, I
think.

And all of a sudden, I hear something in my garage. And as
it turns out, I had left one of the garage doors open. We had
a big store room back there in the garage with lots of canned
food. So I said, "Excuse me for just a second, I need to go out
to the garage for a minute."

And I get out to the garage, and I catch this bad guy breaking into -- with a crowbar, breaking into the storage room. So
I tell him he's under arrest, and he starts fighting. And we're
fighting all over. And there's two cars in the garage, and we're
fighting along. And everyone in the house is oblivious to this,
right? And I finally get him corralled and pinned between my

car and the wall that bumps up against the kitchen, which is a very narrow space.

So I'm, like, hollering into the house, telling Kim Hoang, "Get my gun! Get my handcuffs!" And all of a sudden, these folks, Cuc and her husband -- they're going batshit crazy because they see that there's this huge fight going on.

So I get the guy arrested. And one of the kids -- Sean or Sam or somebody -- runs out to the neighbors and says, "There's a burglar in the house!" So all the people in the cul-de-sac come with literally almost like pitchforks, right? They've come with shovels and guns and weapons and everything, and they're on my driveway. So now I'm having to deal with this lynch mob! (Laughter)

So I call in to get a unit to come and pick this guy up. And one of the funny things about it was -- the guy, when I arrested him, said, "The only thing that could be worse --" Because I had said to him, "Do you know how stupid you are to come and try to burglarize a cop's house?" He said, "I had no idea. The only worse thing could have been if I had been arrested by a woman cop." So when I called in, I said, "Send a female officer." (Laughter)

So meanwhile, while I've got him in handcuffs between the car and the wall, I'm out there reading the riot act to the lynch mob, telling them, "It's okay. I've got it under control. Put your weapons down. Go home. He's under arrest, he's in my custody." And they're yelling, "No, we're gonna kick the shit out of him!" And I said, "No, nobody's gonna come and mess with my prisoner. He's in my custody." So they kind of quietly dispersed, but they're all still standing in front of their houses, waiting for the police unit to arrive.

So the HPD unit gets there, and I'm talking to the officer, and she said, "They said that you requested a female officer?" And I said, "Yeah, because asshole had told me that the only worse thing that could happen to him today was being arrested by a female officer." And she got a big kick out of that. (Laughter) So she came, we took my handcuffs off, she put her handcuffs on, he went away.

And of course, back in the house, poor Cuc and her husband were, like, almost -- I don't know exactly how to put it. It's as if they had been dropped into the pits of Hell. And so, not surprisingly, they decided not to move to Houston. (Laughter)

Dead Body in a Movie Theater

So this is not a real dramatic story, but it actually turns out to be a little bit of a substantive story.

I had an extra job one night, me and another deputy, it was a two-deputy job. There was a church function, and this is in far East Houston. I had no idea even where I was in Houston. But it was far East Houston, somewhere out towards Pasadena or something. And this was in the 70's, maybe early 80's, I don't remember. But that part of -- it was a real depressed area. And everything was shut down.

And there was this church, and they were having some function there, whatever the function was. The other deputy was gonna be working inside the church. I was gonna be outside. And the parking lot for the church was across the street, in the parking lot of this old, long-abandoned movie theater.

So you know, I'm cruising around outside, just looking, making sure nobody's trying to do anything. And I'm walking around the parking lot, and I'm thinking, "I wonder what's in that old movie theater?"

So I get into the movie theater and start poking around. I can see lots of evidence of homeless people that have been living there. And at one point during all of that -- and I wasn't in there the whole time. I would go in, make a little bit of exploration, come back and check the parking lot. And then, you know, when things were kind of boring, I'd go back in.

So ultimately, I came across this dead and long-decayed body. And I'm checking it out, and it looks like a murder. It looks like a homicide. It's mostly decomposed, but the throat had been slit, that was obvious. And there were some other puncture wounds on the body.

Oh, and the other deputy had said, "Whatever you do, just don't go looking for shit." (Laughter)

So I call it in, and they send some homicide detectives out there. One of them was Ray Davis, who I knew real well because I'd worked on other cases with him. He was a good detective, one of my favorite detectives. And he's going through and he says, "Got it. We'll work it. Thanks."

And a few weeks later, I get a call from him, and he said, "This was a murder. We were able to work it up. We caught the person who did this." It was not a random homeless act. It was a serious, some kind or another of retaliation kind of thing.

So I got paid a few extra bucks for working an extra job, and I helped get a murder solved.

Monte Heron Undercover

That first night I was on patrol, I had been riding with Monte Heron. After that night, I lost track of him. He wasn't on my radar screen.

One night, I was on patrol. And, you know, almost all of my shifts in the Sheriff's Department were night shifts -- 95% were nights shifts. So I'm on patrol one night, and I get this call for a suspicious person at this little convenience store in the middle of nowhere in North Harris County off of Hardy Road. So I take the call.

And I get there, and the only information I had from the dispatch was that the suspicious person looked as if he may have had a gun with him. So I get there and I pull up to the store -- oh, and they said that he was on the pay phone on the side of the store. So I pull up on that side of the store. And. I see this guy talking on the telephone, and I pull up and have him in my headlights. He looked like the most wretched person you ever saw. He had this huge beard that was growing out of everywhere, hair that was long. He looked like a turd. (Laughter) That was the nomenclature of that time. (Laughter)

And I get out and I said, "Put the phone down." And he looks at me -- he's got the phone up to his ear -- and he drops the phone and starts to reach for something.

And I pull my pistol. Actually, I already had my pistol out. And I said, "Freeze. Do not even breathe or you die."

And all of a sudden, he says, "Ben?! It's me!" And I said, "Who the fuck are you?!" And he says, "I'm Monte! Monte Heron!" And I said, "Show me some I.D."

And he starts to move and I said, "Stop. Pull your jacket, take your gun out, put it on the ground." And he did. And then he pulled out his badge and I.D. And it was Monte Heron, who was working undercover. And I came so, so close to shooting him.

And how either one of us ever remembered each other's names, I don't know. But when he called me out by name, that was a shock. And I said, "Okay, Monte, come to me. Move to me slowly. Come backwards. I don't want you coming forward." And I got him to come towards me. And I said, "Now, turn around." And I got a good look at him, and yes, I was convinced, it was Monte Heron.

And he said, "Thank you for not shooting me." And I said, "Monte, it came very close." And he said, "It seems like the two times we've ever been together have been very close." (Laughter)

So that was the end of that.

Jimmy Carter

This was while Jimmy Carter was President.

I was in downtown Houston. I don't even remember what I was doing downtown. But I was in some office building, doing a kind of plain-clothes interrogation in some case. One of the older buildings downtown.

And I'm coming out of the door, onto the sidewalk, and literally, Jimmy Carter ran into me. We hit each other, me coming out of the door and him walking on the sidewalk. And he's got all these Secret Service guys with him and everything.

So we stopped. I made myself known to his Secret Service people. I said, "I'm a deputy sheriff. I've got a weapon."

And Jimmy Carter said, "I want to talk to you for a second." He said, "How are you doing? What's going on? Are you policing right now?" And I said, "Yes, Mr. President, actually I was."

But the takeaway from all of that was, I was just stunned that the Secret Service had not vetted every door and alleyway in the area.

But yeah, he was so nice. And of course, I had voted for him and was happy to see him.

Horse Rustling

This was a routine after-the-fact call. And Dimmitt was with me that night. And basically it was these two thoroughbred horses that had been absconded with. And that call lasted over two hours, which is long for an after-the-fact call. But I was intrigued by it.

Dimmitt was antsy, he kept wanting to wrap it up. But I said, "I need more information here." So I am learning everything I can find about these two horses -- you know, questioning the owners and everything. And I take extensive notes for two hours, and I put all of these notes in my report.

And finally we're done. I thought it was a really interesting thing, because I was thinking, "Huh! I've been in the Sheriff's Department for a long time, and this is the first time I've ever had a horse rustling case. And that's what Sheriffs do!" So, that was the end of that.

So, life goes on, and a thousand other things happen after that. At some point, a few years later, when I was a lawyer -- I was at Bankston, Wright and Greenhill at that time, it probably would have been 1990 or 1991 or something like that. I get a call from Dimmitt Johnson. And he says, "The horses were found."

And it was because of the extensive notes that I took -- you know, the birthmarks and other marks on the horses. They found the horses in Oklahoma. And they got them back to their owners, years after I had left the Sheriff's Department. So that was my horse rustling case.

Hostage Negotiation at a Grocery Store

This was a crisis/hostage negotiation at a little grocery store -- a grocery store that was in between a convenience store and a supermarket, in terms of size. And what happened was, there were three bad guys who went into this grocery store in North Harris County. And all of a sudden, the first units rolled up. I wasn't among the first units. And the bad guys had taken everybody in the grocery store hostage.

So I got there probably about 12 or 15 or 20 minutes after the call went out that it was a hostage situation. And of course in that district I was the designated negotiator. And I got there and started making contact with whoever was inside. They were on a landline -- we didn't have cell phones in those days. So we set everything up, I got everything set up. And so I started talking to one guy. I said, "Who am I talking to?"

He said, "Well, I'm not giving you my name, but we've got these people, and if we don't get what we want, and if we don't get out of here, we're killing them all." And I said, "Well, I hear you, but I need to know who I'm talking to." And he said, "Well, you're talking to somebody who can pass it on to somebody else."

And I said, "No. You need to put on whoever it is that is your honcho in all of this. I'll talk to him. I won't talk to anybody else. I'll just send SWAT in." So somebody else gets on the phone, and it turns out this is the honcho. And I said, "Look, here's the deal. You've got people in there. We don't want them to die. We don't want you to die. We don't want anybody to die. But in order for me to help you, you've got to let me know what it is that you really need. I need to see what I can do to help you get out of this mess."

And he started off this list of things. He wanted a helicopter to come in and pick them, take them to Hobby Airport, and put them on a plane, and take them to Cuba, or somewhere in Central America. And I said, "Yeah, I think I can handle all that." (Laughter)

I said, "But, if we're gonna do this, I need to know how many hostages you've got in there and I need to know the condition of the hostages. Is anybody hurt?" He said, "No, nobody's hurt yet. Well, we hit one guy in the head."

"Well," I said, "why'd you do that? What condition is he in?" So I'm going through all this, you know, regular kind of stuff. And I said, "It sounds like he might need a little medical attention, and you've got a number of hostages in there. Why don't you, as an effort of good faith, why don't you send him out here and let us get him taken care of, and you've still got all your other hostages" -- who we were really, really concerned about.

So they send him out. And we get him into EMS, and they haul him off to the hospital. And it was actually a pretty serious wound, now that I reflect on it. It was, at the very least, a concussion. But we got him out of there. So I thought, "Okay, I'm making a little progress here."

So we're talking and I said, "Look, let me check on the helicopter and see where it is. I'll be back with you in a few minutes." And I said, "Oh, feel free to call this number back and it'll put you right through to me."

So anyway, this goes on for hours and hours. So I wind up getting another hostage out of there, because they were freaking out, thought they were having a heart attack or whatever. And I kept saying, "The helicopter's almost here."

And then I had -- I don't remember if the Sheriff's Department had helicopters in those days, but HPD did. So I had HPD start choppering in a helicopter to hover over the place. And I said, "Helicopter's here, it's sitting over you. All you need to do is let the rest of the hostages go, we'll let the helicopter down and we'll get you on a plane to wherever it is that you want to go."

And the idiot on the inside said, "Okay, but we want some kind of assurance that nobody's gonna shoot us while we try to get on the helicopter." And I had established this kind of communication with him. And I said, "I will tell you this. Regardless of anything else that's going on here, I will not let anybody shoot you trying to get from the store to the helicopter. It won't happen."

So I actually had a helicopter land out in the parking lot. And there were about five HPD SWAT people in the helicopter. (Laughter)

So I said, "Once you get everybody in there released, you've got safe passage to the helicopter." And they agreed. And -- these were not the brightest bulbs in the world. I mean, most crooks are not the brightest bulbs in the world. It's not like the movies. I mean, some crooks are brilliant. But these were not brilliant crooks.

So they released all the hostages. And I said, "Okay. Walk out one at a time and get in the helicopter." So each one of them walked out one at a time, got in the helicopter. As soon as they got in the helicopter, they got pulled out of the other side of the helicopter (laughter) by the SWAT team. So boom, boom, boom. (Laughter)

So, yeah, it all ended. Nobody got killed. And only one person was fairly seriously injured, and it was the first hostage that had the head injury. And that was kind of just another typical hostage negotiation scenario.

But I have to tell you, that I think, for me, in that position, those were always the most stressful situations for me. Because I knew that there were one or more lives at stake, and if I made a mistake, it was on me, in my mind. But no mistake was made that night, and everything worked out.

Fight in the Denny's Parking Lot

On this night, Dimmitt and I had arrested some guy. Dimmitt was driving that night. And we were taking him to the substation in Humble. And we pull into the parking lot of the substation, and all of a sudden I see some big disturbance across the street at the Denny's. I see this guy dragging this woman across the parking lot by her feet, banging her head, and slugging her, as he's going across the parking lot.

So I told Dimmitt, "Let me out. Go get this guy in there" -- our prisoner -- "and come back." So I get over there, and I tell the guy -- and there's a huge crowd, I mean a huge crowd, 30 or 40 people. And I tell the guy, "Unhand that maiden," basically, and "You're under arrest." And he says, "I ain't going back to the joint." And the fight was on.

And he had about 10 to 12 friends of his there that night, because he had just gotten out of prison a day or two before, and they were out celebrating. After they got drunk somewhere else, they were at Denny's -- this was at, like, 1 or 2:00 in the morning, right?

So I'm fighting with this guy, and his friends are all jumping into the fray. And I can't pull my pistol because they're all trying to get hold of my pistol. So I've got my right arm down over the flap of my holster, so that nobody can get my pistol, but that only gives me my left hand to be working with.

So I get him down on the ground. I get him turned over. And I can't -- he won't get his arms out from underneath him, which is typical kind of stuff. But I don't have all the usual tools that I need to deal with this because other people are beating on me from the back.

So all of a sudden, he jumps up and he heads for his truck. And somebody said, "He's got a gun in there!" So I get him before he gets to the truck, and I'm fighting with him, and I'm still trying to protect my pistol. And I was not in a position to get down to my ankle pistol. But I am being beat to a bloody fucking pulp. And I'm thinking, "This is not going well. This may be my day to die."

And at some point -- and it seemed like it was forever, but it was probably six or seven or ten minutes at the most -- but then, every police officer, and Texas Ranger, and DPS, and deputy sheriff who was in the substation, come pouring out. And the first guy that comes running over is a Texas Ranger. And one of the people that's beating on me turns around and kicks him in the nuts, and drops him like a sack of, I don't know, potatoes or something.

But finally, the troops were there, and we got everybody arrested that needed to be arrested. And we lined up about 12 or 15 people, all in handcuffs, and marched them from the Denny's, across the street, to the substation. (Laughter) It was insane.

And, you know, the woman that he was beating the shit out of, said, "Please don't kill him! Please don't kill him!" So

I talked to her for a little bit. She said, "I don't want to press charges." I said, "You don't need to." (Laughter) "I've arrested him, I've got my charges." She said, "But he just got out of prison. He just got drunk, he just got out of control." I said, "He's going back to prison." And that's exactly what happened.

But how I survived that little thing, I don't know, because it seemed like -- and quite frankly, if it hadn't have been exigent circumstances, I would have gotten the prisoner in with Dimmitt and then called the troops out. But it looked like he was killing her. So, there was no time, and I just had to make a decision. The decision almost got me killed.

But the most interesting part of the night for me was, once we got everybody under arrest that needed to be under arrest, and we had this line of, like, 15 people who were involved in this, and we're marching them across the street. (Laughter) Yeah, so that was the Denny's deal. And bad guy did go back to prison.

Babies in a Mobile Home Fire

I was on patrol one night and got a call of a fire at a mobile home. So I'm a few minutes away, and I'm the first one there. And there's a woman standing outside, screaming and crying and hollering, as this mobile home was starting to go up in flames. And she's saying, "My babies! My babies!" And from inside the mobile home, I'm hearing all of these babies crying and screaming. A lot of babies, I don't know how many.

So, you know, I'm trying to get her situated and try to figure out what to do. And this was outside the city limits, so the volunteer fire department was showing up. And I'm thinking, when she's screaming about her babies, I'm thinking about running in there and trying to rescue some of these babies.

And I said, "How many babies are there?" She said, "Thirty
or forty." And I said, "What are you talking about?" She says,
"They're kittens! They're cats! They're babies!"

I said, "Okay, thank you. Step back." (Laughter) I'm not running in there to rescue 30 kittens! Although I would love to,
but I'm not gonna do it.

And then the volunteer fire department got there. And you
do not know how fast -- or maybe you do, but most people
don't know -- how fast it takes for a mobile home to burn completely to the ground. It takes about 12 to 15 minutes. I mean,
they are death traps, mobile homes are.

So the volunteer fire department gets there. And I see one
of the volunteer firemen coming out is a guy I know from the
pharmacy. He was a regular in the restaurant, the coffee shop,
of the pharmacy. And I see him run -- I'm watching him. He's
running around the back. And he's running around the back,
and then all of a sudden, boom, he disappears. He's gone. And
I'm thinking, "What the hell just happened?" And it turns out,
this poor schmoe had fallen into an open cesspool, an open
septic tank. It was where everything drained to in the back.

So I'm running back there to deal with him. And he's struggling in this cesspool, and I've got to get down and drag him
out of there. And the woman is still screaming at the top of her
lungs, "My babies! My babies! My babies!"

So I get him out. I get back to her. And by that time, things
were starting to get a little more organized. But that was a total
-- maybe an absolute total of 20 minutes worth of absolute
bedlam, babies crying that weren't babies but they sounded
like babies, the woman just going absolutely crazy for her "babies," and the volunteer firefighter that I knew almost drowning in an open septic tank.

So, yeah, I got the woman away enough from the trailer to
start grasping that her 30 cats or kittens or whatever were done

for. But boy, when I got there, it sounded so much like babies. I almost even without asking ran into that trailer.

It all turned out okay -- except for the kittens. The volunteer firefighter that I knew was a mess, and so was I. She was safe. And so that was the end of that little drama in North Harris County.

Kristy's Birth

This was in 1982. I'd been with the Sheriff's Department for three or four years.

Kim Hoang was pregnant, and it came time for the birth. The same doctor that had birthed Sean and Shane was still her OB/GYN, Dr. Chiu. I liked her. She was a gruff and grumpy old thing, but I liked her well enough.

For Sean, and Shane, and Kristy, I had a $10 bet with Dr. Chiu on the gender of every kid. I kept betting on a girl, because I knew Kim Hoang wanted a daughter. And I lost the Sean bet and I lost the Shane bet. And then I bet on a boy. (Laughter) So I lost again. I lost every bet with Dr. Chiu. (Laughter)

This was in Memorial Northwest Hospital. I was not in the delivery room because Dr. Chiu did not want anybody in the delivery room. I remember when she came out. She didn't say, "It's a girl," she said, "You owe me ten bucks!" (Laughter)

I was in this alliterative period of my life -- Sam, Sean, Shane. I was gonna name her Sharon or Sheila. But no, no, no. Kim Hoang's major program with learning English happened to be American TV, and she was just a nut for Kristy McNichol on whatever show it was. She wanted to name her Kristy. So we did.

She was healthy and smiley. So that was the birth of Miss Kristy. And a joyous birth it was.

Arrest in District Four

Normally speaking, my district was District 2 in Harris County
with the Sheriff's Department. But when other events happened, sometimes we'd get shifted to work other districts to
help out.

There was this huge -- I don't remember if it was a storm,
tornado, hurricane -- I don't remember exactly what it was. But
it was a catastrophic kind of weather event, and they needed
extra help in the next district over, which was District 4, I
think. Out in the 1960 area. District 2 was east of I-45, and District 4 was west of I-45.

So I'm running patrol out there, and all of a sudden get this
call for this gang fight, assault. And one unit rolls up on the
assault victim, and I'm chasing the suspects of the assault. I finally pull that car over on FM 1960 and there's, like, five guys
in the car.

So I'm ordering them all out. And I'm treating them like I
treat every fucking turd in Harris County. Of course, you have
to understand that the turds I worked with were stone-cold
bad-ass turds.

I get these guys out, and they're all teenagers -- you know,
16, 18, 19 years old, or something like that. And I make them
all get out of the car and go lie down spread-eagle on the
ground. And I've got five of them lined up there.

So I arrest all of them, and I pull another couple of units in
to help transport them. Transport them to my substation and
book them.

The arrest itself was not difficult, but the verbal abuse that
I had to endure from these guys -- let's just call them white
privileged guys. And I'm listening to all their shit, and I'm saying "Yeah, yeah, yeah, it doesn't matter to me. Get down on the
ground. You're going to jail."

And the next day or the day after that, I get a call from my supervisor, Drew Warren. So I go over to the substation to talk to him, and he says, "Look, it turns out that the father of one of those guys is a district judge. And he's wanting to file a complaint." And I said, "What for?" He said, "They said that you abused them." I said, "It was a typical arrest." He said, "Yeah, maybe in our district. But that district over there is a little different, more affluent, area. I'm not faulting your police work, I'm just faulting your sensitivity to the situation."

I said, "Well, first of all, I had no idea that any of them had a father that was a judge, but second of all, I wouldn't have given a shit, because these guys were total assholes, every single one of them. And if I had to do it all over again, I'd do it the same way."

And he said, "Yeah, that's kind of the problem. The judge has said that he could probably forgive all of this if he could just get an apology." And I said, "Great! But I'm not gonna give it. If you want to give an apology, you give an apology. But I'm not doing it." And he said, "I thought you were gonna say that. Okay."

So I never gave an apology. Somebody in the Sheriff's Department -- and probably Drew Warren went up one level above himself and had somebody smooth it over. But that was the difference between everything west of I-45 and everything east of I-45.

Arresting a Pharmacy Employee

I didn't work many accidents, as a general rule. But I came up on an accident one night on Airline Drive. So I had to stop and kind of get some order, call in the EMS people, all that kind of stuff. And it was a bad accident, a terrible accident. A fatality.

So I'm working this accident and I'm waiting for other troops to get there. A couple of other units had responded, but

I'm still out there trying to direct traffic around the accident. And all of a sudden this car comes barreling down Airline Drive at about 75 miles an hour. And I'm shining lights at it, I'm doing all this kind of stuff. I almost get killed. I'm almost run over.

So I jump in my vehicle, and turn the scene over to a couple of other deputies that were there, and I chase this car down. Pull the car over. And I get to the car, and I'm talking to the driver, this woman. She was 25, 30 years old, something like that. And I recognized her immediately. She was a cashier that worked at the pharmacy on Airline.

I said, "I need you to step out of the car." And she said, "You look familiar!" I mean, she was drunk -- really, really drunk. And I said, "Cops always look familiar. Step out of the car."

And she gets out of the car, and I place her under arrest. And she says, "Wait a minute, wait a minute! Are you Mr. Cunningham's son?" I said, "Why do you ask?" And she said, "I just think I know you."

And I said, "Well, here's the deal. You almost killed a peace officer. You almost ran into other people. You are super drunk." And she said, "Yeah, but I work for your father." And I said, "That makes no difference. You're going to jail."

So I arrested her and I transported her to jail. And I'm glad I did, because she would have killed somebody that night. And she missed me by inches. I had to dive to get out of the way to keep her from running over me.

By the time she got to jail, she was crying, begging, you know, all this kind of stuff. And I said, "Look. You're gonna be better for this. Because you're gonna learn something about some responsibility. And you're gonna learn that your actions when you're drunk have consequences."

And then of course, the next thing that happened, when she got out of jail, she was terminated from the job. I fired her.

Domestic Violence Case

Obviously, as a cop, you make many, many calls that have to do with physical or sexual assault, especially domestic situations. So no cop is ever a stranger to that sort of stuff. But I was always -- it was something that always bothered me. Because it seemed like the legal system didn't work fast enough to stop the kind of things that would happen. I had seen terrible beatings and homicides, all but for want of a protective order. And even if there was, it made no difference. So I saw that as a huge flaw in the system.

And this particular incident -- I had made this call to a domestic disturbance one night. And it was boyfriend/girlfriend or husband/wife, I don't remember now. But at that time, we did not have -- there was not a statute that allowed us to snatch the bad person out and arrest them based on the circumstances. That came a few years later.

So essentially, I got to this call. It was going on. Bad guy came to the door. He's all fucked up. And he's saying, "Nobody called the cops here!" And I said, "Well, actually, somebody did. I don't know who. But hey, it seems like you're kind of upset. Why don't you come on out for a minute and let's get this all straightened out so you can get to bed early tonight?"

So he steps out on the front porch, and as soon as he does, I arrest him, for public intoxication. (Laughter) Because he was obviously drunk. I couldn't go into his house. And oftentimes, that was our M.O. "Hey, just step out here for a second." And once they were outside the door of that house, they belonged to us.

So I arrested him. And I had another unit transport him, because I wanted to stay there and get a report, and talk to the female. And this had been going on for a long time. And I had armed myself, by that time in my police years, with information -- early on, I learned that I need to know what services and everything is available to people, so I can give them stuff if I can't do anything. And so I gave her this information about getting a protective order. And this wasn't the first time that ever happened -- this was many times. But this was emblematic, I guess, of the whole range of those kinds of encounters in domestic disputes that had to do with either sexual abuse or physical abuse with adults.

So I left her with a couple of pamphlets for who she could call to get help and go to -- you know, safe houses and stuff like that. And I also gave her my card. And I said, "If ever there's another problem, you give me a call. I don't care, night or day. I'll come."

And about three weeks later, I guess it was, I actually get a call from her. I didn't get too many calls from people. I'd give them my card sometimes, but it was rare that anybody would ever call. It was, like, noon-ish one day. And I wasn't on duty. And she said, "He's coming for me! He said he's gonna kill me, and he's gonna kill our baby!"

I said, "Okay. I'm on my way." And I left whatever I was doing at that time. I'm in my personal car, but I put my uniform on, and I'm all geared up.

And I get to her house before bad guy comes. And I'm sitting in my car, kind of hunkered down, and I'm just waiting to see if anything happens. And sure enough, bad guy shows up -- he'd gotten out of jail. And he gets out, and he's got something in his right hand. I can't tell if it's a gun or a knife or whatever, but it was something. And he's obviously on a mission.

And he starts walking up to the house. And we're talking about some little two-bedroom bungalow kind of thing. And he makes it to the porch, and I said, "Hey, remember me?" And he turns around, and I've got my .357 magnum, locked and loaded, aimed at his head. And I said, "Drop whatever you've got in your hands."

And he said, "Hey, I'm just coming to check on the kid." And I said, "No, you're not." Because there was a protective order in place. I said, "You are now being arrested for violation of a protective order."

He said, "I ain't going back to jail." And I said, "Yeah, I think you're right. You're not, because I'm about to shoot you dead, right here on the front porch. So get ready to die."

And he looked at me, and he decided I was serious. He dropped it. And what he had in his hand was a hunting knife. And as I'm arresting him, he's saying, "Fuck you, you fucked this all up. I was gonna kill her. I was gonna kill the baby. And you fucked this all up for me."

And I said, "Hang on a second, let me read you your rights, I want you to tell me what you just said." And he said it all again. And we're driving to the central jail. And I said, "Great. Just know, I'll be testifying at your trial. You are fucking done, dude."

But the good news is, I didn't have to shoot him. The good news is, he didn't kill mama or the baby. And the good news is, he got a number of years on the charges that had been pending. And I thought, "Okay. This isn't perfect. Maybe I should have just dusted his ass." I kind of, even now, decades later, kind of wish I had. Because I never knew what happened after I left the Sheriff's Department. But that's the way that world is.

Attempted Capital Murder of Me

This was in the early 80's. It certainly was before 1985. Between 1980 and 1985.

We were gonna be running a warrant in the middle of the night, and it was a drug dealer and also a guy who had been in prison and was out on parole and busted his parole. So there was a gaggle of people going out on this raid on the house, serving the warrant.

My job was to make my way into the backyard to make sure that bad guy didn't start running out the back when the troops came in the front. There must have been -- I don't remember how many deputies there were in this raid -- but I'm thinking there were at least five or six or seven. I don't know. But they were all coming in the front door.

So before they come busting in the front door, I get back to the back. It's a little suburban house with a patio and a sliding patio door. So I'm standing up against the wall, my back to the wall, and just for the heck of it, I check the door to see if it's locked, so I'll know kind of what the situation is. And the door was not locked.

So the troops come crashing through the front, hollering "Sheriff's Department! Police!" and so on. And all of a sudden somebody's yelling in the house, "He's heading for the back!"

So I open the door a little bit and start going for my gun. I've got a flashlight in the other hand. And as soon as I step around in front of that door, there's bad guy. He's got a .12 gauge shotgun. He sticks it into my belly up underneath my bullet-proof vest. And before I can do anything -- I mean, this happened in a matter of seconds -- he pulled the trigger. And it went "click."

So I -- subdued the suspect (laughter) and gathered up the evidence. Took him into custody and had him transported to the hospital (laughter) because he had some serious flashlight wounds on his head. And I accompanied him to the hospital.

As soon as they fixed him up, I took him back into custody and booked him in the Harris County downtown jail. And since this was a serious felony situation, once I booked him into jail on all of his prior stuff, I walked next door over to the D.A.'s office. Because if it was a felony, you had to get it approved by the D.A.'s intake.

So I went over to D.A. intake. And this was, like, 4:00 in the morning. And I'm sitting there talking to the A.D.A. It's a guy. And I'm explaining to him what was going on. And I showed him my evidence bag with the shotgun shell, that had an indentation of the firing pin on it. And he starts asking me questions.

He says, "Well, was it dark outside?" And I said, "Yeah, it was, like, 2:00 in the morning, it was pretty dark outside." And he said, "How was he supposed to know you were a peace officer?" And I said, "Well, you know, other than the fact that we had half of the Harris County Sheriff's Department crashing through the front door, and I'm standing there with a badge the size of Dallas on my chest, and a gun, and a Harris County Sheriff's Department uniform -- other than that, I don't know." (Laughter)

And he's looking at it, and he's looking at me, and he says, "Eh, I think the best we can do is assault on a peace officer." And I said, "Well, I was thinking more like attempted capital murder of a peace office." And he said, "Nah, with what you've told me, I think this is all we can do." And I said, "Thank you."

I took my bag back, and I went out and sat in my patrol car until a shift change at the D.A.'s office. As soon as the shift change happened, I walked back into the D.A.'s office and that guy's gone. The A.D.A. that replaced him was a female.

So I start explaining the situation to her. I got, like, two minutes into the conversation. And she's sitting there looking at the bag. And she says, "Is that a firing pin indentation on the end of the shotgun shell?" And I said, "Yes, ma'am." And she said, "Sounds like attempted capital murder of a peace officer to me." I said, "Thank you very much." (Laughter) So he got slapped with attempted capital murder of a peace officer.

It could have gone in multiple different directions that night. But since I was a lone ranger in the back of the place, and since I -- I mean, I could not have imagined that he was either lucky enough or smart enough to stick that shotgun in my belly and lift up my bullet-proof vest, and pull the trigger. I think that was one of the top two or three or four times when I should have not made it through the night.

Constables at Denny's

This would have been in about 1985. I was in my first year of law school. I was still with the Sheriff's Department.

So I had some early morning classes to get to. I think the class started at, like, 8:00 or 8:30 in the morning. So I got up and I'm heading into downtown Houston, and I stop at this particular Denny's on the way. Of course, I'm not in uniform or anything, but I always carried my gun, badge, and handcuffs.

So I'm sitting there, in the very back booth. And I glance around the Denny's to see what's going on. There's a couple sitting in the booth in front of me. And there's a couple of deputy constables in uniform at another table.

So I'm not paying too much attention, but all of a sudden, I'm starting to pay attention to the couple, because things are getting a little weird. I hear him muttering, "I'm gonna kill your ass." And she's getting all upset and starting to cry.

And I'm looking at the constables, glancing at them. I see them glance over at the couple. And then it keeps escalating. And I'm just sitting there eating my breakfast, drinking my coffee. And I'm thinking, "Okay, it's getting to a point to where somebody needs to intervene." And I'm thinking, "Okay, constables are there. They're gonna come and intervene."

They ignore it. And it keeps getting worse. And then all of a sudden the constables stand up and walk out. So it's just me.

So I get up, I walk over. And at that moment, he slapped the shit out of her, in front of me. So I put him under arrest and have Denny's call an HPD unit out there to transport him. And the arrest was not an easy arrest. The guy wanted to fight me. I had to throw him across the table.

And I never, ever forgot that. It's an insignificant moment, you would think. But for a cop to see other cops chicken and run -- it really, really upset me. And after the arrest, after school that day, I got hold of the constable precinct they worked for and just read the constable -- the actual constable -- I just read him the riot act on all of that. And he said, "That's unacceptable. I will find out who they are and they will be dealt with."

So, yeah, that kind of ruined my breakfast that day.

Chapter 8

Three More Stories

Peyton's Birth

In every single birth of all my kids, my major concern was, "Please don't let anything go wrong." And nothing ever did.

When Peyton and Colwyn were born, Andi and I decided that we did not want to know the sex of the child. Actually, I didn't know the sex of any of my kids. So it was always a pleasant surprise. But with Peyton, I was practicing law, and there was some kind of little office pool to bet on the sex of the child, which was pretty cool.

My Aunt Icie, whose actual name was Alice -- when she found out Andi was pregnant, she said that she would give us $1,000 if we would name our next girl Alice. Andi about this, we both agreed, "No way."

Also, Kinky Friedman and I wound up on a panel together for something or other. And we kind of bonded a little bit. I was answering legal questions, he was answering musical questions, or whatever. We stayed in contact a little bit. And we were gathered together one time at Liberty Lunch, and Andi was talking about being pregnant. And he came up with some ridiculous name, something screwy like "Golashabosh." Something extraordinarily stupid. And we wisely rejected that name as well. (Laughter)

We wound up naming her Peyton because one of her great-grandfathers was a General named Peyton March. There's an air force base named after him. And I was in the delivery room for Peyton. And I liked that because I felt like I was more in control. And it was very, very cool to see little Peyton come out. But we jokingly called her "Thousand Dollar Alice."

Colwyn's Birth

When Colwyn was born, I was in the middle of lots of heavy duty litigation and trying to bounce back and forth between the hospital and the office. But I was determined to be there.

At some point during Colwyn's birth -- it was early in the morning and Andi had already started having contractions and that sort of thing, but she was asleep. This was, like, six or seven in the morning. And I was thinking how I really wanted a cup of coffee and a donut. And I wondered if I could leave, but I was afraid I might miss the birth. But I decided I had time. So I headed out -- and she wasn't even awake -- and I slipped out of the hospital and got some coffee and a couple of donuts, and scooted back to the hospital. And this was at Seton on 38th Street. At any rate, I had my coffee and ate my donuts, and got back to the hospital just in time to see Colwyn born!

The Colonel -- Andi's father -- kept wanting to name Colwyn "Larry," after him. And neither one of us wanted that to happen. So we bounced back and forth about names. There was a lot of discussion. And finally, she wanted to name him Cole, but we found this name that was this bay in Wales called Colwyn Bay, and I loved that name. So we finally agreed on Colwyn. And just like all the others, he was absolutely perfect.

Kenny and the Order of the Purple Sash

I've not told a lot of stories about my children, for one particular reason. There have been hundreds, if not a thousand or more, stories I could have told about all my kiddos, and even my grandkids. But I thought that those stories belong to my children. So those are their stories to tell. And I didn't want to preempt them or distort them. However they perceive them, is however they were, and I'm good with that, good or bad.

But I did tell the stories of each of their births, and with Kenny, I can't tell his birth story, because he didn't become a part of my family until 15 years ago when he was 7 years old. And that's always an interesting dynamic when another father figure comes into the picture. Kenny's father Jim and I met, and he and I had a good little chat out on the driveway at Bushnell. And basically, Jim was leery of me, as he should have been. And I said, "I'm not here to replace you as Kenny's father, ever. That's you and Kenny." So Jim and I kind of bonded a little bit.

So instead of a birth story, this is a little story that I can tell about Kenny. And this involved Colwyn, too. One of the things that I imposed on both Kenny and Colwyn was after a tiny little exhibition of some aikido martial arts. And I was impressed with both of their abilities. So I put them into the Order of the Purple Sash. I said they would go through some training, and if they passed, they would be awarded a purple sash. And this went on for a few months, and after a few months, they had sufficiently risen to the graduation level that I held a little ceremony to award them both a purple sash! There is no formal school of martial arts that awards purple sashes -- I tried to pick something that was different from the usual sashes and belts. And I don't know if that made any impact on either of them, but it meant a lot to me.

Appendix

Favorite Films
The Big Lebowski
Plan 9 From Outer Space
Shane

Favorite Songs
The Weight by The Band
Hallelujah by k.d. lang
Knockin' on Heaven's Door by Guns N' Roses
Stop Children What's That Sound by Buffalo Springfield
Sixteen Tons by Tennessee Ernie Ford

Favorite Authors
Elmore Leonard
Kurt Vonnegut
Cormac McCarthy
Margaret Atwood

CPSIA information can be obtained
at www.ICGtesting.com
Printed in the USA
LVHW020204021120
670427LV00002B/149

9 780578 756899